LIBERALISM, COMMUNITY,
AND CULTURE

Liberalism, Community, and Culture

WILL KYMLICKA

CLARENDON PRESS · OXFORD

1989

Oxford University Press, Walton Street, Oxford OX2 6DP

Oxford New York Toronto
Delhi Bombay Calcutta Madras Karachi
Petaling Jaya Singapore Hong Kong Tokyo
Nairobi Dar es Salaam Cape Town
Melbourne Auckland

and associated companies in
Berlin Ibadan

Oxford is a trade mark of Oxford University Press

Published in the United States
by Oxford University Press, New York

British Library Cataloguing in Publication Data
Kymlicka, Will
Liberalism, community and culture.
1. Political ideologies: liberalism
I. Title
320.5'1
ISBN 0–19–827599–4

Library of Congress Cataloging in Publication Data
Kymlicka, Will.
Liberalism, community, and culture.
Bibliography   Includes index.
1 Liberalism.   2. Community.   3. Minorities—Civil
rights.   I. Title.
HM276.K96   1989   302.5   88–29649
ISBN 0–19–827599–4

Set by Oxford Text System
Printed and bound in
Great Britain by Biddles Ltd
Guildford and King's Lynn

TO MY PARENTS

Contents

Acknowledgements

THIS book is a revised version of my doctoral thesis. Some of the revisions were made in response to questions raised by my examiners, Professors Ronald Dworkin and Joseph Raz. I am grateful to them, and to the friends, teachers, and colleagues who have commented on parts or all of the manuscript—Alan Gilbert, Leslie Green, J. A. W. Gunn, Amy Gutmann, David Knott, Henry Laycock, Alistair Macleod, Colin Macleod, Debra Satz, Michael A. Smith, C. C. W. Taylor, and Michael Walzer.

I owe a special debt to my doctoral supervisor, G. A. Cohen. He has given unfailing support to this work. The arguments have been improved considerably by his detailed and comprehensive criticisms of a number of drafts.

My greatest debt is to my wife, Susan Donaldson. All of the ideas in this book were developed and clarified in the discussions we have had, and her advice has been invaluable.

Chapter 3 contains material originally published in 'Rawls on Teleology and Deontology', *Philosophy and Public Affairs*, vol. 17 (1988). Chapters 2 and 4 contain material from 'Liberalism and Communitarianism', *Canadian Journal of Philosophy*, vol. 18 (1988). I am grateful for permission to use these articles.

Finally, I should also like to thank the British Council and the Social Sciences and Humanities Research Council of Canada for giving me doctoral and post-doctoral fellowship support.

1

Introduction

LIBERALISM, as a political philosophy, is often viewed as being primarily concerned with the relationship between the individual and the state, and with limiting state intrusions on the liberties of citizens. But, implicitly or explicitly, liberalism also contains a broader account of the relationship between the individual and society—and, in particular, of the individual's membership in a community and a culture. These broader questions are the focus of this book. In the following chapters I shall try to present the liberal accounts of community and culture in a more explicit and systematic way than is usually done, to evaluate their strengths and weaknesses, and to link them to the more familiar liberal views on individual rights and state neutrality.

There are two main motivations for undertaking this project. One is my discomfort with recent communitarian discussions of culture and community, and with the kinds of criticisms they have brought against liberalism. The other is a discomfort with the way liberals have responded with indifference or hostility to the collective rights of minority cultures. In each case, the central debates have suffered from the absence of a systematic discussion of the liberal accounts of community and culture.

A dominant theme of communitarian writings is the insensitivity of liberalism to the virtues and importance of our membership in a community and a culture. There are claims of (at least) three sorts at stake here, all of which require close examination. The first, best exemplified by the work of Michael Sandel, is a claim about the way that liberals have misconstrued the relationship between the self and its social roles and relationships—liberals exaggerate our capacity to distance or abstract ourselves from these social relationships, and hence exaggerate our capacity for, and the value of, individual choice. The second claim, present in the work of Charles Taylor, is that even if liberals have the right account of individuals' capacity for choice, they ignore the fact that this capacity can only be developed and exercised in a certain kind of social and cultural context. Moreover, the measures needed to sustain that context are incompatible with liberal beliefs about the role of individual rights and government neutrality. The third claim, present in a number of recent communitarian, Marxist, and feminist writings, is that the liberal emphasis on justice and rights presupposes, and perpetuates, certain kinds of conflictual or instrumental relationships, relationships that would not exist in a true community.

Any one of these claims would, if sound, pose a serious challenge to liberal beliefs about culture and community. Taken together, they suggest that liberalism is *obviously* inadequate in these matters, that liberals are denying the undeniable, neglecting the most readily apparent facts of the human condition. And this neglect is exacting a high price: liberals, in a misguided attempt to promote the dignity and autonomy of the individual, have undermined the very communities and associations which alone can nurture human flourishing and freedom. Any theory which hopes to respect these facts about the way in which we are socially constructed and culturally situated will have to abandon the 'atomistic' and 'individualistic' premises and principles of liberal theories of justice.

I hope to defend liberalism against these charges. Each of the three criticisms contains important mistakes. In each case, we can distinguish stronger and weaker versions of the communitarian claim. The weak versions advance some true and important claims, but these claims are already recognized by the liberal theories they are supposed to be criticizing, and are not in conflict with liberal premises and principles. The strong versions, which are inconsistent with liberalism, are, I shall argue, mistaken, and contain the potential to justify repressive politics.

So, after presenting what I consider to be the most defensible form of liberal political theory (Chapter 2), and a review of some common confusions over the relationship between the right and the good in liberalism (Chapter 3), I shall examine each of these criticisms in turn (Chapters 4–6). Generally, I hope to show that the liberal view is sensitive to the way our individual lives and our moral deliberations are related to, and situated in, a shared social context. The individualism that underlies liberalism isn't valued at the expense of our social nature or our shared community. It is an individualism that accords with, rather than opposes, the undeniable importance to us of our social world. And, I shall argue, this way of viewing our communal relationships and our relationship to our culture is more in line with our self-understandings than the available alternatives.

The second half of the book focuses on the way that liberals have responded to situations of cultural plurality, where a single country contains more than one cultural community (this is the situation in the vast majority of the world's countries). At first glance, the topic may not seem like a very promising one for a lengthy investigation: contemporary liberals do not, in general, discuss the difference between nation-states and multinational states, and obviously do not think of cultural plurality as raising new or difficult issues for a liberal theory of equality. But that first impression is misleading, for thinking about cultural plurality raises a host of important questions about the nature of liberal individualism and equality.

At the heart of these questions is the idea of cultural membership. What does it mean for people to 'belong' to a cultural community—to what extent are individuals' interests tied to, or their very sense of identity dependent on, a particular culture? And do people have a legitimate interest in ensuring the continuation of their own culture, even if other cultures are available in the political community—is there an interest in cultural membership which requires independent recognition in a theory of justice?

These are all questions which arise most pressingly in a culturally plural country, but they go to the heart of the liberal conception of the relationship between the individual and the community. And they give rise to an important political issue— the rights of minority cultures. This issue has not received the attention it deserves in recent political theory. Liberal philosophers, like Rawls and Dworkin, have entirely neglected it. Minority rights were an important philosophical issue for political theorists before and after World War I, and remain a pressing political issue in many countries. But minority rights policy in these countries tends to be formulated within a theoretical vacuum, with damaging results for those whose rights are at stake.

While political philosophers have neglected the issue, liberal politicians and jurists in many countries have had to confront it directly. The near-universal response by liberals has been one of active hostility to minority rights. There are a variety of reasons for this, but it can only be fully understood in the light of post-war American history. The almost invariable reaction of liberal officials has been to view minority rights in terms of the segregation of American blacks. The legislated differentiation of blacks is taken to be the paradigm case of the unjust treatment of a minority, while the maintenance of a 'colour-blind' constitution is taken as the paradigm case of equal treatment. If the relationship between blacks and whites in the United States is used as the standard of comparison, then schemes which single out minority cultures for special measures will appear irremediably unjust, a disguise for creating or maintaining racial or ethnic privilege.

But the comparison with the segregation of blacks needs to be used more carefully, since it doesn't capture the issue of cultural membership which lies at the heart of most claims by national minorities. And on a closer examination of that issue, I shall argue that cultural membership gives rise to legitimate claims, and that some schemes of minority rights respond to these claims in a way that not only is consistent with the principles of liberal equality, but is indeed required by them.

The example on which I shall primarily be drawing is the case of the special status of the aboriginal peoples of North America, and in particular the recent constitutional debates concerning the aboriginal rights of the Indians and Inuit in Canada. After exploring some of the salient features of the analogy between the segregation of blacks and the special status of aboriginal peoples (Chapter 7), my defence of minority rights will involve two steps: firstly, an argument about the kind of good that cultural membership is, its relationship to individual freedom, and hence its proper status in liberal theory (Chapter 8); and secondly, an account of the ways in which members of a minority culture can be disadvantaged with respect to the good of cultural membership (Chapter 9). This inequality in circumstances faced by the members of minority cultures generates legitimate claims, claims which can be met through certain forms of minority rights. In each step of the argument,

I hope to show how the arguments that liberal theorists like Rawls and Dworkin give for equal rights and resources in a nation-state can be used to defend minority rights in multinational states.

Some liberals will feel unease at such an argument, since hostility to any form of group rights has become deeply entrenched in modern liberalism. But I hope to strengthen the argument, and allay the unease, by showing how minority rights had their place in an earlier liberal tradition (Chapter 10). Minority rights were an integral part of late nineteenth- and early twentieth-century liberalism, both in theory (e.g. Hobhouse) and in practice (e.g. in the League of Nations). The belief these liberals held about the relationship between individual freedom, cultural membership, and minority rights deserves to be recovered and reassessed by modern liberals.

I shall try to bring out the distinctively liberal character of this defence, and hence its limits, by contrasting it with recent communitarian discussions of minority rights (Chapters 11 and 12), and with the system of apartheid, which is often taken to be the logical conclusion of arguments for minority rights (Chapter 13). Finally, I shall try to suggest some of the opportunities and challenges which arise for a liberal theory of justice that makes explicit the role of cultural membership in defining the context of individual freedom (Chapter 14).

I hope to show that the relationship between liberalism and minority rights is more complex, and less antagonistic, than is normally supposed. Here, as elsewhere, the resources available within the liberal view of community and culture have been misdescribed, and underestimated. And I hope to show that an exploration of these resources enriches our understanding of the liberal theory of the self, while also illuminating some of the most persistent and controversial issues facing many liberal-democratic countries.

LIBERALISM

2

Liberalism

IT is a commonplace amongst communitarians, socialists, and feminists alike that liberalism is to be rejected for its excessive 'individualism' or 'atomism', for ignoring the manifest ways in which we are 'embedded' or 'situated' in various social roles and communal relationships. The effect of these theoretical flaws is that liberalism, in a misguided attempt to protect and promote the dignity and autonomy of the individual, has undermined the associations and communities which alone can nurture human flourishing.

My plan, in the next five chapters, is to examine the resources available to liberalism to meet these objections. The term 'liberal' has been applied to many different theories in many different fields, and identifying its defining features can be as controversial as evaluating them. So I should say a few words about the sort of liberalism I'm interested in defending. Firstly, my concern is with liberalism as a normative political philosophy, a set of moral arguments about the justification of political action and institutions. Different critics of 'the liberal tradition' are often attacking different targets—some discussions are directed at the articulated premises of specific liberal theorists, others at the habits and predispositions of liberal-minded politicians and jurists, yet others at some more nebulous world-view which underlies Western culture generally, not just our political culture. These different aspects of the liberal tradition are often in conflict with each other, as they are in any such tradition.

For example, tolerance is considered a cardinal liberal virtue, throughout the whole tradition. But I think there are very different interpretations of this virtue, at different levels of the liberal tradition. In everyday conversation, tolerance is often grounded in a belief about the subjectivity of value. People are often said to be 'liberal-minded' if they do not judge the value of other people's pursuits, if they think that there are no grounds on which to criticize individuals' choices or preferences. But, at another level, many liberal philosophers have argued for tolerance because it provides the best conditions under which people can make informed and rational judgements about the value of different pursuits. Respect for the liberty of others is predicated not on our inability to criticize preferences, but precisely on the role of freedom in securing the conditions under which we can best make such judgements. I will be considering these two interpretations of tolerance at greater length in this chapter, but this is not the only situation in which liberal philosophers have been at variance with everyday perceptions about what it is to be a liberal.

Secondly, my concern is with what liberals *can* say in response to these recent objections, not with what particular liberals actually have said in the past. Still, as a way of acknowledging intellectual debts, if nothing else, I hope to show how my arguments are related to the political morality of modern liberals from J. S. Mill through to Rawls and Dworkin. My concern is with this modern liberalism, not seventeenth-century liberalism, and I want to leave it entirely open what the relationship is between the two. It might be that the developments initiated by the 'new liberals' are really an abandonment of what was definitive of classical liberalism. G. A. Cohen, for example, says that since they reject the principle of 'self-ownership' which characterized one form of classical liberalism (e.g. in Locke), these new liberals should, for some purposes, be called 'social democrats' (G. A. Cohen 1986 p. 79). My concern is to defend their political morality, whatever the proper label.

What is their political morality? It begins with some basic claims about our interests, claims which I hope will be unobjectionable. Our essential interest is in leading a good life, in having those things that a good life contains. That may seem to be a pretty banal claim. But it has important consequences. For leading a good life is different from leading the life we *currently believe* to be good—that is, we recognize that we may be mistaken about the worth or value of what we are currently doing. We may come to see that we've been wasting our lives, pursuing trivial or shallow goals and projects that we had mistakenly considered of great importance. This is the stuff of great novels—the crisis in faith. But the assumption that this could happen to all of us, and not just to the tragic heroine, is needed to make sense of the way we deliberate about important decisions in our lives. We deliberate in these ways because we know we could make mistakes. And not just in the sense of *predicting* wrongly, or of calculating uncertainties. For we deliberate even when we know what will happen, and we may regret our decisions even when things have gone as planned.[1] The inevitability of success in a given project doesn't show that I have a good reason to pursue it (although, of course, the inevitability of failure is a good reason to avoid it). I may succeed brilliantly at becoming the best pushpin player in the world, but then come to realize that pushpin isn't as valuable as poetry, and regret that I ever embarked on that project.

Deliberation, then, doesn't only take the form of asking which course of action maximizes a particular value that is held unquestioned. We also question, and worry about, whether that value is really worth pursuing. As I said, this process of questioning the value of our projects and commitments is the stuff of great literature—we tell stories to ourselves and to others about what gives value to life, from children's fairy-tales to Dostoevskian epics. But they only make sense on the assumption that our beliefs about value could be mistaken. And the concern with which we make these judgements, at certain points in our lives, only makes sense on the assumption that our essential interest is in living a good life, not the life we currently believe to be good. We don't just make such judgements, we worry, sometimes agonize, about them—it is important to us that we not lead our lives on the basis of false beliefs (Raz 1982 pp. 100–2). Some people say that our essential interest is in living our life in accordance with the ends that we, as individuals or as a community, currently hold and share. But that seems a mistake: for our deliberations are not just predictions about how to maximize the achievement of current ends and projects. They are also judgements about the value of those ends and projects, and we recognize that our current or past judgements are fallible.

I mentioned that I hoped these claims would be unobjectionable. But Rawls himself seems to deny them. He often says that our 'highest-order interest' is in our capacity to form and revise our rational plans of life. And Marx says that our highest-order interest is in our capacity for freely creative labour. They both identify our highest-order interest with the exercise of a particular capacity. But, as Dworkin says, this puts the cart before the horse. 'Our highest-order interest is not an interest in exercising a capacity because we find that we have it . . . but rather we develop and train capacities of the sort that [they] describe because we have a certain interest'—namely, an interest in having as good a life as possible, a life that has all the things that a good life should have (Dworkin 1983*a* p. 26). The capacities that Rawls and Marx describe are crucially important— they allow us to examine and change the social conditions in which we live—but our interest in them stems from our higher-order interest in leading the life that is good. Rawls emphasizes deliberating about the value of activities, Marx emphasizes acting on these deliberations; but obviously neither makes sense without the other. In fact both are concerned that individuals not be forced to take current social roles and expectations as 'predetermined yardsticks' (Marx 1858 p. 488) of a valuable life. So I don't think that Marx or Rawls really disagrees with the sketch of our essential interests that I've presented. The claim that we have an essential interest in revising those of our current beliefs about value which are mistaken is not, I hope, an objectionable one.

But while we may be mistaken in our beliefs about value, it doesn't follow that someone else, who has reason to believe a mistake has been made, can come along and improve my life by leading it for me, in accordance with the correct account of value. On the contrary, no life goes better by being led from the outside according to values the person doesn't endorse. My life only goes better if I'm leading it from the inside, according to my beliefs about value. Praying to God may be a valuable activity, but you have to believe that it's a worthwhile thing to do—that it has some worthwhile point and purpose. You can coerce someone into going to church and making the right physical movements, but you won't make someone's life better that way. It won't work, even if the coerced person is mistaken in her belief that praying to God is a waste of time. It won't work because a life only goes better if led from the inside (and some values can only be pursued from the inside).[2]

So we have two preconditions for the fulfilment of our

essential interest in leading a life that is good. One is that we lead our life from the inside, in accordance with our beliefs about what gives value to life; the other is that we be free to question those beliefs, to examine them in the light of whatever information and examples and arguments our culture can provide. Individuals must therefore have the resources and liberties needed to live their lives in accordance with their beliefs about value, without being imprisoned or penalized for unorthodox religious or sexual practices etc. Hence the traditional liberal concern for civil and personal liberties. And individuals must have the cultural conditions conducive to acquiring an awareness of different views about the good life, and to acquiring an ability to intelligently examine and re-examine these views. Hence the equally traditional liberal concern for education, freedom of expression, freedom of the press, artistic freedom, etc. These liberties enable us to judge what is valuable in life in the only way we can judge such things—i.e. by exploring different aspects of our collective cultural heritage.

This account of our essential interest forms the basis of liberal political theory. According to Dworkin, we can restrict our attention to political theories which work from an 'abstract egalitarian plateau', according to which 'the interests of the members of the community matter, and matter equally' (Dworkin 1983a p. 24). Each theory, therefore, must give an account of what people's interests are, most comprehensively conceived, and an account of what follows from supposing that these interests matter equally. According to liberalism, since our most essential interest is in getting these beliefs right and acting on them, government treats people as equals, with equal concern and respect, by providing for each individual the liberties and resources needed to examine and act on these beliefs. This requirement forms the basis of contemporary liberal theories of justice.

That, in the barest outline, is the political morality of modern liberalism. That may not be what people think of as liberalism, for it has become part of the accepted wisdom that liberalism involves abstract individualism and scepticism about the good. The simplest response is that neither of these assumptions enter anywhere in the theories of Mill or Rawls or Dworkin, and it's remarkable how often this accepted wisdom gets passed on without the least bit of textual support. I'll look at just two examples.

The first example comes from Jaggar's discussion of liberalism. She says that

the liberal assumption [is] that human individuals are essentially solitary, with needs and interests that are separate from if not in opposition to those of other individuals. This assumption is the starting point of liberal theory. It generates what liberals take to be the fundamental questions of political philosophy: what are the circumstances in which essentially solitary individuals might agree to come together in civil society, what would justify them in doing so and how might conflict be prevented when they do? (Jaggar p. 40)

Liberals answer these fundamental questions with social contract theories which 'specify the interests individuals have in civil association and limit the legitimate powers of association to fulfilling those interests' (ibid). But, she says, this 'assumption that the essential human characteristics are . . . given independently of any particular social context' has been disproved by empirical research which shows that 'individuals' desires and interests depend on the social context in which they are reared'. This research is a 'challenge to abstract individualism, which takes human nature as a presocial system', and if we accept the research, it 'invalidates the liberal justification of the state, which presupposes that individuals have certain fixed interests' (Jaggar pp. 42–3). If we accept that individuals' goals and interests are the products of various social processes and interactions, like education and socialization, rather than being given presocially, then the liberal concern for individuals' freedom to opt in or out of these social interactions becomes misconceived. A concern for the freedom to opt in or out of these interactions only makes sense on the now disproved thesis that people's interests and goals exist prior to their life in society.

   This is a common enough view of liberalism (see Chapter 5 for similar objections). But Jaggar's criticism rests on a gratuitous inference from what liberals do in fact say. Speaking of liberal feminists, Jaggar says that

implicit in their language of sex-roles, was a strong belief in the possibility and desirability of individual freedom of choice. Sex-role language suggests the abstract individualist belief that human beings exist as actors logically, if not temporally, prior to their entry onto the social stage. When they enter this stage, individuals assume a role that seems appropriate for the time being but that may be discarded at some future date. On this conception of human nature, human beings are not necessarily constituted by society but instead are capable, in principle, of withdrawing from society to redefine their own identity. Thus, an individual is able to throw off the identity imposed by society and can consciously choose her or his own future destiny. (Jaggar p. 86)

Now there are two different claims being attributed to liberals here. One is that people can, and should be able to, question and revise their projects and commitments. The second is that individuals go outside society in order to do this revising, that they somehow can escape being subject to social influence over the formation of their character. This second claim is a completely gratuitous addition to the first claim, for which Jaggar provides no textual support. We all question, at various points in our lives, the projects we have adopted, but we don't go outside society to do this, nor do we suppose we transcend any social conditioning in so doing. Nor do we *need* to exist outside of, or prior to, society for it to be morally important that we have the ability to question our chosen ends. The absurd claims of abstract individualism add absolutely nothing to the moral argument for liberal politics.

On the contrary, if liberals did have such an absurd view of the self, then it would hinder their argument for important parts of the liberal political programme. This, indeed, is precisely how J. S. Mill criticized Bentham. Mill characterized Bentham's ideal as 'that of a collection of persons pursuing each his separate interest or pleasure . . . the prevention of whom from jostling one another more than is unavoidable' is the proper end of government action (Mill 1962 p. 70). But as Mill says, this sort of political theory is of no help to people in the formation of their own character; for it ignores the fact that social interaction modifies our character, and we need to know the way this occurs in order to question and regulate these processes in accordance with our essential interest in leading a good life. Bentham allows for the regulation of outward actions; but without an understanding of, or concern for, the formation of our character, this regulation

must be halting and imperfect . . . for how can we judge in what manner many an action will affect even the worldly interests of ourselves or others, unless we take in, as part of the question, its influence on the regulation of our, or their, affections and desires? A moralist on Bentham's principles may get as far as this, that he ought not to slay, burn or steal; but what will be his qualifications for regulating the nicer shades of human behaviour, or of laying down even the greater moralities as to those facts in human life which are liable to influence the depths of the character quite independently of any influence on worldly circumstances . . . The moralities of these questions depend essentially on considerations which Bentham never so much as took into the account, and *when he happened to be in the right it was always, and necessarily, on wrong or insufficient grounds.* (Mill 1962 p. 71, my emphasis)

Our concern is not only with promoting our current 'worldly interests', but also with the way our 'affections and desires' are formed, with the way our character develops through social interaction. Without this second concern, Mill says, one can only defend rights of person and property, not the traditional liberal concern for civic freedoms, for a public sphere of free expression, and for a liberal education.

This concern for the social formation of our interests, and its relevance to the defence of individual choice and civil liberties, is clear in Rawls as well. Part of his conception of moral personality involves the claim that people

regard themselves as having a highest-order interest in how all their other interests, including even their fundamental ones, are shaped and regulated by social institutions. They do not think of themselves as inevitably bound to, or as identical with, the pursuit of any particular complex of fundamental interests that they may have at any given time, although they want the right to advance such interests (provided they are admissible). Rather, free persons conceive of themselves as beings who can revise and alter their final ends and who give first priority to preserving their liberty in these matters. Hence, they not only have final ends that they are in principle free to pursue or to reject, but their original allegiance and continued devotion to these ends are to be formed and affirmed under conditions that are free. (Rawls 1974 p. 641)

Because our ends are 'formed and affirmed' in society, a liberal society guarantees not only rights of person and property, but also public freedoms.

Neither Mill nor Rawls defends liberal freedoms on the grounds that our interests are fixed presocially. Indeed, Mill insists that you *can't* get liberalism out of such 'abstract individualist' premises. If you treat people's interests as presocial ones, fixed in advance, to which society is only a means, then you can't get the traditional liberal concern for freedom of conscience, freedom of speech, for education and self-education, for any of the conditions which are needed for forming and revising one's character in accordance with what is really valuable.

The second example of a misinterpretation in the accepted wisdom about liberalism concerns scepticism about the good. According to Unger and Jaggar, liberals are sceptics about the rational defensibility of different conceptions of the good. Liberals treat our goals as ultimately arbitrary, incapable of rational criticism or justification. Unger claims that such a moral scepticism underlies the liberal belief in the illegitimacy of governmental interference in the way people lead their lives (Unger pp. 66–7). Jaggar too says that liberals believe

there are no rational criteria for identifying what is good for human individuals other than what those individuals say is good for them. Consequently, individuals' expressed desires are taken as identical with their 'real' needs, wants and interests. Each individual is viewed as the authority on what is good for him or her, and so expressed desires are accepted as unquestionable data, given prior to political theory. (Jaggar p. 194)

Since our ends are held to be arbitrary, the role of reason in liberal psychology is purely instrumental—reason helps us find the most efficient means for the pursuit of our given ends. Indeed, Sullivan claims that 'Instrumentalism, and its corollary, the subjective and finally arbitrary nature of value, is the deepest motif in liberal thinking' (Sullivan p. 39). Liberals are committed to freedom of choice because they 'recognize the moral impotence of reason in liberal psychology' (Unger p. 52), and deny that there are rational grounds for judging the value of different ends (Jaggar p. 174; Sullivan pp. 19–20, 38–40).

Now, as I mentioned at the beginning of the chapter, this

'subjectivist' view of liberalism has resonances in some of the everyday usages of terms such as 'liberal-minded'. But Jaggar and Unger are primarily concerned with locating this view in the dominant philosophical arguments for liberty, and that is a complete misinterpretation. The liberal position in fact rests precisely on the denial of the position attributed to it by Jaggar and Unger. Consider Mill's argument for liberty in both *On Liberty* and *Utilitarianism*. Some projects *are* more worthy than others, and liberty is needed precisely to find out what is valuable in life—to question, re-examine, and revise our beliefs about value (Mill 1972 pp. 114–31; Hobhouse 1964 pp. 59–60; Rosenblum pp. 134–5). This is one of the main reasons why we desire liberty—we hope to learn about the good—and Mill says that our desire should be respected because it is not a vain hope. Liberty is important not because we already know our good prior to social interaction, or because we can't know about our good, but precisely so that we can come to know our good, so that we can 'track bestness', in Nozick's phrase. If we couldn't learn about the good, a crucial premiss in Mill's argument for liberty would collapse. The same is true of Rawls[3] (1971 pp. 206–10), Dworkin (1983*a* pp. 24–30), Nozick (1981 pp. 410–11, 436–40, 498–504), Lomasky (pp. 231–54), and Raz (1986 pp. 291–305). They all argue for a right of moral independence not because our goals in life are fixed, nor because they are arbitrary, but precisely because our goals can be wrong, and because we can revise and improve them.

This sort of liberalism *couldn't* be based on the received wisdom. If abstract individualism or moral scepticism were the fundamental premiss, there'd be no reason to let people revise their beliefs about value, no reason to suppose that people are being made worse off by being denied the social conditions necessary to freely and rationally question their commitments.

Liberalism is not just concerned with the freedom to act on our present desires. That, of course, is not an insignificant freedom. If lives have to be led from the inside, then that freedom alone will justify the traditional liberal prohibitions on coercive paternalism. No one can lead my life for me. But amongst the people who are leading their lives from the inside are people who have been brainwashed into accepting certain ends as their own, and who are discouraged from trying any other ways of life, through the systematic control of socialization, of the press, and of artistic expression. And this is unacceptable to the liberal.[4]

It wouldn't have been unacceptable to Bentham. All he cared about was the freedom to pursue existing ends, which were taken as pre-theoretically given.[5] But for Mill the conditions under which people acquired their ends were important: it mattered whether their education and cultural socialization opened up or closed off the possibility of revising their ends. He believed that this was important because people not only want to act on their choices, they also want to get those choices right. The freedom to examine our ends is worthless if we can't *pursue* our ends, from the inside, but it is not equivalent to the freedom to lead our lives from the inside. It is a distinct concern which is only intelligible on the assumption that our ends are neither arbitrary nor fixed. That is, it is only an intelligible concern if liberals reject the assumptions commonly attributed to them.

Notes

1. See Dworkin 1983*a* pp. 26–7. My argument here, and elsewhere in this and the following chapter, is indebted to Dworkin's writings in ways that are substantial but sometimes difficult to specify. I'd like to acknowledge that debt without implying that he would agree with any of the particular claims being made.

2. This has been the favourite example of liberals from Locke to Rawls. There may be a difficulty in generalizing it, since there is an epistemic requirement to praying that does not always exist. Shklar argues that this 'morality of motives' is insufficient to sustain the full range of liberal freedoms (Shklar pp. 47–50). But it seems to me to be plausible for a broad range of human excellences, from reading poetry and writing novels to friendship, conversation, and social ritual. Value rarely comes in a form that can be injected into a person. It can only come through their beliefs about, and hence their perceptions of, value. See the discussion by Hobhouse (1964 pp. 65–6), Lomasky (pp. 253–4), and Raz (1986 pp. 291–2), who claims this is true of all our non-biological needs or interests.

3. As Buchanan points out, the importance of the revisability of our ends has played a changing role in the way that Rawls describes moral personality, rationality, and our highest-order interests (Buchanan pp. 138–44). In his more recent articles, Rawls has retreated somewhat from the account of the relationship between

liberty and the revisability of our ends that I'm attributing to him. He now says that we accept this account for the purposes of determining our public rights and responsibilities, without necessarily accepting it as an accurate portrayal of our private self-understandings. I discuss these changes, and some questions raised by them, in Chapter 4.

4. As Claude Lefort notes, the right to freedom of speech is essentially 'the right of man, one of his most precious rights, to go beyond himself and relate to others, by speech, writing and thought. In other words, it makes clear that man could not be legitimately confined to the limits of his private wants, when he has the right to public speech and thought' (quoted in Lukes p. 64). Indeed, as Rosenblum notes, the liberal defence of free speech says that the form of speech activity which deserves protection does so 'precisely because [it] is not considered to be a self-regarding activity'. If speech is not 'sufficiently communicative', if it is 'pure self-expression', then it may 'be excluded from First Amendment protection' (Rosenblum p. 62; cf. Hobhouse 1964 pp. 59–67). The importance which liberals have always attached to such rights makes no sense on the interpretation of liberalism offered by Jaggar and Unger.

5. As Bentham said of the children in his envisioned educational programme, who would not be encouraged to develop the capacity for independent choice, 'Call them soldiers, call them monks, call them machines, so long as they be happy ones, I shall not care' (quoted in Gutmann 1982 p. 266 n. 14).

3

The Right and the Good

IT has become a commonplace that most contemporary liberal
theory is 'deontological'; that is, it gives priority to the right
over the good. This is in contrast to its utilitarian predecessors,
which were 'teleological'; that is, they gave priority to the good
over the right. Like so much else in the current vocabulary of
political discourse, this distinction was made prominent by
Rawls's *A Theory of Justice*. Rawls, of course, argues that it is a
great virtue of his theory that it gives priority to the right over
the good. Critics, however, have argued that this is liberalism's
foundational flaw. The criticism is found not just amongst the
old-style utilitarians Rawls was chiefly arguing against, but
also amongst socialists and conservatives, communitarians and
feminists. The desire to give priority to the right over the good
is said to reflect unattractive or even incoherent assumptions
about human interests and human community. The question of
whether the right or the good is prior is now seen as a central
dividing-point for contemporary political theories.

I hope to challenge this view. I don't believe there is a real
issue about which of the right and the good is prior. Critics and
defenders of liberalism share the view that principles of right
are a spelling-out of the requirement that we give equal
consideration to each person's good. This is not a new suggestion.
Ronald Dworkin has argued that Rawls and his critics all share
the same 'egalitarian plateau': they agree that 'the interests of
the members of the community matter, and matter equally'
(Dworkin 1983a p. 24; cf. Dworkin 1977 ch. 6; 1986 pp. 296–
301; 1987 pp. 7–8). In this chapter, I shall support Dworkin's
contention by showing that the contrast Rawls claims to find
between deontological and teleological theories is based on a
serious confusion of two distinct issues, neither of which concerns
the priority of the right or the good. One issue concerns the
definition of people's essential interests. The other issue concerns

the *principles of distribution* which follow from supposing that each person's interests matter equally. Once these issues are distinguished, the debate Rawls claims to find over the priority of the right or the good disappears. I think that this confusion in Rawls is partly responsible for encouraging the kinds of misunderstandings I discussed in the last chapter. Critics may still believe, of course, that liberalism relies on an unattractive view of human interests and community. But we can get a clearer picture of what really separates critics and defenders of contemporary liberalism when we drop the misleading language of the priority of the right or the good.

The first issue that Rawls sees as separating deontological and teleological theories is the issue of distribution. Not all political theories show the same concern with the equitableness of the distribution of the good. Utilitarianism is prepared to contemplate endlessly sacrificing one person's good in order to maximize the overall good. But other theories put constraints on the sacrifices that can be asked of one person in order to promote the good of others—even if the effect of these constraints is to prevent maximization of the overall good. Political theories which take rights seriously will disallow trade-offs which deny some individuals their basic human needs or rights, even if those trade-offs would maximize the good overall.

Rawls claims that utilitarianism fails to provide an adequate account of what it is to treat people as equals. To endlessly sacrifice one person's good because it maximizes happiness overall is to treat that person as a means, not as an end in herself. A proper account of people's moral equality would put constraints on the maximization of utility, constraints like the two principles of justice that Rawls affirms. Treating people as equals requires greater concern for the equality of distribution of the good being pursued than is present in utilitarianism.

What does this have to do with the priority of the right or the good? Rawls claims that the reason utilitarianism allows the good of some to be endlessly sacrificed for the benefit of others is that it gives priority to the good over the right. That is, it has an independent account of the good (happiness), and the right is defined as the maximization of that good. People's rightful claims are entirely dependent on what best promotes the good, and hence the maximization of the good cannot be said to violate people's rightful claims. Rawls calls such theories, which give priority to the good over the right, 'teleological'.

What makes his own theory preferable is that it gives priority to the right over the good. That is, it has an account of people's rightful claims that is not entirely derivative from the maximization of the good. Principles of right are prior to, and constrain, the pursuit of the good. Each person's good matters equally in a way that constrains the pursuit of the good; each person's good should have a standing that puts limits on the sacrifices that can rightfully be asked in the name of the overall good (Rawls 1971 p. 31). Rawls calls such theories, which give priority to the right over the good, 'deontological'.

According to Rawls, then, the debate over distribution is essentially a debate over whether we should or shouldn't define the right as the maximization of the good. But is this an accurate characterization of the debate? Utilitarians do, of course, believe that the right act maximizes happiness, under some description of that good. And that requirement does have potentially abhorrent consequences. But do utilitarians believe that it is right *because* it maximizes happiness? Do they hold that the maximization of the good *defines* the right, as teleological theories are said to do?

I don't think so. But let us first see why Rawls believes they do. Rawls says that utilitarianism is teleological (that is, defines the right as the maximization of the good) because it generalizes from what is rational in the one-person case to what is rational in many-person cases. Since it is rational for me to sacrifice my present happiness to increase my later happiness if it will maximize my happiness overall, it is rational for society to sacrifice my current happiness to increase someone else's happiness if it maximizes social welfare overall. For utilitarians, utility-maximizing acts are right *because* they are maximizing. It's because they are maximizing that they are rational.

Rawls objects to this generalization from the one-person to the many-person case. He believes that it ignores the separateness of persons (Rawls 1971 p. 27). Although it is right and proper that I sacrifice my present happiness for my later happiness if doing so will increase my overall happiness, it is wrong to demand that I sacrifice my present happiness to increase *someone else's* happiness. In the first case, the trade-off occurs *within* one person's life, and the later happiness compensates for my current sacrifice. In the second case, the trade-off occurs across lives, and I am not compensated for my sacrifice by the fact that someone else benefits. My good has simply been sacrificed, and I have been used as a meåns to someone else's happiness. Trade-offs that make sense *within* a life are wrong and unfair *across* lives. Utilitarians obscure this point by ignoring the fact that separate people are involved. They treat society as though it were an individual, as a single organism with its own interests, so that trade-offs between one person and another appear as legitimate trade-offs within the social organism. Scott Gordon echoes this interpretation of utilitarianism when he says that utilitarians adopt the view 'that "society" is an organic entity and contend that *its* utility is the proper objective of social policy'. This view, he says, 'permits flirtation with the grossest form of anti-individualistic social philosophy' (S. Gordon p. 40; cf. Nozick 1974 pp. 31–2).

This, then, is Rawls's major example of a teleological theory which gives priority to the good over the right. His rejection of the priority of the good, *in this context*, is just the corollary of his affirmation of the separateness of persons: promoting the well-being of the social organism can't be the goal from which people's rightful claims are derived, since there is no social organism. Since individuals are distinct, they are ends in themselves, not merely agents or representatives of the well-being of the social organism.

This is why Rawls believes that utilitarianism is teleological, and why he believes that we should reject it in favour of a deontological doctrine. But, as I mentioned earlier, I think Rawls misdescribes utilitarianism, and hence misdescribes the debate over distribution. The most natural and compelling form of utilitarianism is not teleological, and doesn't involve any anti-individualistic generalization from the individual to society. Rawls's characterization of utilitarianism represents, at best, just one interpretation of that doctrine, and misses an important element in many justifications of it, an element that is not teleological at all (Dworkin 1981 pp. 244–6; 1985 p. 274). In fact, Rawls conflates these different elements in utilitarianism, and thereby creates an artificially teleological formulation of utilitarianism. Rawls has legitimate objections to utilitarianism even when presented as a non-teleological doctrine, but those objections are best understood in terms other than the priority of the right or the good.

On one interpretation, utilitarianism is a procedure for aggregating individual interests and desires, a procedure for making social choices, specifying which trade-offs are acceptable. It's a moral theory which purports to treat people as equals, with equal concern and respect. It does so by counting everyone for one, and no one for more than one. This justification of utilitarianism doesn't falsely generalize from what is rational in the one-person case, and hence doesn't fail to respect the distinctness of persons in that sense. (There are other aspects to the question of the distinctness of persons, which will be discussed later in the chapter.) Individuals are of course distinct, with distinct and potentially conflicting preferences. The problem, on this interpretation of utilitarianism, is how to treat distinct people fairly. The standard solution is to give each person's interests equal weight. Each person's life matters equally, from the moral point of view, and hence each person's interests deserve equal consideration. To give some people's interests more weight is to treat others as less than equals. Now this idea of treating people with equal consideration is very imprecise, and it needs to be spelled out if it is to be a real guide for our actions. One obvious, and perhaps initially appealing, way of doing so is to give equal weight to each preference of each person, regardless of the content of the preference or the material situation of the person. That is, we count everyone for one, no one for more than one.

If we decide how to act on this basis, then utility is maximized. But maximization of utility is not the direct goal. Maximization occurs, but as a by-product of a decision procedure that is intended to aggregate people's preferences fairly. Not all utilitarians desire maximization because they treat rational social choice on the model of rational individual choice. On the contrary, it is the concern with equal consideration that underlies the arguments of Bentham and Sidgwick (Bentham pp. xlvi-xlvii; Sidgwick pp. 382–8), and is explicitly affirmed by recent utilitarians like Harsanyi, Griffin, and Singer (Harsanyi pp. 13–14, 19–20, 45–6, 65–7; Griffin 1984 pp. 150–8; Griffin 1986 pp. 167–70, 208–15,

239–42, 295–301; Singer pp. 12–13, 19–23; cf. Haslett pp. 40–3, 220–2). And while this is not his preferred method, Hare too claims that one could defend utilitarianism by reference to a foundational premiss of equal consideration (Hare pp. 106–12). Hare, in fact, along with Harsanyi, finds it difficult to imagine how equal consideration for people could mean anything else (Hare p. 107; Harsanyi p. 35).

I think that utilitarianism, viewed as a theory of equal consideration, is subject to decisive objections. Although from the moral point of view people's interests matter equally, it doesn't follow that the best way of spelling out that idea is to give each preference of each person the same weight, without regard for the content of the preferences or the material welfare of the person. There may be better ways of spelling out the idea (*pace* Hare, who thinks that utilitarianism is logically derivable from it). Rawls's 'original position' is one potential way, as is Dworkin's equality of resources scheme. Rawls believes that his conception of justice is a better way of spelling out the idea that from the moral point of view the interests of each person matter equally, and I agree. Nevertheless utilitarianism is *one* way of spelling out that idea, and it is as 'deontological' as any other, since it views each person as having a distinct and equal standing which must be respected. If people's preferences have not been counted equally, then we have treated them unjustly, as less than equals. Their legitimate claims to equal consideration haven't been met. But, of course, for utilitarians to say that (as many do) they must recognize, rather than deny, that individuals are distinct persons with their own rightful claims. That is, in Rawls's classification, a position that affirms the priority of the right over the good.

Rawls's theory is more egalitarian, at one level, since it puts greater constraints on the differences that can legitimately arise in people's life situations. A theory that favours equal welfare would put even more constraints on such differences. But all these theories are deontological in that they spell out an ideal of fairness or equality for distinct individuals. This, I think, is the best way to characterize the debate between Rawls and utilitarians over distribution: does the difference principle or the utility principle give a better account of what it is to give equal consideration to each person's interests? It is not an issue of deontology versus teleology, since neither side holds that the good is prior to the right in Rawls's sense: neither side defines the right as the maximization of the good.

There is, however, another interpretation of utilitarianism, one that seems more in line with Rawls's characterization of the debate. According to this second interpretation, maximizing the good is primary, and we count individuals equally only because that maximizes value. Our primary duty isn't to treat people as equals, but to bring about valuable states of affairs. As Williams puts it, people are just viewed as *locations* of utilities, or as causal levers for the 'utility network': 'the basic bearer of value for Utilitarianism is the *state of affairs* . . . As a Utilitarian agent, I am just the representative of the satisfaction system who happens to be near certain causal levers at a certain time' (Williams 1981 p. 4). Utilitarianism, on this view, is primarily concerned not with *persons*, but with *states of affairs*.

This second interpretation is *not* merely a matter of emphasizing a different facet of the same theoretical structure. Its distinctness can be made clear in a number of different ways. One difference emerges in utilitarian discussions of population policy, like those of Glover and Parfit. They ask whether we morally ought to double the population, even if it means reducing each person's welfare by almost half (since that will still increase overall utility). They think that a policy of doubling the population is a genuine, if somewhat repugnant, conclusion of utilitarianism. But this conclusion need not be reached if utilitarianism is taken as a theory of treating people as equals. Non-existent people don't have claims—we don't have a moral duty *to them* to bring them into the world. As Broome says, 'one cannot owe anyone a duty to bring her into existence, because failing in such a duty would not be failing anyone' (Broome pp. 7–8; cf. Glover pp. 139–40). So what *is* the duty here, on the second interpretation? The duty is to maximize value, to bring about valuable states of affairs, even if the effect is to make all existing persons worse off than they otherwise would have been.

To put the difference another way: if I fail to maximize utility, by failing to consider the interests of some group of people, then I can be criticized, on both interpretations, for failing to live up to my moral duty as a utilitarian. But on the second interpretation, those whose interests have been neglected have no special grievance against me. I don't have to apologize to them more than to anyone else for my failure to maximize the good, because, on this second interpretation of utilitarianism, my duty isn't to respond fairly to people, each of whom has a right to equal consideration, but to bring about the most valuable state of affairs. The harm done to the neglected persons may be the same in both cases, but there is a difference between being harmed by a wrong act and being wronged. The latter requires that people have legitimate claims to be respected, not just interests that may or may not be advanced.

The distinctness of this second interpretation of utilitarianism is also apparent in Nagel's discussion. He demands that we add a deontological constraint of equal treatment onto utilitarianism, which he thinks is concerned with selecting the *impersonally best outcome* (Nagel p. 127). He thinks we must qualify our moral obligation to maximize the good with the moral obligation to treat people as equals. Obviously his demand only makes sense with reference to this second interpretation of utilitarianism, according to which the fundamental duty is not to aggregate individual interests or preferences fairly, but to bring about the most value in the world. For on the first interpretation, utilitarianism is *already* a principle of moral equality; if it fails as such a principle of equal consideration, then the whole theory fails, for there was no independent commitment to the idea of maximizing utility.

This second interpretation stands the first interpretation on its head. The first defines the right in terms of treating people as equals, which leads to the utilitarian counting procedure, which happens to maximize the good. The second defines the right in terms of maximizing the good, which leads to the utilitarian aggregation procedure, which as a mere consequence treats people's interests equally. As we've seen, this inversion produces important theoretical and practical consequences.

So there is an account of utilitarianism which fits Rawls's characterization. But this interpretation is even less defensible than the first. For it's entirely unclear why maximizing utility, as our direct goal, should be considered a *moral* duty. Whom is it a duty *to*? Morality, in our everyday view at least, is a matter of interpersonal obligations—the obligations we owe to each other. But to whom do we owe the duty of maximizing utility?

Surely not to the impersonal ideal spectator who often figures in such a theory, for he doesn't exist. Nor to the maximally valuable state of affairs itself, for states of affairs don't have moral claims. Perhaps we have a duty to those people who would benefit from the maximization of utility. But if that duty is, as seems most plausible, the duty to treat people with equal consideration, then we are back to the first interpretation of utilitarianism as a way of treating people as equals. Maximizing utility is now just a by-product, not the ultimate ground of the theory. And then we needn't double the population, since we have no obligation to conceive those who would have constituted the increased population.

If we none the less accept that maximizing utility is itself the goal, then it is best seen as a non-moral ideal, akin in some ways to an aesthetic ideal. The appropriateness of this characterization can be seen by looking at the other example Rawls gives of a teleological theorist, namely, Nietzsche (Rawls 1971 p. 25). The good which Nietzsche's theory seeks to maximize is available only to the special few. Others are useful only in so far as they promote the good of the special few. In utilitarianism, the value being maximized is more mundane, something that every individual is capable of partaking in or contributing to (although the maximizing policy may well result in the sacrifice of the good of many). This means that in utilitarian teleology, unlike Nietzsche's, every person's preferences must be given some weight. But in neither case is the fundamental principle to treat people as equals. Rather it is to maximize the good. And in both cases, it's difficult to see how this can be viewed as a *moral* principle. The goal isn't to respect *people*, for whom certain things are needed or wanted, but rather to respect the *good*, to which certain people may or may not be useful contributors. If people have become the means for the maximization of the good, morality has dropped out of the picture, and a non-moral ideal is at work. A Nietzschean society may be aesthetically better, more beautiful, but it is not morally better. (I think Nietzsche himself would not have rejected this analysis. His theory was 'beyond good and evil'.[1]) And if utilitarianism is interpreted in this teleological way, it too has ceased to be a moral theory.[2] This form of utilitarianism does not merit serious consideration as a political morality.

So while there is an interpretation of utilitarianism that fits Rawls's account, it is not the most interesting or compelling form of that doctrine. In fact, Rawls's own discussion reveals that the equal consideration interpretation has to be the more fundamental one, because the 'separateness of persons' criticism makes sense only if it is directed at a deontological, not a teleological, theory. A genuinely teleological utilitarianism *couldn't* be vulnerable to the charge of ignoring the separateness of persons, in the sense that Rawls intends that charge.

That claim requires some explanation. There is a sense in which all teleological theories ignore the distinctness of persons, since the distinctness of persons has no moral significance for such theories. Because the basic bearer of value is the state of affairs, not people, the assessment of value abstracts completely from persons. The assessment is impersonal, indifferent to where the value is located. This is as true of Nietzsche as of the second interpretation of utilitarianism. Both select the option which affords the most of the desired good, regardless of how individuals do. Both theories ignore the distinctness of persons, in this sense.

But that is not the sense that Rawls uses when he claims that utilitarianism ignores the distinctness of persons. For the sense that Rawls has in mind does not apply to Nietzsche. According to Rawls, the reason that utilitarianism in particular ignores the distinctness of persons is that it generalizes from rational decision-making in the one-person case to rational decision-making in the many-person case. In other words, according to Rawls, utilitarians wanted to construct a social choice procedure to rationally aggregate diverse preference-rankings, and they did so by simply generalizing from what is rational in the case of individual decision-making, a generalization that ignores the distinctness of persons. But this is to bring elements of the first interpretation of utilitarianism into what was meant to be an account of the second interpretation. For it is the first, not the second, interpretation that is concerned to provide a social choice procedure for the rational aggregation of each person's preferences and interests. A teleological utilitarianism isn't a decision procedure for aggregating people's preferences or interests, any more than Nietzsche's theory is. The concern of teleological theories is maximizing the good, which may (as in utilitarianism) or may not (as in Nietzsche) come about through respecting each person's interests. Giving equal consideration to people, on this second quasi-aesthetic interpretation of utilitarianism, is a possible by-product of maximizing the good, but it is not the fundamental goal. And whatever its many weaknesses, this sort of utilitarianism doesn't ignore the distinctness of persons in the sense that Rawls intends, since it isn't grounded in any generalization from the one-person to the many-person case. It doesn't conflate the distinct claims of individuals, because in this version of the theory there are no individual claims to conflate.

The claim that utilitarianism ignores the distinctness of persons has become a commonplace, and has been used to explain all the sins of that theory (e.g. Mackie pp. 86–7). But Rawls himself meant it in a much more limited way. His charge centred on his belief that utilitarians defined the morally right act for society in terms of maximization of the good, *and* that they did so because the prudentially right act maximizes the good for the individual. That is, for Rawls utilitarians are moral teleologists because they generalize from the fact that individuals are prudential teleologists. That generalization, which Nietzsche did not make, is the crucial element in Rawls's claim that utilitarianism ignores the distinctness of persons.

But this seems to confuse the two strains of utilitarianism. The first interpretation does seek to define a fair social decision procedure, but, as we've seen, it does not do so by defining the right in terms of maximizing the good, and it does not deny that individuals have distinct claims to equal consideration. The second interpretation does define the right in terms of maximizing the good, but it does not seek to define a social decision procedure by generalization from the case of individual decision-making. The goal is the most valuable state of affairs, impersonally viewed, not the putatively rational aggregation of individual interests.

Rawls seems to have taken the social-choice element of the first interpretation, combined it with the teleological element of the second, and connected them by saying that social-choice utilitarians become teleological utilitarians by generalizing from the case of rational individual choice (a generalization that ignores the distinctness of persons). But that is an artificial reconstruction of utilitarianism. I don't mean to suggest that no utilitarians have confused the two interpretations. Indeed, Rawls cites some

(Rawls 1971 p. 188 n.).[3] But such a hybrid form is incoherent, and any coherent form, even if implausible on other grounds, cannot be said to fail to respect the separateness of persons in the way that Rawls claims.

So the 'separateness of persons' charge makes sense *as a criticism* only if we view 'teleological' utilitarians as having a prior and more fundamental commitment to the principle of equal consideration for persons. Rawls says that utilitarianism is teleological, but his own account conflicts with that claim. If we look closely at his account, the entire interest of utilitarianism as a moral theory (and the interest of the separateness of persons as a criticism of it) depends on viewing utilitarianism as other than a teleological theory. So if we want to treat utilitarianism as a political morality, and not merely a quasi-aesthetic doctrine, then we have to interpret it in the first sense, as a theory of equal consideration.

Viewing utilitarianism as a theory of equal consideration does not remove the dispute over distribution. Rawls has objections to utilitarianism even when interpreted in this first way. The utilitarian principle of distribution does recognize the distinctness of persons, but it still fails to match our intuitions about the difference between trade-offs within a life and trade-offs across lives. We might want to describe this flaw as a failure to recognize the full moral significance of the distinctness of persons. But Rawls thinks that the distinctness of persons *explains* rather than merely *describes* the failure of utilitarianism (Rawls 1971 pp. 26–7). Rawls believes that utilitarians ignore the full moral significance of the distinctness of persons because they ignore the distinctness of persons. That is a mistake. The argument between utilitarianism and Rawls's conception of justice is not over whether people have distinct claims, but over how we give equal weight to each person's claims in formulating principles of justice.

But if this is the argument then it has nothing to do with the priority of the right or the good. In this more compelling form, utilitarianism is a 'deontological' theory, in that the right is not *defined* as the maximization of the good (though it does enjoin maximization of the good for existing individuals), and each individual *is* considered to have a distinct claim to equal consideration. We have to examine utilitarianism as one theory of equality amongst the others, working from the same 'egalitarian plateau', claiming to occupy the same ground that the theories of Rawls and Dworkin occupy. It is a flawed conception of equality, for reasons that Rawls alludes to. But we don't get anywhere towards identifying those flaws by saying that it has an inadequate account of the priority of the right or the good, and the separateness of persons criticism needs to be detached from that misleading context.

The second issue underlying Rawls's contrast of the priority of the right and the priority of the good concerns not the fair distribution of the good, but the proper *definition* of the good. Rawls contrasts perfectionist theories and his own non-perfectionist theory. A perfectionist theory includes a particular view, or range of views, about what dispositions and attributes define human perfection, and it views the development of these as our essential interest. Perfectionists demand that resources should be distributed so as to encourage such development. What one gets depends on how much one needs to pursue, or how much one contributes to, this preferred view of the good life. People are not, therefore, free to choose their own conceptions of the good life, at least not without being penalized or discriminated against by society. People make mistakes about the good life, and the state has the responsibility to teach its citizens about a virtuous life. It abandons that responsibility to its citizens if it funds, or perhaps even if it tolerates, life-plans that embody misconceived views about human excellence.

For Rawls, on the other hand, our essential interests are harmed by attempts to enforce a particular view of the good life on people. He favours the distribution of primary goods, based on a 'thin theory of the good', which can be used to advance many different ways of life. He does this because, as we've seen, he believes that the capacity to examine and revise our plans and projects is important in pursuing our essential interest in leading a good life. Rawls's conception of the person involves the claim that people

regard themselves as having a highest-order interest in how all their other interests, including even their fundamental ones, are shaped and regulated by social institutions. They do not think of themselves as inevitably bound to, or identical with, the pursuit of any particular complex of fundamental interests that they may have at any given time, although they want the right to advance such interests (provided they are admissible). Rather, free persons conceive of themselves as beings who can revise and alter their final ends and who give first priority to preserving their liberty in these matters. (Rawls 1974 p. 641)

The reason why we are not bound to any complex of interests, and why we give first priority to the freedom to revise our ends, is that we may come to question the value of our current ends. Hence our essential interest in living a life that is in fact good requires an ability to revise our ends, and to pursue those revised ends. Perfectionism inhibits this process. If we only have access to resources that are useful for one plan of life, then we shall be unable to act on our beliefs about value should we come to believe that that one preferred conception of the good life is misguided. (Or, at any rate, we shall be unable to do so without suffering some penalization or discrimination in social benefits.) Since lives have to be led from the inside, someone's essential interest in leading a life that is in fact good is not advanced when society penalizes, or discriminates against, the projects that she, on reflection, believes are most valuable for her. Distributing resources according to a 'thin theory of the good', or what Dworkin calls 'resources in the widest sense', best enables people to act on and examine their beliefs about value, and that is the most appropriate way to promote people's essential interest in leading a life that is in fact good.

What does this issue have to do with the priority of the right or the good? Rawls describes the difference between perfectionist and non-perfectionist theories as a conflict over the relative priority of the right and the good. But, as with the issue of distribution, this is altogether unhelpful. Each side has its view about our essential interests and the conditions that are appropriate for their promotion, and hence about how governments should act, given that each person's interests matter equally. Perfectionists identify that essential interest with some particular conception of the good life, and devise a scheme of distribution that promotes that conception, giving equal weight to each person's interest in it. Rawls, on the other hand, emphasizes that since our beliefs about value are fallible, the freedom to revise our projects, as well as the freedom to pursue existing projects, is important for leading a life that is in fact good. Therefore, equal liberty and the distribution of primary goods are the most appropriate conditions for promoting our essential interest, giving equal weight to each person's interests. Rawls doesn't favour the distribution of primary goods out of a concern for the right rather than the good. He just has a different account of what our good is, of what promotes our essential interests, and hence of what it means to give equal weight to each person's interests. Rawls and a perfectionist do not disagree over the relative priority of the right and the good. They just disagree over how best to define and promote people's good.

Not only is it misleading of Rawls to express the debate over perfectionism as a debate over the priority of the right or the good, but it conflicts with his use of these terms in his discussion of the distribution of the good. In discussing the definition of the good, Rawls says that there should be a priority of the right over the good, in the sense that our legitimate entitlements are not tied to the promotion of any particular view of the good life. But this anti-perfectionist sense of the priority of the right over the good has nothing to do with the preceding teleology-versus-deontology sense of that priority. Rawls connects them by saying that perfectionism is a form of teleological theory (Rawls 1971 p. 25)—i.e. perfectionists always wish to maximize their preferred good. But that is a mistake. Some perfectionists may well believe that the good they prefer ought to be maximized (as a by-product of equal consideration for individuals, or for its own sake). But there are also perfectionists (such as Marx, on some interpretations) who would find it unfair to sacrifice one person's pursuit of excellence just because doing so would increase the overall amount of excellence in society. Such perfectionists think that distribution should be determined by its effect on the promotion of that particular good, but they think that the promotion of that excellence in each person is equally important, and that the maximizing procedure fails as an account of what it means to treat each person as equally important.

Conversely, while some anti-perfectionists (such as Rawls) believe that there are constraints on the way we maximize social welfare, others (such as liberal utilitarians) deny that there are any such constraints. After all, Rawls's argument against perfectionism is not affected by whether the parties in the original position choose a utilitarian or a maximin distributive principle. Just as being a perfectionist doesn't commit you to accepting a 'teleological' theory in which there are no constraints on the way that we maximize the desired good, so being an anti-perfectionist does not commit you to accepting 'de-ontological' constraints on the promotion of social welfare.

Two very different concerns, then, underlie Rawls's contrast of the relative priority of the right and the good. The first is that each person's good should be given equal weight, which utilitarianism fails to do adequately. The second is that people's legitimate entitlements shouldn't be tied to any particular conception of the good life. These are real (and controversial) issues, to which Rawls makes important contributions. Unfortunately, neither issue concerns the priority of the right or the good. Moreover, the two issues are not related in the way Rawls claims, as a single unitary contrast. There is not a single choice we have to make here, but a range of possible positions which connect the two issues in various ways.

The results of Rawls's mischaracterizations are apparent in Sandel's discussion of the priority of the right over the good. Sandel accepts Rawls's mistaken claim that there is a single contrast underlying these two issues, and then is faced with the question of what constitutes that single contrast. The answer he gives is that believers in the priority of the right try to formulate principles of justice without any idea of what constitutes human welfare, without any view about our interests. That is why deontologists reject utilitarianism, *and* why they are anti-perfectionist. That is an understandable answer to an absurd question, a question which Rawls unfortunately encourages. There is no single contrast here, but rather two distinct contrasts. And *both* of the positions that Rawls takes on these two issues conflict with the single position that Sandel attributes to him.[4] In neither of the senses in which Rawls says the right is prior to the good is he claiming that we can derive principles of justice without any idea of people's essential interests.

Another result of Rawls's mischaracterization has been to play down an important feature of his principles of justice, namely, that they aim at equality of resources, not equality of welfare.

Rawls presents this as an aspect, or consequence, of affirming the priority of the right over the good (Rawls 1971 p. 31). But this obscures the distinctive argument that Rawls presents for his position here. When explaining his resource-based theory, Rawls says that people's legitimate claims are limited to a fair share of society's resources, determined in advance of their choices about projects and goals. People's decisions about their life-style must be adjusted to what they can rightfully expect. If people come to have projects and aims that require more than their fair share of resources, then there is no claim of justice to the satisfaction of those preferences. Hence a resource-based theory views people as

capable of adjusting their aims and ambitions in the light of what they can reasonably expect and of restricting their claims in matters of justice to certain kinds of things. They recognize that the weight of their claims is not given by the strength or intensity of their wants and desires, even when these are rational. (Rawls 1980 p. 545)

Rawls holds people responsible 'for conforming their conceptions of the good to what the principles of justice require' (Rawls 1971 p. 31). He contrasts this with welfarist theories, in which 'the satisfaction of any desire has some value in itself' (Rawls 1971 p. 30), even if the desires have not been formed in the light of what can rightfully be expected. Hence in a welfare-based scheme, one person's share is always potentially vulnerable to the formation of sufficiently strong desires on the part of others for that share. In a welfare-based scheme, just distributions are adjusted to the pre-existing pattern of ambitions and desires. On a resource-based scheme, people's ambitions and aims are adjusted in the light of the pre-existing pattern of distributive justice.

Rawls calls this an issue about the priority of the right or the good. But the issue here is in fact one of *responsibility*. Some Marxists, for example, claim that since our aims and ambitions are materially determined, people should not be held responsible for the costs of their choices. If some people's aims and ambitions are expensive, and require more than an equal share of resources, they should get more than others, so as to ensure equality of welfare. This subsidy of expensive tastes is not unfair, since otherwise someone is penalized for having the desires which they cannot help having, and which are ultimately not their responsibility (Roemer 1985 pp. 178–9; 1986 pp. 107, 109). Since we are not really in control of the formation of our aims and ambitions, equality cannot be a matter of adjusting our aims to the equal claims of others, as a resource-based theory demands. Equality can only enter into the way that people's existing aims are equally satisfied, as the welfare-based theory demands.

To a liberal like Rawls or Dworkin, on the other hand, people are capable of adjusting their aims, and so are responsible for the formation of their aims and ambitions. Hence subsidizing expensive tastes is simply unfair: it requires that some people pay for the costs of other people's choices. Part of what it means to show equal respect for others is precisely that I take into account the cost of my choice to others, in terms of the resources they have to forgo. Demanding or expecting others to forgo their share of resources in order to subsidize my choices is unfair, and selfish (Dworkin 1981 p. 289). This fairness argument supposes that I am capable of adjusting my ambitions to the rightful claims of others, and responsible in that sense. A resource-based theory incorporates this basic intuition about fairness where attribution of responsibility is appropriate, whereas a welfare-based theory depends for its intuitive fairness on denying responsibility.

So this third issue is essentially one of responsibility.[5] I do not want to defend the liberal view of responsibility here, although I shall in fact employ it in Chapters 9 and 11. Attributions of responsibility are often thought to raise the question of free will, which is certainly beyond the scope of this work. I shall just note that Rawls is aware of the important limits on the extent to which responsibility can be fairly attributed. Clearly no one is responsible for the unequal costs associated with differential natural endowments. Moreover, even those things which are a matter of choice must still be chosen under conditions of material justice and equal liberty. Responsibility for *choices* can only be fairly applied where there are mechanisms to ensure that no one is disadvantaged by their social and natural *circumstances* (Dworkin 1981 p. 303). There are difficulties concerning the proper specification of these limits, but liberals believe that there are, and ought to be, conditions under which individuals accept responsibility for their aims and ambitions.

Rawls says that welfarists and resourcists disagree over the relative priority of the right and the good. But, once again, this is hopelessly confusing. Both sides to the dispute accept that the right involves equal consideration for each person's good. They just disagree over whether equal consideration for others requires holding an individual responsible for adjusting her aims and ambitions in the light of the rightful claims of others.

Moreover, this third use of the priority of the right over the good is not entailed by either of the other two uses of that concept. It is not a simple derivation from the other two issues, but a distinctive feature of a liberal theory of equality, which requires separate attention. One could accept Rawls's anti-utilitarian and anti-perfectionist arguments (i.e. one could affirm the priority of the right in the first two senses), but deny that we should invoke such a principle of responsibility. That is, one could believe, with Rawls, that people should be free to use their resources in accordance with their own conceptions of the good, and that the maximization procedure fails as an account of equal consideration. But one could also claim, against Rawls, that equal consideration requires some people to subsidize the expensive tastes of others, should that subsidy tend to equalize welfare. Many of the Marxists who deny responsibility are likely to fall into this category.

Conversely, one could reject Rawls's anti-perfectionism while accepting his principle of responsibility. That is, one could believe, against Rawls, that distributive principles should be designed so as to promote a particular way of life, giving equal consideration to each person's interest in that good. But one could still agree with Rawls that equal consideration requires that people adjust their pursuit of that good in the light of the equal claims of others.

So the issue of responsibility is conceptually distinct from the other two issues about the priority of the right or the good. It is another important issue which gets obscured by Rawls's description of the contrast between the priority of the right and the priority of the good. These distinct debates raise important issues, issues on which we might disagree with Rawls. We might disagree with his anti-perfectionist account of our essential interests (I shall examine some criticisms of it in Chapter 4), or his anti-utilitarian, pro-responsibility account of what follows from supposing that these interests matter equally (Chapters 5 and 6). But none of these are debates about the priority of the right or the good. Nor, I think, *can* there be a serious debate about that question within political morality. Rawls treats the right as a spelling-out of the requirement that each person's good be given equal consideration. How can one reject that understanding of the right and the good?

There are two ways to reject it, but neither is plausible. Some theories, like Nazism, deny that each person matters equally. But such theories do not merit serious consideration. In any event, it would be misleading to say that they have a different account of the *priority* of the right and the good. For they reject equality, not because they care more about the good than about the right, but because they care more about some people's good than about others'. Conversely, when we affirm equality, it is not because we care more about the right than about the good, but because we think each person's good matters equally.

Some theories, as we've seen, do give priority to the good over the right. In such theories, people's rightful claims are dependent upon what produces the best *state of affairs*, which is the real bearer of value. Nietzsche is an example. He had a vision of a world that was full of his preferred good. But he refused to present it as the vision one gets from the moral point of view, and I think he was right to do so. To define the right as the maximization of the good, and to view people simply as means to the promotion of that good, is not to present an unusual interpretation of the moral point of view. It is to abandon the moral point of view entirely, to take up a non-moral ideal instead. But if we refuse to abandon the moral point of view in developing our political theory, then our disagreements with Rawls, however great they may be, will *not* be disagreements over the priority of the right and the good.

Notes

1. In the first essay of *On the Genealogy of Morals*, Nietzsche compares the moral contrast 'good–evil' with the non-moral contrast 'good–bad'. He ends the essay by saying that he hopes it is sufficiently clear that his 'dangerous watchword . . . *Beyond Good and Evil*, does *not*, at any rate, mean "Beyond Good and Bad" '.
   Notwithstanding Nietzsche's self-description, there may well be

contexts in which it is appropriate and useful to call his theory, or other non-humanistic theories, 'moral'. What matters is not that we use a different label, but that we recognize the very important differences between the two kinds of theories I've outlined. There is a crucial difference between theories which are grounded in equal consideration and theories which are grounded in maximizing the good. The former reflect, I believe, some very deep beliefs we have about the nature and value of morality. The latter conflict with these beliefs. Indeed the latter are closer, in some respects, to our everyday view of an aesthetic theory than to our everyday view of a moral theory. These differences are important to recognize, even if the intuitive classifications I'm using are not useful for all philosophical purposes. (See Harsanyi pp. 35–6, where he proposes for similar reasons that Nietzsche be viewed as having a non-moral 'quasi-aesthetic' theory. Harsanyi goes on to say that this narrowing of the term 'moral' to theories of impartial concern should be used 'at least in systematic moral philosophy, while preferably retaining the wider usage in the social sciences and in the history of moral philosophy' (p. 36).)

2. J. S. Mill sometimes implies that his principle of utility is non-moral (e.g. Mill 1987 ch. 10 sects. 6–7). But this seems to reflect his terminological equation of the 'moral' with those desirable activities which are best elicited by *sanctions*. Hence the principle of utility is prior to, and determines the scope of, the 'moral'. But Mill does not say that utility-maximizing actions are desirable (whether or not they are elicited by sanctions) because the right is defined in terms of maximizing the good, rather than in terms of equal consideration of people's interests. It is, of course, a matter of considerable controversy why exactly Mill did think utility-maximizing acts were desirable. (Sidgwick interprets Mill's argument as relying on an unstated premiss of equal consideration (Sidgwick pp. 387–8).)

3. I think that much of the attraction of utilitarianism comes from tacit or unconscious mixing of the two justifications. The intuitive unfairness of utilitarianism would quickly disqualify it as an adequate account of equal consideration, were it not that many people take its maximizing feature as an additional, independent reason to endorse it. Utilitarians tacitly appeal to the good-maximization standard to deflect intuitive objections to their account of equal consideration. Indeed, it may seem to be a unique advantage of utilitarianism that it can mix these two justifications. Unfortunately, it is simply incoherent to employ both standards in the same theory. One cannot say that morality is fundamentally

about maximizing the good, while also saying that it is fundamentally about respecting the claim of individuals to equal consideration. Some utilitarians seem to accept both positions, without recognizing that the one conflicts with the other. If utilitarians were held to one or other of the standards, then I suspect their theory would lose much of its attractiveness.

Once we recognize how distinct these two strands are, Nagel's proposal to combine an inherently maximizing theory with a theory of equal consideration doesn't sound very promising. It is unclear why Nagel is attracted to the maximizing view. He thinks that maximization is related to moral impartiality, apparently through the idea of epistemological impersonality, but the connection is obscure. Scheffler is similarly unclear on why morality ought to be inherently maximizing (Scheffler 1982 pp. 123–4).

4. The belief that there is a single contrast here also leads Sandel to misinterpret the terminology that Rawls is using. Sandel accepts Rawls's contrast between teleology and deontology, and his self-description as a deontologist (Sandel 1982 p. 3). Rawls uses this contrast in his discussion of the first issue, i.e. about how to aggregate people's interests. But Sandel thinks that this contrast underlies both issues. Thus he uses 'deontologist' as Rawls uses 'non-perfectionist', to designate someone for whom 'first principles are derived in a way that does not presuppose any final human purposes or ends, nor any determinate conception of the human good' (ibid.). A 'teleologist', conversely, becomes a perfectionist. Sandel sets up the second debate using the same terminology which Rawls uses in setting up the first debate.

This wouldn't be a problem if Sandel were aware of the shift in meaning. But he seems quite unaware of it, and this leads him to mislocate the debate between Rawls and Mill. For on this new characterization of teleology (as perfectionism), one would expect that Mill would no longer be a teleologist. On Sandel's usage, Rawls and Mill should both be considered deontologists, since they both oppose perfectionism. What Rawls means by Mill's 'teleology' (and what he objected to) is his *interest-maximization*, not his account of our interests. Sandel misses this because he accepts Rawls's false claim that there is only one debate here. Ian Shapiro makes a similar mistake in his discussion of Rawls and utilitarianism (Shapiro 1986 pp. 213–17, 255–7).

Apart from this terminological confusion, Sandel cites no evidence that Mill and Rawls disagree about the nature of our essential interests, or about their importance in determining principles of justice. Nor does he explain why Rawls endorses the essential elements of Mill's argument for a principle of liberty (Rawls 1971 pp. 209–10), an endorsement that seems incompatible with Sandel's interpretation. Mill and Rawls both say that the good is the satisfaction of informed desire, and both give similar accounts of the value of liberty in promoting that good. Where they differ is on how to promote fairly these essential interests. That difference, while important, does not support Sandel's claim that Rawls differs from Mill in attempting to derive principles of justice without any account of people's interests.

5. It is not solely an issue of responsibility, however. There are some Marxists who reject resource-based theories without denying responsibility, since they are concerned with the possible consequences of a resource-based theory for political equality and self-respect. But they are worried by the intuitive unfairness of welfarism in the case of expensive tastes (Nielsen 1985 pp. 298–301; Elster pp. 231–2). Conversely, there are some liberals who would reject welfarism, even if people lacked responsibility, since there may be no single standard of welfare that every person can accept as defining their well-being. But they are worried by the intuitive unfairness of resourcism in the case of unchosen expensive tastes (Dworkin 1981 part 1). So even those who invoke other considerations to help decide the welfare-versus-resource issue still concede that the respective claims to fairness rest on differing attributions of responsibility.

COMMUNITY

4

Communitarianism and the Self

THE preceding two chapters presented an interpretation of liberalism, and defended it against some common mis-interpretations. I now want to look at recent communitarian discussions of the view I've just presented. In this chapter, I shall look at criticisms of the liberal account of the self and its interests. In the next chapter, I shall look at criticisms of the way that liberals seek to promote those interests politically.

In the writings of communitarians, one can identify a number of arguments that attempt to explain why the liberal view of the self is inadequate. The five arguments I shall discuss can be summarized this way: the liberal view of the self (1) is empty; (2) violates our self-perceptions; (3) ignores our embeddedness in communal practices; (4) ignores the necessity for social confirmation of our individual judgements; and (5) pretends to have an impossible universality or objectivity.

Firstly, the emptiness argument. Being free to question all the given limits of our social situation, to question all our social roles, is self-defeating, Taylor says, because

complete freedom would be a void in which nothing would be worth doing, nothing would deserve to count for anything. The self which has arrived at freedom by setting aside all external obstacles and impingements is characterless, and hence without defined purpose, however much this is hidden by such seemingly positive terms as 'rationality' or 'creativity'. (C. Taylor 1979 p. 157)

True freedom must be 'situated', Taylor argues. The desire to subordinate *all* the presuppositions of our social situation to our rational self-determination is finally empty, because the demand to be freely self-determining is indeterminate: it 'cannot specify any content to our action outside of a situation which sets goals for us, which thus imparts a shape to rationality and provides an inspiration for creativity' (ibid.). We must accept the goal that our situation 'sets for us'—if we don't, then the quest for self-determination leads to Nietzschean nihilism, the rejection of all communal and cultural values as ultimately arbitrary: 'one after the other, the authoritative horizons of life, Christian and humanist, are cast off as shackles on the will. Only the will to power remains' (C. Taylor 1979 p. 159). MacIntyre too sees Nietzsche's nihilism as the logical consequence of this absolute self-determination view of free individuality, this view which denies that communal values are 'authoritative horizons' (MacIntyre ch. 9).

But this argument misconstrues the role that freedom plays in liberalism. According to Taylor, liberals teach us that the freedom to form and revise our projects is inherently valuable, something to be pursued *for its own sake*, an instruction that Taylor rightly rejects as empty. Instead, he says, there has to be some project that is worth pursuing, some task that is worth fulfilling. But the concern for freedom within liberalism doesn't take the place of these projects and tasks. On the contrary, the liberal defence of freedom rests precisely on the importance of those tasks and projects. Liberals aren't saying that we should have the freedom to select our projects for its own sake, because freedom is the most valuable thing in the world. Rather, it is our projects and tasks that are the most important things in our lives, and it is because they are so important that we should be free to revise and reject them, should we come to believe that they are not fulfilling or worthwhile. Our projects are the most important things in our lives, but since our lives have to be led from the inside, in accordance with our beliefs about value, we should have the freedom to form, revise, and act on our plans of life. Freedom of choice, then, isn't pursued for its own sake, but as a precondition for pursuing those projects and practices that *are* valued for their own sake.

Of course, some liberals have believed that the exercise of such freedom of choice is also inherently valuable, something to be valued for its own sake. It is the exercise of an inherently satisfying capacity. Larmore attributes this position to Kant (Larmore pp. 77–9), and Isaiah Berlin attributes it to Mill (Berlin p. 192). And indeed Mill does suggest that we should exercise our capacity for free choice because it is our 'distinctive endowment' (Mill 1972 p. 116). But Mill immediately goes on to say that exercising that capacity is important not for its own sake, but because without it we gain 'no practice in discerning or desiring what is best' (ibid.). Ladenson cites a number of other passages which suggest that Mill is best understood as having 'attached the greatest importance not to the mere exercise (or existence) of the capacity for choice, but to certain states of affairs and conditions which he believed are the consequences, under favourable conditions, of its free exercise' (Ladenson p. 171).

Claiming that freedom of choice is intrinsically valuable may seem like a direct and effective way of defending a broad range of liberal freedoms. But the implications of that claim conflict with the way we understand the value in our lives in at least two important ways.

(*a*) Saying that freedom of choice is intrinsically valuable suggests that the more we exercise our capacity for choice, the more free we are, and hence the more valuable our lives are. But that is false, and indeed perverse. It quickly leads to the quasi-existentialist view that we should wake up each morning and decide anew what sort of a person we should be. This is perverse because a valuable life, for most of us, will be a life filled with commitments and relationships. These, as Bernard Williams has argued at length, give our lives depth and character. And what makes them *commitments* is precisely that they aren't the sort of thing that we question every day. We don't suppose that someone who has made twenty marriage choices is in any way leading a more valuable life than someone who has no reason to question or revise their original choice. Only someone incapable of attachment or commitment would think that the best thing about her goals was that they were readily replaced. A life with more autonomous choices is not even *ceteris paribus* better than a life with fewer such choices.

(*b*) Saying that freedom of choice is intrinsically valuable suggests that the value we attempt to achieve in our actions is freedom, not the value internal to the activity itself. This suggestion is endorsed by Carol Gould. She accepts that action is directed at achieving the purposes internal to a given project, and that 'one is *apparently* acting for the sake of these purposes themselves posited as external aims' (Gould p. 118). But she goes on to say that truly free activity has freedom itself as the ultimate end: 'Thus freedom is not only the activity that creates value but is that for the sake of which all these other values are pursued and therefore that with respect to which they become valuable' (ibid.).

But this is false. Firstly, as Taylor points out, telling people to act freely doesn't tell them what particular free activities are worth doing. But even if it provided determinate guidance, it would still present a false view of our motivations. If I am writing a book, for example, my motivation isn't to be free, but to say something that is worth saying. Indeed, if I didn't really want to say anything, except in so far as it is a way of being free, then my writing wouldn't be fulfilling. What and how I write would become the result of arbitrary, indifferent, and ultimately unsatisfying choices. If writing is to be intrinsically valuable, I have to believe that writing is worth doing for its own sake. If we are to understand the interest and value people see in their projects we have to look to the ends which are internal to them. I do not pursue my writing for the sake of my freedom. On the contrary, I pursue my writing for its own sake, because there are things which are worth saying. Freedom is valuable because it allows me to say them.

The best liberal defence of individual freedoms is not necessarily the most direct one. The best defence is the one which best accords with the way that people on reflection understand the value of their own lives. And if we look at the value of freedom in this way, then it seems that freedom of choice, while central to a valuable life, is not the value which is centrally pursued in such a life.[1]

So no one disagrees that tasks and projects have to be our primary concern and goal—that is just a red herring in the debate. The real debate is not over whether we need such tasks, but over how we acquire them and judge their worth. Taylor seems to believe that we can acquire these tasks only by treating communal values and practices as 'authoritative horizons' which 'set goals for us' (C. Taylor 1979 pp. 157–9). Liberals, on the other hand, insist that we have an ability to detach ourselves from any particular communal practice. No particular task is set for us by society, and no particular cultural practice has authority that is beyond individual judgement and possible rejection. We can and should acquire our tasks through freely made personal judgements about the cultural structure, the matrix of understandings and alternatives passed down to us by previous generations, which offers us possibilities we can either affirm or reject. Nothing is 'set for us', nothing is authoritative before our judgement of its value.

Of course in making that judgement, we must take something as a 'given'; someone who is nothing but a free rational being or a freely creative being would have no reason to choose one way of life over another (Sandel 1982 pp. 161–5; C. Taylor 1979 p. 157; Phillips pp. 153–61; Crowley pp. 204–5). But liberals believe that what we put in the given in order to make meaningful judgements can not only be different between individuals but also can change within one individual's life. If at one time we make choices about what's valuable given our commitment to a certain religious life, we could later come to question that commitment, and ask what's valuable given our commitment to our family. The question then is not whether we must take something as given in making judgements about the value of our activity. Rather, the question is whether an individual can question and possibly substitute what is in the given, or whether the given has to be set for us by the community's values. Taylor's emptiness argument fails to show anything in support of the claim that the given *must* be the authoritative horizons of communal values. There is nothing empty or self-defeating in the idea that these communal values should be subject to individual evaluation and possible rejection.

One can weaken the communitarian objection by arguing that even if we *can* get our purposes this way, unset by the community, we none the less *should* treat communal ends as authoritative. We should do this because the liberal view relies on a false account of the self. The liberal view, as we've seen, is that the self is, in an important sense, prior to its ends, since we reserve the right to question and reappraise even our most deeply held convictions about the nature of the good life. Sandel, however, argues that the self is not prior to, but rather constituted by, its ends—we can't distinguish 'me' from 'my ends'. Our 'selves are at least partly constituted by ends that we do not choose, but rather *discover* by virtue of our being embedded in some shared social context. Since we have these constitutive ends, our lives go better not by having the conditions needed to select and revise our projects, but by having the conditions needed to come to an awareness of these shared constitutive ends.

Sandel has two different arguments for this claim, which are worth separating; I've called them the self-perception argument and the embedded-self argument. The self-perception argument goes like this: the Rawlsian view of the 'unencumbered self' doesn't correspond with our 'deepest self-understanding' in the sense of our deepest *self-perception*. According to this objection, if the self is prior to its ends, then we should, when introspecting, be able to see through our particular ends to an unencumbered self. But as Nozick and Sandel note, we don't perceive our selves as being essentially unencumbered: Rawls's conception of the self as 'given prior to its ends, a pure subject of agency and possession, ultimately thin', is 'radically at odds with our more familiar notion of ourselves as being "thick with particular traits"' (Sandel 1982 pp. 94, 100, quoting Nozick). If we were Rawlsian selves, 'to identify any characteristics as *my* aims, ambitions, desires, and so on, is always to imply some subject 'me' standing behind them, at a certain distance' (Sandel 1984*a* p. 86). There would have to be this thing, a self, which has some shape, albeit an ultimately thin shape, standing at some distance behind our ends. To accept Rawls, I would have to see myself as this propertyless thing, a disembodied, rather ghostly, object in space, or as Rorty puts it, as a kind of 'substrate' lying 'behind' my ends (Rorty p. 217). In contrast, Sandel says that our deepest self-perceptions always include some motivations, and this shows that some ends are constitutive of the self.

But the question of perception here is at best misleading. What is central to the liberal view is not that we can *perceive* a self prior to its ends, but that we understand our selves to be prior to our ends, *in the sense that no end or goal is exempt from possible re-examination*. For re-examination to be meaningfully conducted I must be able to envisage my self encumbered with different motivations than I now have, in order that I have some reason to choose one over another as more valuable for me. My self is, in this sense, perceived prior to its ends, i.e. I can always envisage my self without its *present* ends. But this doesn't require that I can ever perceive a self totally unencumbered by any ends—the process of ethical reasoning is always one of comparing one 'encumbered' potential self with another 'encumbered' potential self. There must always be some ends given with the self when we engage in such reasoning, but it doesn't follow that any *particular* ends must always be taken as given with the self. As I said before, it seems that what is given with the self can, and sometimes does, change over the course of a lifetime. Thus there is a further claim that Sandel must establish: he must show not only that we can't perceive a totally unencumbered self, but that we can't perceive our self without some *specific* end or motivation. This requires a different argument, which I call the embedded-self argument.

This third argument contrasts the communitarian view of practical reasoning as self-discovery with the liberal view of practical reasoning as judgement. For Sandel, as for MacIntyre, the relevant question is not 'What should I be, what sort of life should I lead?' but 'Who am I?'. The self 'comes by' its ends not 'by choice' but 'by discovery', not 'by choosing that which is already given (this would be unintelligible) but by reflecting on itself and inquiring into its constituent nature, discerning its laws and imperatives, and acknowledging its purposes as its own' (Sandel 1982 p. 58). For example, he criticizes Rawls's account of community, because 'while Rawls allows that the good of community can be internal to the extent of engaging the aims and values of the self, it cannot be so thoroughgoing as to reach beyond the motivations to the subject of motivations' (Sandel 1982 p. 149). On a more adequate account, Sandel claims, communal aims and values are not just affirmed by the members of the community, but define their identity. The shared pursuit of a communal goal is 'not a relationship they choose (as in a voluntary association) but an attachment they discover, not merely an attribute but a constituent of their identity' (Sandel 1982 p. 150). The good for such members is found by a process of self-discovery—by achieving awareness of, and acknowledging the claims of, the various attachments they 'find'.

But surely it is Sandel here who is violating our deepest self-understandings. For we don't think that this self-discovery replaces or forecloses judgements about how to lead our life. We don't consider ourselves trapped by our present attachments, incapable of judging the worth of the goals we have inherited (or ourselves chosen earlier). We do indeed find ourselves in various roles and relationships, but we may not like what we find. The roles and relationships may be oppressive or demeaning, they 'may be experienced as suffocating rather than embracing' (Rosenblum p. 156). No matter how deeply implicated we find ourselves in a social practice or tradition, we feel capable of questioning whether the practice is a valuable one—a questioning which isn't meaningful on Sandel's account (how can it *not* be valuable for me since the good for me just *is* coming to a greater self-awareness of these attachments and practices I find myself in?). The idea that practical reasoning is completed by this process of self-discovery (rather than by judgements of the value of the attachments we discover) seems pretty facile.[2]

Communitarians often say that they wish to replace Kantian *Moralitat* with Hegelian *Sittlichkeit*. But it's not clear that Hegel would have accepted Sandel's suggestion. For Sandel seems to want a *Sittlichkeit* without a *Moralitat*. But Hegel thought that *Sittlichkeit* without *Moralitat* only worked if individuals asked neither 'What sort of life should I lead?' nor 'Who am I?'—i.e. it only worked if people were essentially unquestioning about the leading of their lives (Hegel p. 317 n. 64). Hegel realized what his followers have missed, that if the self engages in reflection at all, it takes the form of 'determining itself in accordance with universal and rational laws', for that is the only way in which we can reflectively understand ourselves (Hegel pp. 33–6, 103–4, 314 n. 49). Hegel's concern wasn't to *replace Moralitat* with *Sittlichkeit*, but rather to give *Moralitat* some content, which he thought was lacking in Kant's formulation of it. The point wasn't to get people to stop asking 'What sort of life should I lead?', but rather to give them genuine reasons for answering that question in a way that harmonized with the existing traditions and practices of the community. He thought that in Kant's theory, any answer to the question 'What sort of life should I lead?' would be unsupportable, resulting in the destruction of existing practices without the construction of anything new. But his solution wasn't to change the question; rather it was to show that existing practices provided rationally supportable answers to it. We have good reasons for endorsing the values which are internal to those practices, but it is still a matter of endorsing or rejecting those values, rather than taking them as given. A *Sittlichkeit* rooted in, and content with, its own particularity is impossible for us, since there is no conscious route back from reflectiveness (Williams 1985 pp. 163–4). This may have been what Marx had in mind when he said that we can't return to the conditions of ancient Greece because of their *naïveté* (Marx 1858 p. 111). We've lost the naïve faith necessary to consciously let the community set goals for us (Hegel p. 317 n. 64).

In places, Sandel admits that practical reasoning isn't just a matter of self-discovery. He says that the boundaries of the self, although constituted by its ends, are none the less flexible and can be redrawn, incorporating new ends and excluding others. In his words, 'the subject is empowered to participate in the constitution of its identity'; on his account 'the bounds of the self [are] open . . . and the identity of the subject [is] the product rather than the premise of its agency' (Sandel 1982 p. 152). The subject can, after all, make choices about which of the 'possible purposes and ends all impinging indiscriminately on its identity' it will pursue, and which it will not (ibid.). The self, constituted by its ends, can be 'reconstituted', as it were—and so self-discovery isn't enough. But at this point it's not clear whether the whole distinction between the two views doesn't collapse entirely.

There are apparent differences here: Sandel claims that the self is constituted by its ends, and that the boundaries of the self are fluid, whereas Rawls says that the self is prior to its ends, and its boundaries are fixed antecedently. But these two differences hide a more fundamental identity: both accept that the *person* is prior to her ends. They disagree over where, within the person, to draw the boundaries of the 'self'; but this question, if it is indeed a meaningful question, is one for the philosophy of mind, with no direct relevance to political philosophy. For so long as Sandel admits that the *person* can re-examine her ends— even the ends constitutive of her 'self'—then he's failed to justify communitarian politics. He's failed to show why individuals shouldn't be given the conditions appropriate to that re-examining, as an indispensable part of leading the best possible life. And amongst those conditions should be the liberal

guarantees of personal independence necessary to make that judgement freely. So long as a person is prior to her ends, then Sandel
has failed to show why the liberal view of the self is wrong, and
hence why liberal political morality is wrong. Sandel trades on
an ambiguity in the view of the person that he uses in defending
communitarian politics. The strong claim (that self-discovery
replaces judgement) is implausible, and the weak claim (which
allows that a self constituted by its ends can none the less be
reconstituted), while attractive, fails to distinguish his position
from the liberal view.[3]

MacIntyre's argument in *After Virtue* suffers from a similar
ambiguity. Sometimes he argues for an 'embedded self' view:
'we all approach our own circumstances as bearers of a particular
social identity. I am someone's son or daughter, someone else's
cousin or uncle; I am a citizen of this or that city, a member of
this or that guild or profession; I belong to this clan, that tribe,
this nation. Hence what is good for me has to be the good for
one who inhabits these roles' (MacIntyre pp. 204–5). Since
my good is determined by the roles I occupy, 'the key question
for men is not about their own authorship; I can only answer
the question "What am I to do?" if I can answer the prior
question "Of what story or stories do I find myself a part?" '
(MacIntyre p. 201). MacIntyre's argument against liberal individualism is similar to Sandel's. It rests on the claim that 'the
story of my life is always embedded in the story of those
communities from which I derive my identity' (MacIntyre
p. 205), so that deciding how I should live is just a matter of
coming to an awareness of the various 'histories' or 'stories' I'm
'embedded' in, and interpreting the goods specified in them. He
contrasts this with the liberal individualist standpoint, according
to which 'I am what I myself choose to be. I can always, if I
wish to, put in question what are taken to be the merely
contingent social features of my existence' (ibid.).

MacIntyre rejects the possibility that our membership in these
communal roles can be put in question. But like Sandel, he also
says that the fact that the self has to find its moral identity in
these communal traditions, practices, and roles 'does not entail
that the self has to accept the moral *limitations* of the particularity
of those forms of community' (ibid.). He says that the good life
is one spent in search of the good life, and this search apparently

can involve rejection of any of the particular roles I find myself in: 'rebellion against my identity is always one possible mode of expressing it' (ibid.). But if we can, after all, put in question the 'rightful expectations and obligations' of the roles and statuses we inhabit, if we can reject the value of the goods internal to a given practice, then it's not clear how MacIntyre's view is any different from the liberal individualist one he claims to reject. MacIntyre's defence of communitarian politics requires that my good be the good of someone in the social roles I currently occupy, but that's implausible, since we believe that we can question the value of such roles and statuses. When MacIntyre allows for such questioning, his argument against the liberal view collapses.[4]

MacIntyre and Sandel both say that liberalism ignores the way we are embedded or situated in our social relationships and roles. Communitarians emphasize that as reflective, 'self-interpreting beings' (Sandel 1984*a* p. 91) we can interpret the *meaning* of these constitutive attachments. But the question is whether we can reject them entirely should we come to view them as inherently trivial or even degrading. On one interpretation of communitarianism, we can't, or at any rate, we shouldn't. On this view, we neither choose nor reject these attachments, rather we find ourselves in them; our ends and goals come not by choice, but by self-discovery. A Christian housewife in a monogamous, heterosexual marriage can interpret what it means to be a Christian, or a housewife—she can interpret the meaning of these shared religious, economic, and sexual practices. But she can't stand back and decide that she doesn't want to be a Christian at all, or a housewife. I can interpret the meaning of the social roles and practices I find myself in, but I can't reject the roles themselves, or the goals internal to them, as worthless. Since these attachments and ends are constitutive of me, as a person, they have to be taken as given in deciding what to do with my life; the question of the good in my life can only be a question of how best to interpret their meaning. It makes no sense to say that they have no value for me, since there is no 'me' standing behind them, no self prior to these constitutive attachments.

It's unclear which, if any, communitarians hold this view consistently. It isn't a plausible position, since we can and do make sense of questions not just about the meaning of the roles and attachments we find ourselves in, but also about their value. Perhaps communitarians don't mean to deny that; perhaps their idea of our embeddedness isn't incompatible with our rejecting the attachments we find ourselves in. But then the advertised contrast with the liberal view is a deception, for the sense in which communitarians view us as embedded in communal roles incorporates the sense in which liberals view us as independent of them, and the sense in which communitarians view practical reasoning as a process of self-discovery incorporates the sense in which liberals view practical reasoning as a process of judgement and choice. The differences would be merely semantic.[5]

Given the weakness of the communitarian critique, the recent changes in Rawls's views are somewhat surprising. Faced with challenges such as those of MacIntyre and Sandel, Rawls has retreated somewhat from the account of the relationship between liberty and revisability that I have been attributing to him. He now says that we accept this account for the purposes of determining our public rights and responsibilities, without necessarily accepting it as an accurate portrayal of our private self-understandings (Rawls 1980 p. 454; 1985). But he gives no real examples of people whose self-understandings are bound to a particular complex of ends, nor does he give a compelling explanation of why, if there are such people, they would agree to give up their private self-understandings in the public sphere. Why, for example, would people with constitutive attachments be interested in Rawls's scheme of primary goods? Note that under the new interpretation Rawls gives of that scheme, primary goods are not to be viewed as essentially all-purpose means for the pursuit of people's final ends (as they were in Rawls 1982 pp. 165–7). Rather they are viewed as means for 'developing and exercising the two moral powers', including the 'capacity to form, revise and rationally to pursue a conception of the good' (1980 p. 525). But if people (in their deepest self-understandings) view themselves as finding a conception of the good which is set for them, rather than forming and revising their own conception, then what is their interest in agreeing to a public distribution intended to promote the development of a capacity they do not use or value?

I have similar questions about Larmore's recent attempt to

defend liberalism as a *modus vivendi* amongst people who are assumed to have constitutive attachments. He argues that the revisability view of the relationship between the self and its ends is controversial, and indeed unattractive. But that is at least in part because he takes the revisability view to be claiming that we can revise our ends 'with equanimity' (Larmore p. 96), and that revision would leave us 'untouched by the experience' (Crowley p. 206). He says this is the view in Kant (Larmore pp. 77–8), and in the Kant-inspired sections of Rawls (Larmore pp. 120–1). But Rawls's claim that we are not identified with any particular complex of ends, and that we are concerned to preserve our liberty in revising our ends, does not commit him to the view that we can revise our ends with equanimity, and indeed Rawls never endorses that view (see e.g. Rawls 1982 pp. 180–1). As I mentioned earlier in this chapter, and in Chapter 2, revising our ends is often a matter of a crisis in deeply felt beliefs and commitments.

Larmore (along with the more recent Rawls) hopes to defend liberalism as essentially a principle of tolerance between members of different and sometimes conflicting beliefs and faiths, even if these people are bound to their various ends. The defence of personal liberties is founded not on the revisability of each person's ends, but on the plurality of different people's ends. So long as different people have differing ends, then mutual respect requires that the government ought not to favour one group over another. Hence the members of each group should be free to practice their shared life-style without government penalty, as provided by the liberal principle of freedom of association. But can plurality do all the work that Larmore and Rawls require of it? Can it defend the traditional liberal principle of freedom of association? I don't think so. As Rosenblum notes, there are two aspects to the liberal conception of freedom of association. Liberalism 'encourages both access to groups in which one has a "voice" and the possibility of "exit" from them as equally important parts of freedom of association'. Liberals have historically insisted 'that the public sphere should limit not only the political power of religious groups but also the power private groups exercise over their own members' (Rosenblum p. 60). Tolerance defends the first of these components of freedom of association, but not the second.

Let us assume that the members of different groups are bound to their present ends. Representatives of each group meet and attempt to come to an 'overlapping consensus' (Rawls), or a '*modus vivendi*' (Larmore). Each group would agree to let the members of the other groups engage in their practices. But why would either group demand that individuals be free to convert from one group to another, or that individuals have state protection of their rights to dissent and to non-discrimination within their current group (rights which the American Supreme Court has often recognized and protected; see Rosenblum p. 64). The freedom of individuals to dissent and convert isn't needed to ensure tolerance between groups.

And even if the legal freedom of individuals to question and revise their ends is adequately defended, why would the members of either group be concerned with the cultural conditions in which these revisions are made? Why would freedom of expression and other cultural freedoms be given the importance they are in liberal societies? There might be some cosmopolitan people who wish to learn about other life-styles, but there might be other people who would prefer that certain kinds of information not be publicly available. There seems no reason why the freedom to publicly debate the merits of competing conceptions of the good life would have any special role in a society of people with competing but constitutive attachments. Plurality, divorced from revisability, may require that current adherents of different faiths be allowed to practise their creed. But I don't yet see why it would require, or even support, either the right to publicly defend your creed to non-believers, or the right to hear what the members of other groups can say in their defence. The importance liberal societies attach to freedom of expression is only explicable, I think, if the assumption of plurality is accompanied by the view of revisability I have been defending. (We don't need revisability to defend *political* expression, since that is a requirement of a functioning democracy, but then again we don't need plurality either. The question is how to defend the full liberal conception of freedom of expression.) Plurality and mutual respect do not seem sufficient to defend the full range of liberal freedoms, and Rawls has not yet explained how he would defend these broader aspects of freedom of association to people with constitutive ends.

In any event, as I mentioned above, I don't believe that either Rawls or Larmore (or Sandel and MacIntyre) have given us genuine examples of people in our society who reject the revisability view of our ends. If the account I'm attributing to Rawls is not his current view, I think it is none the less his most compelling account, and his retreat from it in the face of communitarian criticisms is unmotivated.

The fourth argument I want to consider is the social confirmation argument. This argument does not deny that we understand ourselves as sovereign moral agents (i.e. as having the capacity, and indeed the task, of judging the value of the purposes we could pursue), but claims that we need considerable social confirmation of that judgement in order to have any confidence in it. Government should encourage certain communal values, and discourage non-conforming values, in order to try to ensure that our judgements are confirmed by society. Liberalism, at least of the sort envisaged by Rawls and Dworkin, 'provides little concrete moral reassurance or guidance on worthy courses of action' (R. Smith p. 170). This point is suggested by Williams and Unger, but I think it is a powerful motivation for many communitarians, and it has certainly been a worry for many liberals.[6] The point isn't that unconstrained individual choice is logically empty (as in Taylor) or that it presupposes a mistaken self-understanding (as in Sandel). Rather the concern is that this vaunting of 'free individuality' will result not in the confident affirmation and pursuit of worthy courses of action but rather in existential uncertainty and anomie, in doubt about the very value of one's life and its purposes. To put it melodramatically, the tragedy of the human situation is that we do indeed think of ourselves as morally sovereign—we alone can make these judgements of value, others can't make them for us. But at the same time, we can't believe in our judgements unless someone else confirms them for us. No one's life goes well if led according to values she's chosen but doesn't really believe in, and the confirmation of others is needed for firm belief.

Now no one disputes the importance of securing the social preconditions of self-respect, i.e. the conditions which give a person 'the secure conviction that his conception of the good, his plan of life, is worth carrying out' (Rawls 1971 p. 440).

Rawls, for example, calls self-respect the most important primary good (ibid.). Liberals believe that self-respect is best secured by providing the conditions for freely judging and choosing our potential ends. Some people, however, think rather the opposite—that is, we only have confidence in our moral judgements if they are protected socially from the eroding effects of our own individual rational scrutiny. We lack faith in our own judgements, and social confirmation must come in to guide or even limit individual reflection and choice.

This is a very difficult question to which there are no easy answers. While some people obviously can sustain a sense of the worth of their purposes despite an absence of social confirmation (e.g. a woman who in a traditionally sexist society none the less believes women and men are equals), it's also likely that the spread of the idea of individual self-determination has generated more doubt about the value of our projects than before. But it's worth noting one important difference between the two positions. The liberal view operates through people's rationality—i.e. it generates confidence in the value of one's projects by removing any impediments or distortions in the reasoning process involved in making judgements of value. The alternative view operates behind the backs of the individuals involved—i.e. it generates confidence via a process which people can't acknowledge as the grounds of their confidence. We have to think we have good *reasons* for our confidence. We'd lose that confidence if we thought our beliefs weren't rationally grounded, but rather merely caused. As Kant says,

we cannot possibly conceive of a reason as being consciously directed from outside in regard to its judgements; for in that case the subject would attribute the determination of his power of judgement, not to his reason, but to an impulsion. Reason must look upon itself as the author of its own principles independently of alien influences. (Kant p. 116)

We can see ourselves as having come to a judgement for external causal reasons, but we can't stay with it unless we endorse it as independently valid (Raz 1986 p. 300). Williams correctly says that it is a social or psychological, not philosophical, question what forms of socialization and public discourse help foster confidence in moral judgements (Williams 1985 p. 170). But if confidence is fostered by giving people causal reinforcement—causes rather than reasons, as it were—then it must do so behind the backs of people. This seems ironic, given Williams's vehement critique of 'Government House' utilitarianism for precisely such manipulation of people's moral beliefs, and his desire for transparency in ethical practices (Williams 1985 pp. 108–10, 199). In any event, this solution is in conflict with the liberal view, which desires a society that is transparently intelligible—where nothing works behind the backs of its members, and where the causes of our actions are the considerations we have recognized and affirmed as reasons for action.[7] Liberals clearly wouldn't then support a programme for increasing moral confidence by a process that distorted conscious reasoning, i.e. that causally influenced judgements independent of reasons.

Since the attempt to promote social confirmation through communitarian politics involves working behind the backs of people, it is incompatible with the liberal vision of an undistorted, transparent community. Of course, that hardly settles the issue, since it might be that one values undistorted transparency only if one has a prior commitment to the liberal view of the relationship between individual purposes and communal values. But it does mean that communitarianism can only be endorsed from the third-person perspective. As sociologists, we can agree that people's lives might go better if they had the moral confidence which comes when communal practices and traditions are taken as 'authoritative horizons' and critical reflection on them is discouraged. And Williams is right to castigate those who extol uncertainty rather than accept that possibility (Williams 1985 p. 169). But from the inside, from the first-person perspective, I can't endorse the aim that my own life be made to go better in that way. The confidence we desire in our moral judgements is, therefore, essentially a by-product: it supervenes on thought activity directed towards another end (i.e. making the right judgement in the light of good reasons). It cannot be directly pursued.

The fifth and final argument I want to consider is that which accuses liberals of having an untenable account of morality as transcultural and ahistorical. Or, more accurately, it accuses 'Kantian' liberals (like Rawls and Dworkin) of this, as contrasted

with 'Hegelian' liberals (like Dewey) who recognize that a
political morality can only be defended by reference to the
shared values of a particular historical tradition or interpretative
community. This is Richard Rorty's argument. But this criticism,
and the contrast it's based on, are distressingly obscure in Rorty.
In fact, Rorty conflates four different ways of drawing the
contrast, and it's not clear that any of them is persuasive when
made to stand on its own. The first way he describes the contrast
focuses on the relationship between the self and its ends. Here
he cites, and repeats, Sandel's claim that we should

> think of the moral self, the embodiment of rationality, not as one of
> Rawls's original choosers, somebody who can distinguish her *self* from
> her talents and interests and views about the good, but as a network
> of beliefs, desires, and emotions with nothing behind it—no substrate
> behind the attributes. (Rorty p. 217)

Now this argument stands or falls—I think falls—with Sandel's
embedded-self argument. But I mention it just to distinguish it
from the next way that Rorty draws the contrast, a way that
he thinks is equivalent to the first, or is, at any rate, a 'corollary' of it. He goes on to accuse Kantian liberals of an 'account
of "rationality" and "morality" as transcultural and ahistorical'
(p. 216), and advises liberals to drop these 'Kantian buttresses'.
Instead, liberals should try to convince our society that it 'need
be responsible only to its own traditions, and not to the moral
law as well' (p. 217). Rather than appealing to any ahistorical
theory of justice, 'the moral justification of the institutions and
practices of one's group . . . is mostly a matter of historical
narratives . . . rather than of philosophical metanarratives' (Rorty
p. 218).

But Rorty doesn't urge this on us because we've adopted a
Sandelian view of the self (although Rorty presents it as a
'corollary'). On the contrary, Sandel's view of the self, as much
as any other, could provide *philosophical* grounds for questioning
entire sections of our historical narratives—for example, those
Kant-inspired sections according to which 'the sharing of values
is without ethical significance' (Unger p. 68), or which encourage
people to 'put in question what are taken to be the merely
contingent social features of [their] existence' (MacIntyre p. 205).
According to Unger and MacIntyre, these aspects of our historical

tradition, which they both say run very deep in our culture, and are embedded in our everyday life and institutions, have disastrous consequences for our ability to sustain a sense of individual integrity and shared community. These are criticisms of our historical tradition on the basis of that philosophical view of the self that Rorty has endorsed. It's just not true that restricting moral justification to historical narratives is a corollary of Sandel's view of the self.

The real reason Rorty rejects 'philosophical metanarratives' is that he believes there *are* no such things—that is, there are no reasons which aren't reasons internal to a historical tradition or interpretative community; and he believes this is true whatever the relationship is between the self and its ends. The reason we have to drop the Kantian buttresses of a 'transcultural and ahistorical' account of rationality and morality (Rorty p. 216) is not the truth of any moral theory about whether our ends are or are not constituents of the self. Rather, the Kantian buttresses have to be dropped because of an *epistemological* theory which says that 'rational behaviour is just adaptive behaviour of a sort which roughly parallels the behaviour, in similar circumstances, of the other members of some relevant community' (p. 217). For Rorty, this epistemological theory applies as much to physics as it does to ethics.

But is it true that Kantian liberals have some unacceptable view about transcultural moral truth? Rorty gives the example of liberals who responded to the Vietnam War by 'attempting to rehabilitate Kantian notions in order to say, with Chomsky, that the war not merely betrayed America's hopes and interests and self-image, but was *immoral*, one which we had no *right* to engage in in the first place' (Rorty p. 219). But what kind of Kantian notions are involved in making such claims, and why should we give them up in favour of Hegelian notions about appeals to historical tradition? There are in fact three possible Kantian notions involved here, three different ways of drawing this contrast, which Rorty runs together.

Firstly, there is the question of the *meaning* of our moral language. When we say things like 'Slavery is wrong', do we mean 'We don't do that around here', or do we mean something which isn't tied in this way to our current social practices? Rorty thinks the former: when a person appeals to morality, she appeals to a shared consciousness of beliefs and emotions 'which permit her to say "WE do not do this sort of thing". Morality is, as Wilfred Sellars has said, a matter of "we-intentions" ' (Rorty p. 218). Unfortunately for Rorty, Sellars was wrong to say that. When a Muslim woman in Egypt says 'Sexual discrimination is wrong', she does *not* mean 'We don't do that around here.' On the contrary, she is saying this precisely because it *is* done around there, and always has been done, and is very firmly embedded in all the myths, symbols, and institutions of their history and society. She might also say 'Discrimination is wrong (although it is approved around here).' Now if Rorty were right about what moral language *meant*, then she would be contradicting herself. She'd be saying 'We don't do that around here, although we do do that around here.' But of course we know what she means, and she is not contradicting herself. So it's just not true that when we say 'X is wrong', we *mean* 'We don't do X around here.'

Rorty does allow that we sometimes denounce the values of our own community. He thinks such denunciations take the form of appealing, in the very meaning of our language, to the values of some *other* specific community. But while the Muslim woman may well gesture at some other community as a moral example, her claim that discrimination is wrong doesn't mean 'The Y's don't do it in their community.' If she stopped gesturing to that community (because, for example, they begin to discriminate), and instead appealed to some other example, the meaning of her claim wouldn't have changed at all. She wouldn't now mean 'The Z's don't do it in their community.' She hasn't made two different claims which have different meanings. Any theory of meaning that says she has changed the meaning of her claim is simply mistaken. The meaning of our moral language isn't tied in this way to claims about the values of any particular community. When we criticize or defend the values of our community, the meaning of our claims is not captured by statements like '*We* do this' or '*They* don't do that'. If *this* is the contrast between Kantian and Hegelian liberals, then Hegelian liberals are simply wrong.

But perhaps the contrast isn't in their theory of meaning, but in their account of *philosophical method*. Once we know what people mean by their moral statements, how do we go about examining those statements? What criterion or test do we apply? Perhaps the difference between Kantian and Hegelian liberals is this: Hegelian liberals start with our intuitions and institutions, our shared values and community standards; Kantian liberals, on the other hand, start by fashioning an objective and ahistorical standpoint, and ask what is valuable from there. Or so says Michael Walzer, whom Rorty approvingly cites:

One way *to begin the philosophical enterprise*—perhaps the original way— is to walk out of the cave, leave the city, climb the mountain, fashion for oneself (what can never be fashioned for ordinary men and women) an objective and universal standpoint. Then one describes the terrain of everyday life from far away . . . But I mean to stand in the cave, in the city, on the ground. (Walzer 1983 p. xiv, emphasis added)

But if *this* is meant to be the crux of the matter then the debate is simply a non-starter, for this contrast is wholly spurious. 'There are certainly serious disagreements about the enterprise of political philosophy. But it is wrong to say that they are importantly about where "to *begin* the philosophical enterprise" ' (J. Cohen p. 467). Plato and Kant, the philosophers most commonly viewed as endorsing the mountain-top view of philosophy, in fact agree with Walzer that philosophy *starts* on the ground. We start with such local and particular ethical opinions as that justice is 'truth and returning what one takes', but we are 'impelled to go outside its sphere and to take a step into the field of practical philosophy in order to escape from the perplexity of opposing claims' (Kant, quoted in J. Cohen p. 467). Starting from the ground, we are *led* to philosophy. Of course the real target here is Rawls, and his 'original position' (Walzer 1983 pp. 5, 79). But the criticism is just as misplaced against him. Rawls also starts on the ground, with our widely shared intuitions about fairness. He notes that these intuitions are vague, incapable of providing guidance in those cases where help is needed. We need some way of teasing out their mean- ing and implications. This is where, and why, he invokes the device of the original position. We start with commonly shared intuitions about sources of unfairness in determining principles of justice—for example, that people shouldn't be able to use advantages in power to affect the selection process in their favour—and construct a decision-making process which 'incorporates these commonly shared presumptions' (Rawls 1971 p. 18). Hence we 'should not be misled . . . by the somewhat unusual conditions which characterize the original position. The idea here is simply to make vivid to ourselves the restrictions that it seems reasonable to impose on arguments for principles of justice' (ibid.)—i.e. the restrictions imposed by our shared intuitions. The premiss of Rawls's argument isn't the original position, as some sort of transcendental standpoint from which we survey the moral landscape, and choose all our moral beliefs. On the contrary, we *start* with the shared moral beliefs, and then describe an original position in accordance with those shared beliefs, in order to work out their fuller implications. We are to look at the original position 'as an expository device which sums up the meaning of these [intuitions] and helps us to extract their consequences' (Rawls 1971 p. 21). It is a device for working through the meaning and consequences of our shared moral beliefs.

So the idea that there is some great difference between Hegelian and Kantian liberals on this question of where to *begin* the moral conversation is spurious, and is simply a way of avoiding the need to examine the arguments of Kantian liberals (Bernstein pp. 551–2). Where there may be a difference isn't in their beliefs about where to begin the philosophical enterprise, but about where that enterprise must *end up*. For Walzer and Rorty, 'the notions of community and shared values mark the *limits* of practical reason', not just its point of departure (J. Cohen p. 467).

Now if this were just a *prediction* about the limits of practical reason, then it wouldn't be objectionable. It would be just speculation, and we'd have to wait and see how far the reasons and arguments had taken us at the end of the day. We'd have to see whether there are standards of rational persuasion which can lead us to reject a particular historical tradition. Perhaps, at the end of the day, the only reason we can give for our actions is 'this is what we do around here'—an appeal to localized and particular standards, not shared by others.[8] This is certainly possible, and Dworkin allows for it (Dworkin 1985 p. 176). In *After Virtue*, MacIntyre says that the best reason we have to reject transcultural accounts of rights is the same reason we have to reject the existence of witches, i.e. that every attempt to show that they do exist has failed (MacIntyre p. 67). Now that is the right *kind* of argument, and if it were true, and if it could be generalized to other sorts of transcultural moral theories, then we'd have good reason to accept that Rorty's prediction about the limits of practical reason had turned out to be true. But notice that this isn't an objection to trying to give Kantian arguments; on the contrary, it is one of the things we can *conclude* from such arguments at the end of the day. MacIntyre's claim is based on an examination of these arguments, and he concludes (what was an open question at the beginning of the day) that none of these arguments is compelling. The only weakness in MacIntyre's argument, of course, is that his examination of the arguments is so incomplete, his conclusion far too hasty. It's too early in the day to draw such conclusions, and any predictions are rather idle ones at this point.

But Rorty and Walzer aren't just predicting that there are such limits to practical reasoning. They claim to *know* such limits exist—they claim to know this *in advance of the arguments*. They claim to know that reasons will only be compelling to particular historical communities, before those reasons have been advanced. Now this, unlike the question of where to begin the conversation, certainly does distinguish Rorty from Kantian liberals who don't accept that we can know in advance what are the limits to practical reason. This way of drawing the contrast between Hegelian and Kantian liberals is very different from the other ways, despite Rorty's conflation; in order to distinguish it clearly we can call it, to use a neutral phrase, the dogmatic objection to Kantian liberalism. There are no grounds for deciding in advance what the limits of practical reasoning are. Rorty and Walzer simply presuppose what MacIntyre attempts to show— that Kantian liberal theories won't work. If MacIntyre is too hasty in his examination, Rorty has decided he doesn't even have to examine the theories—and that is just dogmatism.

So Rorty's Hegelian argument against the Kantian notions involved in Rawls's and Dworkin's view of morality can be taken in three ways. The first, about the meaning of moral language, is false; the second, about the starting-point of moral conversation, is spurious; and the third, about the limits of moral conversation, is dogmatic. There may be other, more defensible moral objections to the view of the self that I've tried to outline and defend, or to the broader political theory which is based on it. But we get nowhere towards identifying these problems by invoking old slogans about 'abstract' or 'atomistic' individualism, slogans which have stood in the way, or taken the place, of serious analysis. Progress will only be made when the rhetoric is dropped.

Notes

1. I am here agreeing with Roger Smith's claim that the best way to defend liberalism (and perhaps the only intelligible way) is to adopt

   > an essentially psychological or even phenomenological approach to the ultimate character of the human self and human will, appealing to our practical experience of our selves as enduring beings with some apparent capacities for self-direction . . . this basic sense of our selves, however illusory, is our inescapable starting point in moral and political reflection and the standard against which we judge rival interpretations. (R. Smith p. 202)

   But I disagree with Smith's claim that this phenomenological approach will reveal that 'the enhancement of our understanding and powers of self-direction [is] in itself something we should, after sufficient reflection, judge to be our highest delight' (R. Smith p. 204). The limitations of this view have been discussed elsewhere (Scheffler 1979 p. 295; Perry pp. 212–19; Larmore pp. 77–8, 120–1), although most of these critiques mistakenly attribute the position being criticized to Rawls.

2. Sandel's idea of constitutive relationships is particularly unattractive if, as Green believes, it is intended to apply to the relationship between citizens and political authorities. For if it's said that one can have no conception of oneself outside of one's authority relations,

   > It would mean that at the core of one's very self-understanding lie the commands of another. This is much more than the normal surrender of judgment characteristic of any obedience to authority. There, an independently constituted subject surrenders his judgment, usually for limited time and purposes. In the political communitarian view, however, the person has lost any conception of himself apart from what others tell him to do. (L. Green p. 214)

   Green thinks that this communitarian view of the self does not give an accurate picture of authority relations. But, like Rawls in his recent work, Green believes it could apply to our more private relationships (ibid. p. 213).

3. Sandel's claim, that Rawls's view of the relationship between the self and its ends violates our self-understanding, gets much of its force, I think, from being linked to the further claim that Rawls views people as being essentially *disembodied*. According to Sandel, the reason Rawls denies that people are entitled to the rewards which accrue from the exercise of their natural talents is that he denies that natural talents are an essential part of our personal identity. Natural talents are mere possessions, not constituents, of the self (Sandel 1982 pp. 75–94; Larmore p. 127). But this is a misinterpretation. The reason Rawls denies that people are entitled to the fruits of the exercise of their natural talents is that no one deserves their place in the lottery of natural talents, no one deserves to have more natural talents than anyone else. Differential natural talents, and corresponding differential earning power, are undeserved, and undeserved inequalities should be compensated for. This position is entirely consistent with the claim that natural talents are constituents of the self. The fact that natural talents are constitutive of the self does nothing to show that a gifted child deserved to be born with greater talents than a handicapped child. Many liberals would not in fact accept the claim that *all* our natural attributes are constituents of the self (Dworkin 1983*a* p. 39), and I myself am unsure where to draw the line. But this question does not threaten to undermine the liberal view that natural disadvantages should be compensated for. Rawls's theory is quite capable of recognizing our essential embodiment in whatever way best accords with our deepest self-understandings. In any event, the fact that we are essentially *embodied* does nothing to support Sandel's conception of the ways in which we are socially *embedded*.

4. Taylor's argument in *Hegel and Modern Society* suffers from a similar ambiguity in its view of the person. He says that we need to recover a 'situated' sense of freedom based on a 'defining situation' which 'sets goals for us' and provides us with 'authoritative horizons'. He then goes on to say that this involves 'the notion of a bent in our situation which we can either endorse or reject, reinterpret or distort' (C. Taylor 1979 p. 160). But if we can affirm or reject this bent (and not merely interpret it), I fail to see the sense in which goals are set for us, or the sense in which communal practices are authoritative horizons. Our communal situation does provide us with a horizon in the sense of a range of options, but

liberals don't deny that. Taylor's view of freedom seems distinctive in claiming that our goals are set for us by the authoritative horizons of the community's practices. But it turns out that the sense in which he views our goals as set for us includes the sense in which liberals view our goals as freely chosen. And the sense in which he views communal practices as authoritative horizons includes the sense in which liberals view communal practices as open to challenge and possible rejection.

5. See Rosenblum's discussion of the convergence of liberal freedom of association and what she calls 'pluralist communitarianism' (as distinct from the stronger positions which she calls 'latent community' or a 'community of direct relations' (Rosenblum ch. 7)). She notes that on this weaker view, 'communitarianism becomes an outgrowth of the fundamental liberal freedom of association' (p. 157). The 'conventional pluralist framework of liberalism is preserved', but 'recast' so as to emphasize the way in which associations are 'expressive', and not simply arenas for the pursuit of shared interests (p. 158). As she also notes, this 'pluralist communitarian' recasting is 'surprisingly modest, in light of their severe attacks on abstract personhood' (p. 163), and fails to deliver on the advertised contrast with contemporary liberal views, which do not deny this 'paler' view of our embeddedness in associations (ibid.). While the advertised contrasts between contemporary liberals and communitarians may be false (if communitarians are advancing this weaker version of their position), it is undoubtedly true that the two schools have reached their shared position in different ways (see Rosenblum, *passim*).

6. For liberal worries about the relationship between individual judgement and social confirmation, see Rawls 1971 pp. 441–2, 450, 536, 543–4; R. Smith pp. 188–91, 217–19; Dworkin 1987 pp. 16–17; Galston 1980 pp. 44–5. For an interpretation of MacIntyre's communitarianism which makes this worry a central motivation, see Kateb. According to Kateb, MacIntyre seeks

> to construct a world in which every feature cooperates to one purpose: glorifying the *bounded* individual . . . [MacIntyre seeks] to persuade us of the beauty of living a life that is made more firm by being greatly reduced in self-consciousness. I think that self-consciousness is really, for MacIntyre, the greatest vice of modernity. How, MacIntyre furiously asks, can society go on when the temptations, uncertainties, possibilities, opportunities, powers, and instruments of life multiply to such an extent as to deprive every self of a sense of knowing himself or his world— of knowing his place? (Kateb p. 436)

This is probably an exaggeration, but so, I think, is Gill's contrary claim that MacIntyre is *encouraging* critical individual reflection (Gill pp. 122–3).

7. For contrasting views of the importance of transparency for a liberal society, see Waldron (pp. 134–5, 146–50), who puts transparency at the very centre of liberal doctrine, and Gray (ch. 9), who sees the desire for transparency as evidence of a 'hubristic rationalism' which liberals ought to abandon. Government attempts to build confidence in certain values non-rationally may indirectly give us genuine and affirmable reasons for action. If more people come to believe more strongly in certain shared values or practices then their chances of achieving solidarity are improved, which could be a perfectly good reason for action. But having an increased opportunity to achieve solidarity is distinct from having increased confidence in the value of the goods being pursued in solidarity, and it is the latter which the government policy would be intended to achieve. (And without the latter, the former may be unattainable; see Ch. 6 below.)

8. It is worth noting that this is not the same as accepting the relativist theory of meaning discussed above: 'This is what we do around here' would be given as a *reason* for the moral claim, not part of the *meaning* of the moral claim.

5

Taylor's Social Thesis

THE arguments of the preceding chapter defended liberalism's emphasis on our capacity to distance ourselves from particular communal roles and practices, and to choose the plan of life that is most valuable for us. But there are other issues raised by the communitarian critique of liberalism. Many criticisms centre not on the liberal idea of the self and its interests, but on the 'individualistic' way that liberals seek to promote those interests politically. Liberal politics is said to neglect the social preconditions for the effective fulfilment of those interests.

As we've seen, Charles Taylor rejects the liberal view of the self (discussed in Chapter 4). But he also says that even if liberals are right about our capacity for choice, they ignore the fact that that capacity can only develop in society, in and through relations and interactions with others. Liberals emphasize choice, to the neglect of the social preconditions that allow choice. This is a common enough criticism, often linked to criticisms of liberal social science, whose methodology is supposed to be idealist and individualistic, rather than materialistic and holistic. Liberals overemphasize choice in the explanation of events, neglecting the social determinants of action. Now there's no doubt that liberal social science has often been sociologically naïve, as contrasted with, say, conservative functionalism, Marxist class-analysis, or feminist gender-analysis. It is a commonplace that sociology, as a discipline, arose as a response to the overemphasis on rational individual choice by liberals. Does this problem also damage liberal political morality? Are the principles of justice advanced by recent liberals based on a false view about the social preconditions of individual action? Taylor thinks so. He claims that many liberal political theories are based on 'atomism', on 'the utterly facile moral psychology of traditional empiricism', according to which individuals are self-sufficient outside of society and hence not in need of the cultural context of choice in order to exercise their 'moral powers' (e.g. to choose a conception of the good life). The liberal individual, in such an atomistic theory, is 'concerned purely with his individual choices . . . to the neglect of the matrix in which such choices can be open or closed, rich or meagre' (C. Taylor 1985 p. 207). Taylor argues instead for the 'social thesis', which says that these capacities can only be developed and exercised in a certain kind of society, with a certain kind of social and cultural surrounding.

Now Rawls, Dworkin, and Mill are not atomists in this sense (as Taylor himself agrees). Their arguments notice, and indeed emphasize, our dependence, as individuals, on our cultural structure and community. Thus Rawls talks about how we decide our life-plans, not *de novo*, but rather from examining the models and ways of life of those who have preceded us (Rawls 1971 pp. 563–4). Likewise Dworkin talks about the importance of the cultural structure in providing the conditions necessary to make imaginative decisions about how to lead our lives, a structure which can be enriched or diminished in the opportunities it provides (Dworkin 1985 pp. 230–3). These liberals do not deny that the free individual is only possible within a culture of freedom.

Taylor, however, thinks that a full acceptance of the social thesis would require abandoning a central tenet of liberalism, which he calls the 'primacy of rights'. I think that the term 'primacy of rights' is unhelpful, at least for our purposes.[1] Taylor is referring to the moral view that individual rights have primacy over other moral notions like individual duties, or virtue, or collective good. But I don't think that contemporary liberal theories are best understood in this way. It is true that Dworkin, at one point, claimed that liberalism is 'rights-based', in contrast to other theories which are 'goal-based' or 'duty-based' (Dworkin 1977 pp. 169–73). But this was an unfortunate schema, which he has subsequently withdrawn; he now emphasizes the derivative nature of the concept of rights within a theory of justice (e.g. Dworkin 1983*a* pp. 34–5). None of these moral notions are of the right sort to be morally primary, and the use of these terms in describing political theories often results in misdescriptions.

This doesn't dissolve the debate between Taylor and liberals. For there are particular kinds of duties which Taylor believes liberals ignore, because of their inadequate attention to the social thesis, and particular kinds of rights that they overemphasize. These criticisms are the subject of this chapter. But the debate would go better if we dropped the question of whether rights in the abstract have primacy over duties in the abstract, and instead just asked whether there are *particular* rights, goals, virtues, or duties which are inadequately recognized or affirmed in liberalism.

Why does Taylor think that there are particular duties or goods which are inadequately recognized in liberalism? One of the features of liberalism which Taylor feels is inadequate is its insistence on 'neutral political concern'.[2] The idea is that people are entitled to 'neutral concern' from the government—that is, equal concern regardless of their conception of the good (so long as it does not violate the rights of others), whether it is approved or disapproved of by the majority in society, or by state officials. This entitlement includes the right to veto the collective pursuit of the ends shared by the majority, where that pursuit violates my claim to equal neutral concern (for example by denying my freedom to choose and pursue dissident religious or cultural activities). Rights are, therefore, part of the liberal political programme—they put constraints on the pursuit of these shared ends. But rights are not morally primary, and they do not define what is of moral significance. Rather they protect and promote those interests which are of moral significance.

According to Taylor (and Sandel), such a politics of neutral concern should be abandoned for what they call a 'politics of the common good' (C. Taylor 1986; Sandel 1984*b*). But that too is a little misleading. After all, a liberal state can be said to promote the common good, since its policies aim at promoting the interests of the members of the community. The process of combining individual preferences into a social choice function is often said to determine the common good for a liberal society. Thus it might promote the common good to build a new airport or highway, if a fair process of counting preferences yields that result.

The real difference is in the way the common good is envisioned. In a liberal society, the common good is the result of a process of combining preferences, all of which are counted equally (if consistent with the principles of justice). All preferences have equal weight 'not in the sense that there is an agreed public measure of intrinsic value or satisfaction with respect to which all these conceptions come out equal, but in the sense that they are not evaluated at all from a [public] standpoint' (Rawls 1982 p. 172). As we saw in Chapter 3, this anti-perfectionist insistence on state neutrality stems from Rawls's belief that since lives have to be led from the inside, my essential interest in leading a good life is not advanced when society penalizes, or discriminates against, the projects that I, on reflection, believe are most valuable for me. Hence in a liberal society the common good is adjusted to fit the pattern of preferences and conceptions of the good held by individuals.

In a communitarian society, on the other hand, the common good is conceived of as a substantive conception of the good which defines the community's 'way of life'. This common good, rather than adjusting itself to the pattern of people's preferences, provides a standard by which those preferences are evaluated. The community's way of life forms the basis for a public ranking of conceptions of the good, and the weight given to an individual's preferences depends on how much she conforms or contributes to that common good. The public pursuit of the shared ends which define the community's way of life is not, therefore, constrained by the requirement of neutral concern. It takes precedence over the claim of individuals to the liberties and resources needed to choose and pursue their own ends. Individuals are no longer able to veto the pursuit of these shared ends whenever it violates neutral concern. Individuals may be able to exercise such a veto on some occasions—communitarians are not always clear (or agreed) on when, if ever, individuals would be able to veto majority decisions.[3] But whatever the variations within communitarianism, the fact of shared values has greater weight among communitarians than liberals, and the possible existence of dissent from those values is treated as less of a constraint on state action.

Since both liberals and communitarians can be described as promoting a common good, it would be helpful to have another term to describe communitarian politics. Unfortunately, the term 'politics of the common good' seems entrenched in the literature, and so I shall continue to use it. Why should we prefer a politics of the common good over a politics of liberal neutrality? One communitarian argument, discussed in the previous chapter, is that liberalism exaggerates our ability to question the shared values which are embodied in communal practices. But that argument is, I've claimed, mistaken. I shall now consider whether the social thesis provides any grounds for preferring a politics of the common good to the liberal politics of neutral concern.

Communitarians give both conceptual and empirical arguments for connecting the social thesis to communitarian politics. Conceptually, it is sometimes argued that once liberals admit that the capacity for individual choice can only be developed and exercised in a certain sort of society, and accept the necessity of promoting and protecting such a society, then they have already accepted a politics of the common good. For the promotion of such a society, which we can call the liberal common good, must be prior to the rights of individuals within that society. It would be incoherent to put the rights of individuals above the good of creating a society where those rights can be exercised.

But if we use the term 'politics of the common good' this broadly, then we can no longer say that we must choose between a politics of the common good and a politics of neutrality. For the liberal common good is a good precisely because it secures for individuals the capacity for free choice in conceptions of the good life, and this requirement constrains the pursuit of shared ends; whereas the common good for communitarians is precisely the pursuit of these shared ends, which constrains the freedom of individuals to choose and pursue their own life-style. There's nothing incoherent in saying that the common good for liberals is to bring about a society governed by a politics of neutral concern.

The conceptual argument against liberal neutrality depends for its force on a series of conflations. Taylor's social thesis shows that liberals are committed, on pain of self-contradiction, to sustaining a certain kind of society. This is often rephrased as a commitment to a certain kind of 'community', then a kind of 'form of life', from which it is a short step to a 'way of life', and finally to certain 'conceptions of the good'. But these notions are ambiguous, and a lack of conceptual precision allows communitarians to exaggerate the support they can derive from the social thesis. Both traditions can be described as promoting a certain kind of community as their common good, but further argumentation is needed to show why the community should be a communitarian one, and why the common good should be a particular conception (or a defined range of conceptions) of the good. We need more than conceptual arguments to establish that.

If we accept the liberal picture of our essential interests, then the social thesis provides us with no conceptual reason to give up our liberal principles. However, Taylor believes that the social thesis creates *empirical* doubts about the possibility of the liberal politics of neutral concern. These empirical concerns centre on the perceived insecurity of the 'culture of freedom' which liberals admit is required in view of the social thesis. Since our possible projects and goals come from a cultural structure, and since that structure can deteriorate under certain conditions, Taylor says that we have an obligation 'to belong to or sustain' this kind of cultural community. Given that we are dependent on the culture of freedom for our individual liberty, we must have not only 'negative' duties of non-interference, but also 'positive' duties to sustain that culture. The empirical fact of cultural vulnerability requires that we go beyond a politics of neutral concern. As Cragg puts it, worthwhile freedom requires cultural pluralism, and yet

Any collective attempt by a liberal state to protect pluralism would itself be in breach of liberal principles of justice. The state is not entitled to interfere in the movement of the cultural market place except, of course, to ensure that each individual has a just share of available resources to exercise his or her moral powers. The welfare or demise of particular conceptions of the good and, therefore, the welfare or demise of social unions of a particular character is not the business of the state . . . any attempt to halt or reverse a slide into cultural homogeneity will generate injustice, given a liberal perspective. (Cragg p. 47)

But the existence of such positive duties is not denied by liberal theorists. Thus while Rawls doesn't include such an obligation in his two principles of justice, he argues that the operation of the two principles would in fact protect the culture of freedom, and he obviously considers that to be a precondition for the acceptability of his theory (Rawls 1971 pp. 331, 441–2, 522–9). Dworkin is even more explicit. Taylor's obligation to sustain such preconditions is very similar to Dworkin's duty to protect the cultural structure from 'debasement or decay' (Dworkin 1985 p. 230). Indeed, Taylor and Dworkin have much in common here: they both talk about how the capacity to form an imaginative conception of the good life requires, for example, specialized debate among intellectuals who attempt to define and clarify the alternatives facing us, or the presence of people who attempt to bring the culture of the past to life again in the art of the present, or who sustain the drive to cultural innovation (C. Taylor 1985 pp. 204–6; Dworkin 1985 pp. 229–32). All of this spells out the social conditions required for individuals to have the sort of freedom of choice which liberal politics seeks to promote. Liberals recognize the importance of duties to protect and promote such social conditions, and accept those duties precisely because they promote, rather than conflict with, the aims of liberal politics.

The importance of such duties is stressed by another liberal, Joseph Raz. But he differs from Rawls and Dworkin in claiming that these duties cannot be discharged by the government without violating the central tenet of neutral concern—that governments should not use the superiority (or inferiority) of anyone's conception of the good as their reason for any state action. According to Rawls and Dworkin, governments are not allowed to use controversial judgements about the nature of human excellence or perfection in deciding how to promote the social conditions of individual freedom. Raz, however, argues that appeal to perfectionist ideals is unavoidable. He recognizes that citizens may not want government officials to act on controversial perfectionist ideals, since it implies that they have greater insight into the nature of the good life. But he believes that if governments are to ensure the social conditions of freedom, they must invoke perfectionist ideals:

Whatever else can be said about this argument one point is decisive. Supporting valuable ways of life is a social rather than an individual matter . . . perfectionist ideals require public action for their viability. Anti-perfectionism in practice would lead not merely to a political stand-off from support for valuable conceptions of the good. It would undermine the chances of survival of many cherished aspects of our culture. (Raz 1986 p. 162)

But this is hardly a decisive point against supporters of neutral concern. For, as Raz himself emphasizes, public support of the cultural structure is valuable for all people, and should be supported by all, regardless of their differing conceptions of the good life. This is so because everyone has an interest in having an adequate range of options when forming their aims and ambitions, and even those who experiment with or leave behind the conventional ways of life in society draw none the less on the social stock of meanings and beliefs in developing their alternative life-styles. Both Cragg and Raz claim that the necessity of public support for the cultural structure requires some controversial public ranking of the intrinsic merits of competing conceptions of the good. Yet in both cases, their 'decisive' argument for public support relies on the non-controversial value of a secure cultural pluralism for people in developing their varying conceptions of the good (Raz 1986 p. 162; Cragg pp. 47–50). And so there is no reason to suppose that governments couldn't develop a decision procedure for public support of the culture of freedom that respected the principle of neutral concern, that was endorsable as fair by everyone in society.[4] For example, the state could ensure an adequate range of options, not by contributing to the ways of life it finds valuable, but by providing tax incentives for private citizens to contribute to the ways of life they find valuable (Dworkin 1985 ch. 11).

So the necessity of public support for various aspects of the culture of freedom does not by itself undermine the possibility of liberal neutrality. But Taylor's empirical doubts go deeper: public support will only be forthcoming if public institutions are stable and effective, and that in turn requires that the institutions have legitimacy in the eyes of the citizens who must bear the burdens imposed by those institutions. Taylor believes that political institutions governed by the principle of neutral concern will, empirically, be incapable of sustaining legitimacy, and hence will be incapable of sustaining the culture of freedom.

He sees two problems with the effects of neutral concern on legitimacy. (1) The possibility that certain ways of life have to be discouraged in order to ensure a political culture of the right sort and of sufficient strength to preserve the conditions of individual liberty:

since the free individual can only maintain his identity within a society/culture of a certain kind, he has to be concerned about the shape of this society/culture as a whole. He cannot . . . be concerned purely with his individual choices and the associations formed from such choices to the neglect of the matrix in which such choices can be open or closed, rich or meagre . . . It is even of importance to him what the moral tone of the whole society is—shocking as it may be to libertarians to raise this issue—because freedom and individual diversity can only flourish in a society where there is a general recognition of their worth. They are threatened by the spread of bigotry, but also by other conceptions of life—for example, those which look on originality, innovation, and diversity as luxuries which society can ill afford given the need for efficiency, productivity, or growth, or those which in a host of other ways depreciate freedom. (C. Taylor 1985 p. 207)

(2) The possibility, much discussed of late, that Western liberal democracies are undergoing a 'legitimation crisis', which has arisen because the welfare state is demanding more from its citizens, but the citizens no longer see the state, and political community generally, as the focus of any identification or allegiance. Citizens will identify with the state, and accept its demands as legitimate, if 'the common form of life is seen as a supremely important good, so that its continuance and flourishing matters to the citizen for its own sake and not just instrumentally to their several individual goods or as the sum total of these individual goods' (C. Taylor 1986 p. 213). But this identification has been undermined, in part because we now have a political culture of rights in which individuals are free to choose their goals independently of this 'common form of life', and to trump the pursuit of this common good should it violate their rights. In contrast to such an identification with the common form of life,

the rights model goes very well with a more atomist consciousness, where I understand my dignity as that of an individual bearer of rights. Indeed—and here the tension surfaces between the two—I cannot be too willing to trump the collective decision in the name of individual rights if I haven't already moved some distance from the community which makes these decisions. (C. Taylor 1986 p. 211)

This 'distancing' from the community's shared form of life, this lack of identification with its common good, means we become unwilling to shoulder the burdens of a just liberal-democratic order, and instead view its demands as illegitimate.[5]

The first problem for liberal neutrality, then, is that some options about the good life must be *discouraged* in order to ensure a political culture that supports and defends the value of liberal freedoms. The second problem is that certain shared forms of life must be *encouraged* in order for the political culture to accept the demands of liberal justice. What lies behind the two problems is the claim, which strikes at the heart of liberalism's political practice, that the stability of a just liberal society is not secured by the public recognition of certain principles of right or justice, but also requires some recognition and acceptance of principles of the good life. That, I believe, is meant as an empirical, not conceptual, claim about the preconditions for the kind of stable community required by the social thesis.

Rawls and Dworkin, on the other hand, would say that a person can and should be free to choose any conception of the good life as long as she doesn't actively violate the principles of justice, no matter how little that conception itself values freedom or equality—as in the case of an élitist who believes that giving equal status to the masses has lowered cultural sensibilities and made the best in human existence impossible to sustain. Such conceptions are allowed, so long as their adherents recognize the equal right of others to choose their conception of the good life. These conceptions can be tolerated because the public recognition of principles of justice is sufficient to ensure stability even in the face of such conceptions (Rawls 1985 p. 245). The élitist will respect the rights of the masses, not because it promotes his interests, but because it promotes their interests, and they have an equal claim to consideration. Respecting the rights of the masses is a command of justice, not of his own conception of the good. Likewise, people in a well-ordered society will accept the burdens of welfare redistribution as legitimate, because they will recognize and respect the claims of other citizens to their fair share of resources.

Taylor presumably would say this is sociologically naïve: people will not respect the claims of others unless they are bound by certain shared conceptions of the good, by common forms of life—unless they identify with a communitarian form of political community. I say 'presumably' because he is sometimes attacking the (unnamed) 'atomists' who believe that the exercise of our capacity for choice isn't dependent on any public recognition or affirmation at all.[6] Against such people, he is sometimes content merely to emphasize the necessity of a 'common good' in the sense of publicly recognized principles of justice. But if that is all Taylor means, then he adds nothing to Rawls and Dworkin who also affirm that necessity (e.g. Rawls 1971 pp. 177–82).[7] Usually, however, Taylor clearly means common acceptance of particular conceptions of the good life, and hence communitarian politics.

Why does Taylor believe that liberal politics cannot sustain legitimacy? One answer seems to be that civic participation is needed for legitimacy, and liberal politics doesn't involve participation. He describes 'two package solutions emerging out of the mists to the problem of sustaining a viable modern political polity in the twentieth century', which roughly correspond to the liberal and communitarian conceptions of community, and claims that there are

severe doubts [about] the entire long-term viability of the rights model as a safeguard for the dignity of the modern free agent. Can it really substitute for the sense of having a say in the common decision? Could the increasing stress on rights as dominant over collective decisions come in the end to undermine the very legitimacy of the democratic order? (C. Taylor 1986 p. 225)

But his rejection of the liberal conception rests, as is evident in this passage, on saddling it with a lot of extraneous baggage. He plausibly claims that the demise of participation is caused by political centralization and 'bureaucratic tutelage', so that the citizen no longer feels any dignity in her status as a political participant. But I see no empirical or theoretical warrant for claiming that liberalism requires centralization or bureaucratization. From the fact that individuals are allowed to trump rights-violating majority decisions, it doesn't follow that decisions are not after all made by electorates but by bureaucrats, or that decisions must be made by centralized authorities rather than decentralized ones. Political participation may well be a precondition of legitimacy, and hence of stability. But the need for political participation, like that for the public recognition of principles of justice, fails to show why the *communitarian* conception of political participation, or of justice, is the only viable one.

I don't think that Taylor is saying that liberal politics is theoretically inconsistent with an emphasis on decentralization and participation. It's rather, I think, that participation has less meaning in liberal regimes, since it is disconnected from the collective pursuit of shared ends, which is the real ground of legitimacy. We participate less because politics has lost its meaning, and this is why we've allowed centralization and bureaucratization. The lack of participation is an effect of the loss of a politics of the common good.

But that still leaves us with the question of why legitimacy is necessarily bound up with communitarian politics. There is no clear answer to this question in Taylor. But I think one answer lies in a romanticized view of earlier communities in which legitimacy was freely given and earned, based on the effective pursuit of shared ends. The suggestion is that we could recoup the sense of allegiance and legitimacy that was present in earlier days if we just accepted a politics of the common good, promoted the renewal of civic republicanism, and encouraged everyone to participate freely in it.

But that historical picture ignores a very important fact. Eighteenth-century New England town governments may well have had a great deal of legitimacy amongst their members in virtue of the effective pursuit of their shared ends. But that is at least partly because women, atheists, Indians, and the propertyless were all excluded from membership. Had they been allowed membership, they would not have been impressed by the pursuit of what was a racist and sexist 'common good'. The usual way in which legitimacy was ensured amongst all members was to exclude some people from membership.

Now, communitarians are not advocating that legitimacy be secured by denying membership to those groups of people in the community who have not historically participated in shaping and defining the 'common way of life'. Communitarians believe there are certain communal ends and practices that everyone can endorse as the basis for a politics of the common good. But what are these practices? Surely not the traditional ends that were the focus of earlier communities. One can try to pursue those ends without excluding the historically subordinated groups. But no legitimacy will be gained that way. Communitarians often write as if the historical exclusion of various groups was just *arbitrary*, so that we can now include them and proceed forward.[8] But the exclusion of women, for example, wasn't arbitrary. It was done for a reason—namely, that the ends being pursued were sexist, defined by men to serve the interests of men. If women are to have a sense of allegiance to the community, they have to be given the power to define their own interests, rather than merely accepting the identity that men have defined for them. We can't avoid this by saying that women's identities are constituted by existing roles and relationships. That is simply false: women can, and have, rejected those roles, which in many ways operate to deny and submerge their separate identities. This was also true in eighteenth-century New England, but legitimacy there was preserved by excluding women from membership. We must find some other way of securing legitimacy, one that doesn't continue to define women in terms of an identity that others created for them.

Now Taylor is right that the mere extension of rights has failed so far to engender a sense of legitimacy amongst many women or blacks or gays. And that is a problem. The liberal response has to be to give disadvantaged groups more power to define and develop practices that promote their ends. That too may fail. But the communitarian response seems much worse. Sandel and Taylor say that there are shared ends that can serve as the basis for a politics of the common good which will be legitimate for all groups in society. But they give no examples of such ends or practices—and surely part of the reason is that there are no such shared ends.[9] They say that these shared ends are to be found in our historical practices and roles, but they do not mention that those practices and roles were defined by a small portion of the society—propertied, white men—to serve the interests of propertied, white men. These practices remain gender-coded, race-coded, and class-coded, even when women, blacks, and workers are legally allowed to participate in them.

Attempts to promote ends of this kind reduce the level of legitimacy in society, and further exclude and alienate marginalized groups in society (Gutmann 1985 pp. 318–21; Herzog pp. 481–90; Bernstein pp. 550–1; Hirsch pp. 435–8, 441–4; Rosenblum pp. 178–81). Indeed, just such a loss of legitimacy seems to be occurring amongst many elements of American society—blacks, gays, single mothers, non-Christians—as the right wing tries to implement its agenda based on the Christian, patriarchal family. Many communitarians undoubtedly dislike the Moral Majority's view of the common good, but the problem of the exclusion of historically marginalized groups is endemic to the communitarian project. As Hirsch notes, 'any "renewal" or strengthening of community sentiment will accomplish nothing for these groups'. On the contrary, our historical sentiments and traditions are 'part of the problem, not part of the solution' (Hirsch p. 424).

I think the problems here are exhibited in the one concrete issue offered by Sandel—the possible regulation of pornography by local communities. This example needs careful scrutiny, since it may seem to contradict what I have been arguing. The regulation of pornography has been a common demand of women's groups, and it has been demanded precisely as a precondition for women to be able to define their own identities, especially their sexuality. Women have been one of the groups excluded from the process of defining historical traditions and practices, including sexual practices, and regulation of pornography may be needed if women are to be able to reject the view of female sexuality defined by men over the years. Given that Sandel supports the censorship of pornography, doesn't that show that communitarians support the ability of subordinated and marginalized groups to define their own practices and identities?

Unfortunately, Sandel's reason for allowing the regulation of pornography has nothing to do with the ability of women to define their own identities. His argument is that pornography can be regulated by a local community 'on the grounds that pornography offends its way of life' (Sandel 1984*b* p. 17). This argument, far from supporting the right of women to define their own identity, is ultimately incompatible with it, and can be used to restrict the ability of women and other marginalized groups to reject the aims and ambitions which have been defined for them by others.

The feminist argument for regulating pornography concerns its possible social role in promoting violence against women, and in perpetuating the subordination of women to male-defined

ideas of sexuality and gender roles (e.g. MacKinnon chs. 13–14).
Anyone concerned with sexual equality needs to take this
argument seriously, for the evidence is significant, and the trends
concerning the incidence and effects of sexual violence are
appalling. But if pornography does in fact play this role in the
subordination of women, it does so not because it 'offends our
way of life', but precisely because it conforms to our cultural
stereotypes about sexuality and the role of women. In fact, as
MacKinnon notes, from a feminist standpoint the problem with
pornography is not that it violates community standards, but
that it enforces them. (MacKinnon says that the view of
pornographers as intrepid dissidents challenging conventional
views of sexuality in the face of a repressive state is a liberal
myth, but apparently it is a myth also believed by Sandel.)

This is the best argument for regulating pornography, and it
relies on the familiar premiss about harm to others. MacKinnon
claims that the evidence concerning the harms of pornography
is as good or better than the evidence which liberals have
accepted elsewhere for state regulation of speech. If so, then we
have a plausible (and recognizably liberal) argument for regulation of pornography: it is needed to provide women with the
liberty and security needed to define their own identity.

Sandel's argument, however, is in fundamental opposition to
the argument concerning women's autonomy. The problem
with Sandel's defence can be seen by comparing it to the question
of homosexuality. Homosexuality has been, and continues to be,
'offensive to the way of life' of many Americans. Indeed,
measured by any plausible standards, more people are offended
by homosexuality than by pornography. Would Sandel therefore
want communities to be able to criminalize homosexual relations,
or perhaps the public affirmation of homosexuality? If not, what
distinguishes it from pornography? Sandel gives us no answer.
For liberals, the answer is that homosexuality does not harm
others, and the fact that others are offended by it has no moral
weight. The majority in a local (or national) community does
not have the right to enforce its 'external preferences' concerning
the practices and personalities of those people who are outside
of the mainstream way of life (Dworkin 1985 ch. 17). But this
is precisely what Sandel cannot say: on his argument, members
of marginalized groups have to adjust their personalities and

practices so as to be inoffensive to the dominant values of the community. Nothing in Sandel's argument gives members of marginalized groups the power to reject the identity that others have historically defined for them.

Likewise, in the case of pornography, Sandel is not recognizing the importance of giving disempowered women the ability to reject the male view of female sexuality, and to define their own sexuality. On the contrary, he is saying that pornography can be regulated because one male-defined view of sexuality (the pornographers') conflicts with another male-defined view of sexuality (the 'way of life' of the community). Regulating pornography on these grounds may have the side-effect of reducing one set of male-defined pressures on the definition of female sexuality, but it does so on the basis of another set of male-defined values. And, of course, nothing guarantees that the men who are offended by pornography won't have a different but equally oppressive definition of female sexuality. However the community decides, women will have to adjust their identities and aims to male-defined expectations concerning female sexuality (and gender roles in general). The same problem will face gays, blacks, immigrants, and other people who have not been a part of the defining of the community's 'way of life'. This is no way to develop feelings of legitimacy and attachment amongst members of marginalized groups.

Sandel concludes his book by saying that when politics goes well 'we can know a good in common that we cannot know alone' (Sandel 1982 p. 183). But surely, given the inherent diversity of modern societies, and their exclusionary pasts, we should say instead that politics goes well precisely when we don't use state power to promote particular conceptions of the good life. Increasing the level of state legitimacy may well require greater civic participation by the marginalized, but, as Dworkin notes, it only makes sense to invite people to participate in politics (or for people to accept that invitation) if they will be treated as equals (Dworkin 1983a p. 33). And that is incompatible with defining people in terms of roles they did not shape or endorse.

Making the basic structure of society legitimate in the eyes of the marginalized and alienated is not an easy task, and mere extension of the franchise is not enough. Communitarians are right to worry about this. But the communitarian solution to the problem is no solution at all. It rests on a romanticized view of how legitimacy was created in earlier days, and on a naïve view of how our dominant practices have been defined. If legitimacy is to be earned, it won't be by strengthening communal practices and sentiments that have been defined by and for others. It will require empowering the oppressed and dominated to define their own practices and ends. Liberalism may not do enough to develop a sense of attachment amongst the marginalized, but as Herzog succinctly puts it, 'If liberalism is the problem, how could republicanism be the solution?' (Herzog p. 484; cf. Rosenblum p. 179).

How should marginalized groups be enabled to define their own identities and practices? It will undoubtedly involve some modification in the way we view certain institutions which have heretofore been viewed as relatively benign by most liberals, such as welfare-state capitalism, and the traditional family. This undoubtedly poses a challenge to liberal political practice, a challenge that has not been seriously faced by most liberal theorists. William Connolly says that 'current liberalism cannot be defined merely through its commitment to freedom, rights, dissent, and justice. It must be understood, as well, through the institutional arrangements it endorses' (Connolly p. 233). The two aspects of liberalism, he claims, 'can be united as long as it is possible to believe that the welfare state in the privately incorporated economy of growth can be the vehicle of liberty and justice' (ibid.). Unfortunately, the demands of the economy, which finances the welfare state, are now seen to conflict with the principles of justice that underlie the policies of the welfare state. The welfare state is said to need a growing economy to support its redistributive programmes, but the structure of the economy is such that growth can only be secured by policies inconsistent with the principles of justice that underlie those welfare programmes (Connolly pp. 227–31). Thus there are cut-backs in funding (or no funding at all) for day care, abortion clinics, direct payments to homemakers, etc.—things that are prerequisites for women to be able to decide their own fates, but which the welfare state, dependent on corporate capitalism, cannot afford.

According to Connolly, this has led to a 'bifurcation of

liberalism'. One stream clings to the traditional institutions of liberal political practice, and exhorts people to lower their expectations concerning justice and freedom. The other stream (in which he includes Dworkin) reaffirms the principles, but 'the commitment to liberal principles is increasingly matched by the disengagement from practical issues . . . this principled liberalism is neither at home in the civilization of productivity nor prepared to challenge its hegemony' (Connolly p. 234). While Connolly's explanation of the economics of the welfare state is open to doubt, I think he has accurately described the condition of current liberalism. The principle of neutral concern is a compelling one, and it can serve as the basis for state legitimacy in the culture of freedom. But the enforcement of that principle requires reforms that are much more extensive than Rawls or Dworkin has explicitly allowed. As Connolly says, neither has challenged the 'civilization of productivity', whose priorities and main-tenance have perpetuated, and often exaggerated, entrenched inequalities of class and gender.

It might be that a full implementation of the principle of neutral concern would move us much closer to market socialism than to welfare capitalism. Many people have claimed that Rawls's 'difference principle' is best fulfilled under market socialism (Buchanan pp. 124–31, 150–2; DiQuattro), and Dwor-kin's auction scheme may be even more egalitarian. It is an implication of Connolly's definition of liberalism that endorsing socialism is necessarily abandoning one's liberalism. But that seems unduly restrictive. After all, John Stuart Mill, whose liberal credentials cannot be questioned, was prepared to call himself a socialist. And as Hobhouse put it, liberalism 'when it grapples with the facts, is driven no small distance along Socialist lines' (Hobhouse 1964 p. 54). The two traditions have borrowed from each other throughout their history, and 'in the give and take of ideas with socialism, [liberalism] has learnt, and taught, more than one lesson' (Hobhouse 1964 p. 115; cf. Gutmann 1980 pp. 63–8, 70–86, 145–56). I think there are still lessons to be learned, and taught.

In any event, the reform which is perhaps most needed has not been adequately addressed by either tradition—namely, the critique of gender. Throughout both traditions, while men are viewed as having (autonomously chosen) ends, women are

viewed as having (biologically given) functions.[10] While liberals
from Locke through Mill to Rawls have officially proclaimed
that their theories are based on the natural equality of individuals,
they have in fact taken the male-headed family as the essential
unit of political analysis; women's interests are defined by, and
submerged in, the family, which is taken to be their 'natural'
position (Okin 1987 p. 43). The resultant devaluation of women's
contributions is evident in the fact that while women 'perform
nearly two-thirds of all working hours, [they] receive only
one-tenth of the world income, and own less than one per cent
of world resources' (D. Taylor p. 82). In the United States and
Canada, the extent of job segregation in the lowest-paying
occupations is increasing (David-McNeil). And the 1981 President's Advisory Council on Economic Opportunity warned that
if present trends continue, then by the year 2000 the population
in the United States below the poverty line will be composed
solely of women and children. Needless to say, such a mal-
distribution does not match the results of freely made choices
in either Rawls's original position or Dworkin's auction. Yet
neither theorist has anything to say about how this systematic
devaluation of the role of women can be removed. Indeed,
Rawls defines his original position (as an assembly of 'heads
of families'), and his principles of distribution (as measuring
'household income'), in such a way that questions about the
justice of arrangements within the family are ruled out of court
by definition (Okin 1987 p. 49). And while Dworkin doesn't
invoke the usual assumptions about the role of women in the
family, he doesn't say anything about fighting gender-bias at
all.

It's unclear what institutions and practices would constitute
the best non-sexist spelling-out of the ideals underlying the
principle of neutral concern. The assumptions of women's
inferiority are deeply embedded in many of society's institutions,
from the teaching of sex roles to children to the public
devaluation of domestic labour. Removing them will require
changes not only in the access women have to social positions,
but also in their ability to shape and define those positions. These
reforms have not on the whole been endorsed by liberals, even
by liberal feminists. Liberal feminist political groups like the

National Organization of Women have concentrated on increasing access to the predominantly male spheres of government and business, without seeking to challenge the systematic devaluation and segregation of the predominantly female spheres of work (e.g. domestic work and the service sector). Jaggar in fact takes it as a defining characteristic of liberal feminism that it accepts the existing definitions and valuations of social roles as given, and seeks only to ensure equality of opportunity in the competition for those roles (Jaggar p. 177). Just as favouring the elimination of class-based inequalities may bring liberals closer to the traditional socialist programme, so favouring the elimination of gender-based inequalities may bring liberals closer to the radical feminist programme. Some people, again, will view such reforms as an abandonment of liberalism. But those reforms are consistent with, and indeed required by, the ideals of liberal equality.

Rawls and Dworkin often write as if the most obvious or likely result of implementing their conceptions of justice would be to increase the level of transfer payments between occupants of existing social roles (e.g. Dworkin 1981 p. 321; 1985 p. 207). But we have every reason to suppose that another important result would be to change the way existing roles are defined. As they both recognize, an important component of the primary goods or resources available to a person is opportunity for skill-development, for personal accomplishment, and for exercising responsibility. These are predominantly matters not of the material rewards for a given job, but of the power relations entailed by the job. People would not choose to enter social relations that deny these opportunities, that put them in a position of subjection or degradation, if they were able to choose from a position of equality. From a position of equality, women wouldn't have agreed to a system of social roles that defines 'male' jobs as superior to, and dominating over, 'female' jobs. We have every reason to believe this, since those gender roles were created not only without the consent of women, but in fact required the legal and political suppression of women.

For example, the roles of male and female health practitioners were coercively redefined by men, to fit their interests, against the will of women medical workers (Ehrenreich and English). With the rise of the medical 'profession', women were squeezed out of their traditional health-care roles (e.g. as midwives in Canada), and forced into the role of nurse—a position defined by male doctors for their own benefit. Health-care roles were redefined to create the position of nurse, a role which is subservient to, and financially less rewarding than, the role of doctor. And then the exclusion of women affected the way that the role of doctor was defined *vis-à-vis* the world of domestic labour (e.g. it became impossible to combine doctoring with motherhood). These changes presupposed the exclusion of women, and would not have arisen had there been a situation of genuine equality. More generally,

If a group is kept out of something for long enough, it is over-whelmingly likely that activities of that sort will develop in a way unsuited to the excluded group. We know for certain that women have been kept out of many kinds of work, and this means that the work is quite likely to be unsuited to them. The most obvious example of this is the incompatibility of most work with the bearing and rearing of children; I am firmly convinced that if women had been fully involved in the running of society from the start they would have *found* a way of arranging work and children to fit each other. (Radcliffe Richards pp. 113–14)

The same sort of injustice is present in the exaggerated distinction between 'mental' and 'manual' labour in our society. We have every reason to believe that people in a position of initial equality would not have created such a system, since the implementation of the 'scientific management' system, for example, was opposed by the workers, and would have been stopped if workers had the same power as capitalists (Braverman). Dworkin says that increased transfer payments are justified because we can assume that the poor would be willing to do the work in higher-paying jobs, if they entered the market on an equal footing (1985 p. 207). But we can also assume that if the poor entered the market on an equal footing, they wouldn't accept relations of unequal power and domination. We have as good evidence for the latter as for the former. Liberals, therefore, should seek not only to redistribute money from doctors to nurses, or from capitalists to workers, but also ensure that doctors and capitalists don't have the power to define relationships of power and domination. Justice requires that people's circumstances be evaluated, not only in terms of income, but also in terms of power relations.

As Dworkin says of the egalitarian premiss underlying Rawls's (and his own) theory, 'it cannot be denied in the name of any more radical concept of equality, because none exists' (Dworkin 1977 p. 182). That premiss may have more radical implications for the critique of class and gender inequality than Rawls or Dworkin envisage (Nielsen 1985 pp. 298–302). Socialists and feminists correctly point out failures in traditional liberal institutions, but they are often wrong in supposing that these failures express or reflect problems inherent in the liberal conception of the person, or of social justice. On the contrary, these institutions are failing because they *don't* properly express or reflect these liberal ideals.

These comments are, of course, far too brief to do justice to the issues at stake. But they help sketch a possible response to Taylor's charge that liberalism is atomistic and fails to recognize the full implications of the social thesis. Taylor is right to emphasize the importance of his social thesis, and hence the importance of a secure social context, of public principles of justice, and of civic participation. All these are of unquestionable importance. But that is just the problem. No one does question their importance (Rosenblum pp. 161–2). Liberal principles of justice may be misconceived, but not because they deny any of these obvious truths about our social situation.

Whether liberal politics would in fact sustain civic participation and a sense of public legitimacy is a complex question which is hard to answer, since liberal principles remain to be properly implemented. But I have tried to argue that the egalitarian principle of neutral concern is the most likely political principle to secure public assent in societies like ours, which are inherently diverse, and historically racist and sexist.[11] Inviting people to participate in political life on any other understanding is not likely to be successful. As Mill said, a feeling of commitment to a common public philosophy is a precondition of the culture of freedom, and 'the only shape in which the feeling is likely to exist hereafter' is an attachment to 'the principles of individual freedom and political and social equality, as realized in institutions which as yet exist nowhere, or exist only in a rudimentary state'

(Mill 1962 pp. 122–3). Those principles are still our only option, and they still remain largely unrealized in practice.

Moving closer to these liberal principles might well, as Connolly predicts, involve moving away from some traditional liberal institutions. But I now want to see whether this movement would take us 'beyond justice', as some Marxists claim.

Notes

1. Taylor's idea of the 'primacy of rights' does perhaps apply to some contractualist theories, like those of Hobbes and Gauthier, which seek to derive morality out of rational self-interest. But this is the sort of contract theory which Rawls excludes from the liberal social contract tradition (Rawls 1971 p. 11 n.). In any event, Taylor's arguments pose a challenge to theories beyond those which maintain the 'primacy of rights' in the strict sense, and I shall be considering this broader challenge.

2. The term was coined, I believe, by Raz (1982), although I am using it to refer to what he calls the 'exclusion of ideals', not what he calls 'neutral concern'. In Raz's terminology, the 'exclusion of ideals' principle says that governments cannot use as their justification for any action the fact that one person's way of life is more or less worthy than another's. The 'neutral concern' principle says that government action should seek to be neutral in its *effects* on people's ability to pursue their different conceptions of the good. These two principles conflict if, as in Rawls, Nozick, and Dworkin, people are held responsible for the costs of their choices (i.e. those with expensive tastes will be less able to advance those ends than others with more modest tastes).

   I continue to use the term 'neutral concern' for the exclusion of ideals since that is clearly what Rawls, Nozick, and Dworkin meant by neutrality, and their theories are the focus of current debates over neutrality. Raz claims that Rawls endorses neutral concern in Raz's sense, and that both Nozick and Dworkin confuse the two principles. But none of them ever express any sympathy for Raz's neutral concern. They all deny that their theories are neutral in their effects, and indeed they all have principled reasons for wanting their theories not to be neutral in their effects. The very reason they give for the exclusion of ideals (that individuals are responsible for their ends) is also reason to hold people responsible for the costs of their choices, and to deny that people are obligated to subsidize the costs of other people's choices (which is what Raz's neutral concern sometimes requires).

In endorsing the principle of neutral concern, I am adopting what is in fact a controversial position, even within liberalism. Some of those who put forward what they consider to be liberal theories deny that liberalism should be neutral in this way between competing conceptions of the good, and some neutrality-respecting liberals ground their neutrality in scepticism about the rational defensibility of conceptions of the good (e.g. Ackerman 1980 p. 11). The view I'm here adopting, however, grounds this neutrality in the egalitarian requirement discussed above: government neutrality is part of what it is to treat people as equals, given the view of our interests that I defended in Ch. 2. For liberal doubts about this project see Raz 1982, 1986; Galston 1982, 1986*b*; Haksar; Barry 1973 pp. 126–7; Rodewald; Alexander and Schwarzschild; R. Smith; Spragens; Neal; Thigpen and Downing. Although I can't discuss all these objections, I don't believe that any succeed in showing that governments should or must act on the basis of controversial judgements about the good life.

3. Some commentators give a very unattractive picture of a communitarian society that has rejected a politics of neutral concern for a politics of the common good. For example, Ackerman says that we must make sure that we don't 'find ourselves lost in the primeval communitarian ooze' (Ackerman 1983 p. 62; cf. Barry 1984 p. 525). He is obviously assuming that communitarianism intends or allows drastic departures from liberal principles. That may be a misinterpretation. But my concern is whether the social thesis gives us reason to deviate *at all* from a politics of neutral concern.

4. The point is not that diversity and complexity in the cultural environment are valued equally in different conceptions of the good. Rather, as Dworkin puts it, 'Since our intellectual environment provides the spectacles through which we identify experiences as valuable, it cannot sensibly be put on the scales as one of the experiences it identifies to be weighed against others and found more or less valuable than they' (Dworkin 1985 p. 228). The importance of cultural pluralism for a theory of liberal equality lies below, or prior to, the value attached to it in any of the particular conceptions which are contained in the culture.

5. One extreme version of this argument is found in Oldenquist's recent book, *The Non-Suicidal Society*. He argues that a society without such a common good would be suicidal (a condition he takes the contemporary United States to be in). This common good needs to be publicly affirmed, not only in principles of justice, but in all manner of grand ceremonies, rituals, and monuments

(Oldenquist 1986 ch. 14). This need comes from the fact that we are essentially 'tribal' creatures, and it is part of our 'Pleistocene inheritance'. Given the failure of liberal individualist attempts to stop the disintegration of American society, Oldenquist says 'it is time to take seriously biologically-based hypotheses about the collectivist, communitarian side of human beings' (p. 240).

6. Taylor does name Nozick as someone who denies we have any obligation to sustain the social conditions in which our capacities can develop (C. Taylor 1985 p. 206 n.). But he doesn't claim that Nozick denies the social thesis. Why would Nozick accept the social thesis yet not accept an obligation to protect the community? Taylor says it is a 'paradox' of Nozick's theory that he puts so much emphasis on free choice, and so little on the context from which we choose. But that is being too generous to Nozick. For this is not the only place in which Nozick sacrifices meaningful choice in order to protect the sanctity of property-rights. Nozick also rails against the evils of paternalism, when it would involve restricting people's rights, but he cheerfully invokes paternalism when it helps generate property-rights in the state of nature (G. A. Cohen 1985 p. 103). As Cohen puts it, 'Nozick cannot claim to be inspired throughout by a desire to protect freedom, unless he means by 'freedom' what he really does mean by it: the freedom of private property-owners to do as they wish with their property' (G. A. Cohen 1985 p. 104). Taylor doesn't name anyone who denies an obligation to the community *because they deny the social thesis*.

7. While Rawls and Dworkin do affirm the necessity of publicly recognized principles of justice, they do not give an adequate account of the way in which these principles, and the dispositions to obey them, are learned in society. This, in turn, raises the broader question of the nature of liberal education and child-rearing. These questions have been almost entirely neglected by recent liberal philosophers. For discussions of some aspects of these issues from a liberal perspective, see Strike (1982), De Lue (1986), and Gutmann (1982). It is not at all obvious that the required moral education is compatible with traditional notions of family autonomy and the domestic division of labour. For a discussion of the tensions created in Rawls's theory by his reliance on the family as a school of moral education alongside his neglect of the question of the justice of the family itself, see Okin (1989b). Although Taylor himself does not focus on this issue in his discussion of the empirical preconditions of a stable 'culture of freedom', it clearly is one of the most important preconditions, and the absence of a proper

account of moral education is a serious lacuna in contemporary liberal theory.

8. One remarkable example is MacIntyre's description of the 'shared ends' embodied in the classical tradition of virtues. MacIntyre claims that these ends were truly shared amongst, and furthered the good of, the members of the community as a whole, even though they were defined solely by one small part of the community. He recognizes that the community was defined to exclude slaves, and that women lacked political equality. But he none the less thinks that the 'common good' embodied in these traditions included the whole community. He thus ignores the obvious implications of the fact that women's virtues are defined in relation to the good of men, in a way that men's virtues are not defined in relation to the good of women (see the critique of MacIntyre in Okin 1989a; cf. MacIntyre pp. 116, 119).

9. As Herzog says, communitarians 'owe us an account of what commitments should bind us, what *content* the communal attachments that should transcend our individual projects should have, what exactly the common good should be' (Herzog p. 187). Without such an account, 'politics appears as a *deus ex machina*' in communitarian writings (Wallach p. 528). For other criticisms of the lack of political specifics in communitarian writings, see Gutmann 1985 pp. 318–19; Shapiro p. 297; Rosenblum pp. 157, 163, 179, 182.

10. See Okin 1979 ch. 9 for this assumption in Mill, and Jaggar ch. 4 for its role in Marx's thought.

11. I develop this argument at greater length in 'Liberal Neutrality and Liberal Individualism', *Ethics*, vol. 99 (1989).

6

Marxism and The Critique of Justice

MARXISTS and communitarians often employ the same rhetoric and imagery in their critiques of liberalism, and many people have supposed them to have similar grounds for rejecting its conception of community. However, the common rhetoric obscures important differences in their relationship to the liberal ideal. As I suggested in Chapter 2, I believe that Marx was in general agreement with the liberal view of our essential interests, and would have had no sympathy for the communitarian critique of it. His objections were to the way that liberals answered the second question involved in Dworkin's egalitarian plateau, about treating people as equals. Marx thought that liberal theories of justice and rights failed to describe a genuine community, a failure that he thought was inherent in any attempt to create a community of equals through the implementation of a theory of justice. A good community is beyond justice, since justice is a remedial virtue, a response to some flaw in the community that can and will be overcome. Marx's critique of justice has many strands, and raises some interesting questions about the implementation of a theory of justice. But this central claim about the remedial nature of justice is, I believe, mistaken. If it is dropped, it is unclear where or how the Marxist account of community differs from recent liberal egalitarian accounts.

We can get a better understanding of Marx's concerns about justice if we look at why he would have disavowed communitarianism. Communitarians, we've seen, reject the liberal account of our essential interests. They deny that our essential interest in having a good life can be conceived of as potentially different from our interest in the goods internal to the communal relations and practices we're currently situated in. Rather, our good just is the good internal to these practices, since they are constitutive of our personal identity. As MacIntyre puts it, 'what is good for me has to be the good for one who inhabits these roles' (MacIntyre p. 205). If we accept these social roles, and the goods internal to them, then community can be restored, as can the human fulfilment which can only occur inside these role-governed practices.

Now Marx too believed, of course, that human fulfilment would only occur when community was restored, and that capitalist societies denied this community: 'Only in community [with others has each] individual the means of cultivating his gifts in all directions; only in the community, therefore, is personal freedom possible' (Marx and Engels 1846 p. 83). But as that quote shows, the ultimate value for Marx, to which community provides the means, is the all-sided development of individuals, and this automatically excludes the communitarian solution to community. For Marx makes it clear that it is a requirement of any adequate solution to the problem of community that the individual not be limited in her activities by any pre-existing social roles (and corresponding expectations). Her truly human relations to others and to the community are not to be mediated by any social roles. The individual under communism paints or hunts just as she pleases, without ever being a painter or hunter (Marx and Engels 1846 p. 54), i.e. without ever adopting a social identity of the sort that sets boundaries to development, that sets a predetermined range of goals for her. For Marx, this was a sign of the incompleteness of historical development (Marx and Engels 1846 p. 86; Marx 1858 pp. 161–2), to be replaced by the universal development of individuals who freely reproduce themselves as a 'totality' without any 'predetermined yardstick' (Marx 1858 p. 488), exercising their 'capacity to enjoy the all-sided production of the whole earth' (Marx and Engels 1846 p. 55).

The dispute here isn't that MacIntyre, for example, stresses the value of a life of 'integrity' based on dedication to a single project that is definitive of our social role (MacIntyre ch. 15), whereas Marx envisions people pursuing accomplishment in several projects. To be sure, Marx would have considered such single-minded devotion to one project as evidence of reified, not truly free, activity (Elster pp. 78–82). And surely not every person, or every project, benefits from such unity of purpose in life. But the real issue is not how many projects we pursue, but rather whether those projects, however numerous, are given to us in virtue of our being embedded in certain communal roles, or whether, in contrast, our activities and projects are to be unconstrained by the existence of such roles. And for Marx, the value of communism lies precisely in its liberating people from the sorts of social roles which, for communitarians, are the bases of our personal identity and moral deliberations. (Of course, communitarians might agree with Marxists about the importance of liberating people from the alienating nature of many roles as they are interpreted under capitalism. But communitarians would free people by reinterpreting and strengthening the communal nature of these identity-defining roles, whereas Marx would free people by eliminating identity-defining roles.)

The existence of a set of socially defined roles means that 'man's own deed becomes an alien power opposed to him, which enslaves him instead of being controlled by him. For as soon as the distribution of labour comes into being, each man has a particular, exclusive sphere of activity, which is forced upon him and from which he cannot escape' (Marx and Engels 1846 pp. 53–4). Communism ends this 'fixation of social activity', this 'consolidation of what we ourselves produce into an objective power above us' (ibid.). In communist society, far from having my activity set for me by my social position, I may 'hunt in the morning, fish in the afternoon, rear cattle in the evening, criticise after dinner, just as I have a mind, without ever becoming hunter, fisherman, herdsman or critic' (ibid.). We do as we choose, in accordance with our beliefs about value, without ever adopting the sort of social identity that communitarians say should be the basis of that choice.[1]

Now it's interesting to note how similar this is to the liberal view of our choices and interests, a similarity that some communitarians draw attention to. Taylor, for example, mentions that both Kant and Marx had the 'absolute freedom' view which he argues is empty. Both 'wanted to go beyond the given altogether' (C. Taylor 1979 p. 156), to master and subordinate, and make over according to our purposes, all the presuppositions of our social situation. Both felt that individuals should not be forced to take the roles and expectations of society as pre-determined yardsticks of a valuable life. Indeed, the 'emptiness' objection I considered in Chapter 4 was directed more at Marx than at liberals.

That, of course, doesn't show that Marx and liberals share the same account of our essential interests. They might share the same commitment to individual freedom of choice, but for different reasons. And Marx does seem to give a different basis for his endorsement of free choice. Marx argued that freely chosen activity is our essential interest because this is what differentiates us from other species—i.e. it's what defines us *as humans*. But this 'differentia' argument is, of course, a *non sequitur*, notwithstanding its venerable roots in Western thought. Asking what is best in a human life is not a question 'about biological classification. It is a question in moral philosophy. And we do not help ourselves at all in answering it if we decide in advance that the answer ought to be a single, simple characteristic, unshared by other species, such as the differentia is meant to be' (Midgley p. 204). Exaltation of freely chosen creative activity 'is a particular moral position and must be defended as such against others; it cannot ride into acceptance on the back of a crude method of taxonomy' (ibid.). If other animals had exactly the same capacities that Marx discusses, it would do no harm to his claim about our essential interests. But nor does the absence of such animals provide any support for his claim. The idea of a human differentia does not work in an argument about our essential interests.

Another problem with Marx's argument is the one that Taylor points to in his emptiness objection. If we try to pursue free creativity for its own sake, we are left without any direction to our life, for the idea of such freedom provides us with no determinate criterion for deciding what to do. It doesn't tell us what is *worth* doing in a freely creative way. Telling someone to be 'creative' is an empty instruction. Taylor thinks that this emptiness shows that free creativity can't be of inherent value. But another explanation may be available. Free creativity may be one of those values that only arise as a by-product of action directed at some other end. A classic example of such a value concerns the in-process benefits of collective action. One can achieve a valuable sense of solidarity and belonging from participation in a political movement, but one can't pursue that value directly, because solidarity supervenes on the activity of people *who are dedicated to some other end.*

The same situation applies to the value of free creativity. One only gets the satisfaction of free creativity in one's activity if there is something one independently believes to be worth creating for its own sake. Creating clothes, for example, is only worth while if clothes are worth producing, and we will only get satisfaction from freely creating them if we believe them to be worth creating for their own sake, prior to and independently of their status as an instance of free creativity. If we produce clothes, not because we believe they have any intrinsic value, but because it's simply a way of being freely creative, then the activity will not be very satisfying. We have to *care* about the thing we are doing, and believe in its worth, in order to get the satisfaction of freely creating it. As Elster says, 'In a society geared towards self-realization no one should be concerned with self-realization. They should be concerned with the tasks at hand—writing books, making embroideries or playing chess' (Elster p. 523).

Marx's differentiation argument doesn't tell us whether the value of our 'distinctive' capacities can be directly pursued or not. According to Gould's interpretation, Marx felt that we should pursue free individuality for its own sake. After saying that self-realization comes about through fulfilment of one's purposes, she goes on to say that in Marx's view

one is *apparently* acting for the sake of these purposes themselves posited as external aims. But insofar as the fulfilment of these purposes is self-fulfilment or is an activity of self-realization, the end that these purposes serve and the ultimate value achieved in this activity is self-realization, that is, freedom. When this self-realization is consciously taken as the end in itself of these activities, freedom becomes manifest as the end in itself. Thus freedom is not only the activity that creates value but is that for the sake of which all these other values are pursued and therefore that with respect to which they become valuable. (Gould p. 118)

But self-realization is only achieved if the 'external aims' are valued in themselves, not just as means to freedom. To be fair to Gould, Marx does seem to make this mistake in one passage. He asks: What is wealth but a situation where man 'strives not to remain something he has become, but is in the absolute movement of becoming?' (Marx 1858 p. 488). If he means that people in communism will *in fact* be 'in the absolute movement of becoming' since their activity won't be constrained by a 'predetermined yardstick' (ibid.), and so the activities they find valuable will be indefinitely various and developing, then I have no objection. But if he means, with Gould, that people will be 'striving' to be in that absolute movement of becoming, and will view any activity as simply a means to that movement, then their striving will be self-defeating. Freely creative labour may be inherently satisfying, but that satisfaction isn't something that can be directly pursued for its own sake.

Marx seems to recognize this in another passage of the *Grundrisse*, where he's criticizing Adam Smith for equating tranquillity with freedom and happiness:

It seems quite far from Smith's mind that the individual, 'in his normal state of health, strength, activity, skill, facility', also needs a normal portion of work, and of the suspension of tranquility. Certainly, labour obtains its measure from the outside, through the aim to be attained and the obstacles to be overcome in attaining it. But Smith has no inkling whatever that this overcoming of obstacles is in itself a liberating activity—and that, further, the external aims become stripped of the semblance of merely external natural urgencies, and become posited as aims which the individual himself posits—hence as self-realization, objectification of the subject, hence real freedom, whose action is, precisely, labour. (Marx 1858 p. 611)

Labour, he says, always gets its measure from the outside, through the aim to be attained. What makes this activity really free, and inherently satisfying, is that these aims are posited by the individual for the inherent value found in them, rather than being pursued under pressure of 'merely external natural urgencies', or what he elsewhere calls the 'pressure of extraneous purpose', like the need to make money to survive in conditions of material scarcity, or to fulfil certain socially given role expectations. Exercising our capacity for free choice is both a precondition for getting the value of our activities, and has some inherent value of its own; but the goal we are always pursuing (really pursuing, not merely *apparently* pursuing) is the value of whatever project or activity we are engaged in. 'Really free working' (ibid.) is self-realizing, but that self-realization is neither the aim nor the measure of such work.

But if this is the story that Marx wishes to stand by, then the idea of species-differentiation has dropped out entirely, and the story isn't fundamentally different from the liberal story I described in Chapter 2. Just as Mill says free choice is valuable because of the value of the things being chosen, so Marx says that free creativity is valuable because of the value of the aims we creatively pursue. And in each case, the projects only have value if freely chosen, if the aims are freely posited by the individual, since we have to lead our lives from the inside.

Marx may have thought that the fact that humans alone have the capacity for free creativity was relevant to its value. But that is a mistake, and in any event, it doesn't really explain *how* it is supposed to be valuable for human lives. If we look beneath the argument about species-differentiation to his account of how freedom matters to us, we find an answer that is not that dissimilar to the liberal view.

But if Marxists and liberals share this view of the self, and of our essential interests, then why do they not have the same theory of justice? If Marx shared this view, he should have been equally concerned that the social conditions of individual freedom be secured for the members of the community. Yet it seems clear that Marx, unlike liberals, didn't make these conditions something that individuals could claim, *as rights*, within a theory of *justice*.

But this, I believe, does not show that Marx had a different view of our essential interests. Rather he had a different view about the second question raised by Dworkin's egalitarian plateau—that is, about what follows from supposing that these interests matter equally. For liberals, this second question has an obvious answer: we promote the *moral* equality of people by formulating a theory of *juridical* equality, which attempts to secure for each individual the conditions which promote her essential interest in a life that is in fact good. Since liberals believe that all individuals are to be treated as equals by the government, justice requires that the liberties and resources necessary to examine and act on our beliefs about value be secured for each individual equally.

Marx however was quite averse to this liberal answer to the second question. Some people say that Marx was averse to the whole question. According to Wood, Marx was 'no friend to the idea that "equality" is something good in itself' (Wood 1979 p. 281). He denies that Marx believed in communism because he was 'a believer in a society of equals' (Wood 1981 p. 195). In Wood's view, Marx would have rejected the 'abstract egalitarian plateau' which underlies the second question.

But I think Wood is mistaken here. The idea of treating people as equals is fundamental to Marx. It often appears in Marx in the same form that it appears in Kant, i.e. as the requirement that we should treat people as ends not means. This requirement underlies both his critique of capitalism and his defence of communism. He thought that capitalism failed to treat people as ends, not means, in two main areas (at least).

(1) *The relations of production.* Marx condemns the capitalist labour process as dehumanizing, reducing the worker to the status of a thing, an instrument, a part of the machine. Proletarians are treated as a factor of production along with inanimate machines and resources, to be exploited by the capitalist. Workers are the 'conscious linkages' of the production process whose activity 'merely transmits the machine's work, the machine's action' (Marx 1858 p. 692). In this production process, labour (our conscious purposive activity) no longer governs the process: 'Labour appears, rather, merely as a conscious organ, scattered among the living workers at numerous points of the mechanical system; subsumed under the total process of the machinery itself, as itself only a link of the system' (Marx 1858 p. 693). Workers become not only appendages to the machine, but are used up, slowly destroyed, just as machines are used up and thrown away.

(2) *The relations of exchange.* In the market-place, we view others merely as means to our enrichment. We produce things not to fulfil the needs of others, but as the only way to advance our interests. As the president of General Motors once said, his job wasn't to make cars, but to make money. Car buyers, and their transportation needs, weren't his concern. He didn't see himself as responding to the worthwhile claims and needs of others. Rather, he saw their needs as something he could exploit to further his interests and needs. As Buchanan puts it, when people meet in the market, 'Each views the *needs* and *desires* of the other not as needs and desires, but rather as levers to be manipulated, as weaknesses to be preyed upon' (Buchanan p. 39).[2]

So 'some of Marx's most trenchant criticisms of alienation in capitalism focus on the ways in which social interaction in capitalism fails to recognize, or even subverts, the distinction between persons and mere things' (Buchanan p. 78). This idea, as Buchanan notes, is the Kantian way of rendering vivid the requirement of moral equality, of equal concern and respect, and it is basic to Marx's moral position.

So Marx does accept the basic assumption of moral equality, and the question of how to treat people as equals. What he rejects is that the answer to it should take the form of a theory of *juridical* equality. I think this is made clear in the very passages that Wood cites. The crucial one is the Gotha Programme passage where Marx attacks the ideas of 'equal right' and 'fair distribution' as 'obsolete verbal rubbish' (Marx 1875 p. 321). In this passage, Marx accepts the principle of moral equality, but denies that it can be spelt out in terms of a system of rights. The passage involves a critique of the 'contribution principle', i.e. the claim that labourers have a right to the products of their labour. Marx says that the contribution principle is an 'equal right' in that 'measurement is made with an *equal standard*, labour'. However, some people are more naturally talented, so this 'equal right is an unequal right for unequal labour':

it tacitly recognizes unequal individual endowment and thus productive capacity as natural privileges. *It is, therefore, a right of inequality, in its content, like every right.* Right by its very nature can consist only in the application of an equal standard; but unequal individuals (and they would not be different individuals if they were not unequal) are measurable only by an equal standard in so far as they are brought under an equal point of view, are taken from one *definite* side only, for instance, in the present case, are regarded *only as workers* and nothing more is seen in them, everything else being ignored. (Marx 1875 p. 320)

He is here endorsing a principle of equal regard, but denying that any 'equal right' ever captures it because rights only work by defining one limited viewpoint from which individuals are to be regarded equally. In reality, the number of viewpoints relevant to the fullest expression of equal regard is indefinite, or in any event, can't be specified in advance. But notice that this description of 'equal right' is only a *criticism* if people *are* owed equal concern and respect. The way in which Marx thinks individuals are necessarily unequal has nothing to do with, and lends no support to, the idea that there should be any inequality in the moral status of people, any inequality in the concern and respect shown people. On the contrary, the claim that rights are necessarily unequal is only a criticism if people are owed equal consideration. Trying to enforce equal regard through a limited number of equal rights both ignores relevant moral differences and, we may imagine, distorts human development, since it specifies a 'predetermined yardstick' according to which individuals will be rewarded, whereas Marx felt individuals should develop freely, unconstrained by such prior social determinants. Marx rejected the idea of equal right, not because he wasn't a friend to the idea of treating people as equals, but precisely because rights failed to live up to that ideal.[3]

What distinguishes Marx from liberals, then, is his refusal to enforce the moral equality of the members of communist society through a theory of juridical equality. This is one reason that Marx was such a challenging theorist. The egalitarian tradition in Western thought is a deep one, but Marx questions many of the traditional assumptions and expectations about how to implement such equality. He denies that equality can be captured in any theory of fair distribution, or of equal rights. He considered such ideas to be 'obsolete verbal rubbish' which obscured the real issues and changes that were needed.

The good society, communist society, will be beyond justice, not defined or governed by theories of fair shares or equal rights. This is in stark contrast to Rawls, for example, who says that 'justice is the first virtue of social institutions' (Rawls 1971 p. 3). For Marx, justice represents the failure to achieve truly virtuous social institutions, or a truly good community.

He has a number of different reasons for rejecting the idea of juridical equality. I'll discuss three minor arguments against justice, and one major one, which underlies the others. The first minor one, we've seen, is that he thinks equal rights necessarily have unequal effects, since they only specify a limited number of the morally relevant standpoints. But that argument is very weak, both because we have no reason to think that the relevant viewpoints are in fact indefinite, and, more importantly, because even if they were, it wouldn't follow that the best way of treating people with equal regard is by not specifying any viewpoints at all. Even if a schedule of rights can't fully model equal regard, it may do so better than any other alternative, especially if there is a back-up general right to equality. It may be true that even our best attempt to specify the viewpoints which the general right to equality makes morally relevant will be imperfect. But we could have a back-up right to equality for those who fall into categories not covered by our schedule of specific rights.

This is roughly the way that Dworkin interprets the relationship between the Fourteenth Amendment of the American Constitution, guaranteeing equal protection of the law to all citizens, and the more specific rights that individuals are held to have (Dworkin 1977 pp. 113 n., 321 n.). If the specific rights fail to fully respect people as moral equals, due to their limited viewpoints, then people can appeal to the general right to equality itself as a final resort. That is, we can build into our judicial theory, and our judicial institutions, some mechanism for recognizing and correcting the flaws which Marx says attach to any specific schedule of rights.

The second minor objection Marx has to the idea of justice also appears in his *Critique of the Gotha Programme*. Theories of fair distribution concentrate too much on *distribution*, rather than on the more fundamental questions of *production* (Marx 1875 p. 321). If all we do is redistribute income from those who own productive assets to those who don't, then we shall still have classes, exploitation, and hence the kind of contradictory interests that make justice necessary in the first place. We should instead be concerned with changing the relations of production, transferring ownership of the means of production themselves. When this is accomplished, questions of fair distribution become obsolete.

Now this is surely of the utmost political importance, and it remains a common objection to liberal theories of justice today (e.g. I. Young; Wolff pp. 199–208). Many proposals made in the political arena suffer from just the flaw that Marx notices. Our concern *should* be with ownership, since it constitutes both wealth and power.[4] Ownership allows people not only to accrue greater income, but also gain a substantial measure of control over other people's lives. People care not only about the disposable income that they have, but also about the power relations that they are involved in. A scheme of redistributive taxation may leave a capitalist and a proletarian with equal incomes, but it would still leave the capitalist with the power to decide how the worker spends much of her time, a power that the proletarian lacks in relation to the capitalist.

As an objection to the idea of justice, however, Marx's complaint fails. There's nothing in the idea of justice that limits it to questions of income. On the contrary, both Rawls and Dworkin include productive assets as one of society's resources to be distributed in accordance with a theory of justice. If both of them tend, when discussing the practical implementation of their theories, to look at schemes of income redistribution, rather than any fundamental redistribution of wealth, that is not the fault of their concern for justice. On the contrary, productive assets, as much as income, are meant to be distributed equally, unless inequalities are to the benefit of the least well-off (Rawls), or reflect differences in choices, not differences in circumstances (Dworkin). The entrenched inequalities of class and gender obviously don't meet Rawls's and Dworkin's criteria, and their failure to question those inequalities is a failure to live up to their own stated ideals. Nothing in their theories warrants their inattention to questions about the distribution of productive assets.

Marx's third minor objection to justice is a strategic one. Appeals to justice tend to divide people, and lead to needless sectarian arguments and confusions. As he says, 'Do not the bourgeois assert that the present-day distribution is "fair"? . . . Have not also the socialist sectarians the most varied notions about "fair" distribution?' (Marx 1875 pp. 317–18). Since different groups have different conceptions of justice, appealing to justice only hinders the unity of the socialist movement.

This pessimistic view of the efficacy of appeals to justice didn't trouble Marx because he believed there was a natural unity in the socialist movement. That is not a belief that is easy for us to share. His belief in that pre-existing unity reflects a too narrow view of the alternatives available to us, which in turn reflects a mistaken view about the development of capitalism. Marx thought that capitalism would be plagued by recurring and worsening crises, and that in such crises, the choice of action would be clear. It would be a choice, as Rosa Luxemburg put it, between socialism and barbarism. If that were our choice, or even if we could be sure that it would become our choice, then it is likely that most or all workers would agree on socialism, notwithstanding their disagreements over justice. But that has never been our choice, nor can we safely predict that it will become our choice. There has always been a much larger range of options, different strategies as well as different goals, and the justice of these different options is a question we face, whether or not we use justice as our rallying cry.

Marx thought that justice was, in a certain sense, epiphenomenal. It could be dropped without damage to the movement, since the movement would be carried forward anyway by the flow of historical events which put people in positions of little or no choice. But history has not pushed everyone into the same corner with the same limited choice. We, as individuals or as groups, have to decide which of the many options available to us are the most important, which are the most beneficial. These things are by no means obvious, even when we are agreed on the facts of the situation. How does our obligation to the racially oppressed relate to our obligation to those oppressed by sex, or class? These struggles developed separately, sometimes in opposition. Unity won't be restored by asking everyone to give up their appeals to justice, for there is no pre-existing unity to be restored. It is up to us to *build* unity in the struggle for a society of equals—history won't do it for us. And appeals to justice may be one of the most effective means of building that unity, either by finding common ground within the different conceptions of justice, or by persuading others that our conception is more defensible. Once we recognize that there is no pre-existing unity to the socialist movement, then appeals to justice, far from undermining that unity, may be needed to create it. At any rate, Marx has given us no reason to believe that justice is more divisive than any other way of rallying people for progressive social change.

So none of these three minor objections to justice are compelling. At best, they point to limitations in the way that some people have developed and implemented their conceptions of justice. But these minor objections do not really get to the heart of Marx's critique of the liberal conception of *community*. Marx had a deeper objection to the very idea of a juridical community, and it is one which he shares with the communitarians. They both believe that justice is a remedial virtue, a response to some defect in community, some incompleteness in the development of community, which can and should be overcome. Justice, far from being the first virtue of social institutions, is something that the truly good community has no need for. Justice is appropriate only if we are in the 'circumstances of justice', circumstances which create the kinds of conflicts between people that require principles of justice to resolve. These circumstances are usually said to be of two main kinds: differing goals, and limited material resources. If people all shared the same goals and ends, then people wouldn't make conflicting claims on scarce social resources, since they would all agree on how those resources should be utilized. Or even if people differed in their projects, conflicts wouldn't arise if there was an abundance of resources for all. If either of these circumstances of justice were eliminated, then we'd have no need for a theory of juridical equality, and be better off for it.

But while both Marxists and communitarians believe in the supersession of justice, as an aspect of the development of a higher form of community, they concentrate on different problems. For communitarians, the defect to be overcome is conflicting conceptions of the good. Sandel, following Hegel, takes the family as an example of a social institution which is non-juridical, where there is an identity of interest and ends, in which people respond spontaneously to the needs of others out of love, rather than responding on the basis of rightful obligations and claims, or calculations of one's own advantage (Hegel pp. 110–12; Sandel 1982 pp. 30–5). If the community as a whole also had an identity of interests and affective ties, then justice wouldn't be needed, because to conceive of oneself as a bearer of rights is to 'view oneself as a potential party to interpersonal conflicts in which it is *necessary* to assert claims and to "stand up" for what one claims as one's due' (Buchanan p. 76). If, as in the family, we fulfilled each other's needs out of love, or out of a harmony of interests, then there'd be no occasion for such a concept of rights to appear.

Some people think that Marx also believed in this vision of an affectively integrated community with an identity of interests. Of course, Marx didn't accept that the family is an example of such a community, because he believed that the family is in fact a microcosm of the exploitation and alienation of the larger class-divided society, not a sphere of identical interests and genuinely reciprocal need-fulfilment (Marx 1858 p. 50; 1844*b* pp. 88–90). As a result, 'Marx cannot argue, as other socialists have, that the harmonious family provides a preview of the affectively integrated, nonegoistic life' of the members of communist society (Buchanan p. 13).

Now I think, *contra* Buchanan and other commentators, that Marx not only didn't endorse using the family as the model of the affectively integrated life of communist individuals, he also didn't endorse the very idea of an affectively integrated community, and, *a fortiori*, didn't use that idea as a solution to the circumstances of justice. I think it is material abundance which allows communist society to overcome the need for justice.

That is a controversial claim, and requires some explanation. Marx does say that life in communism would be a 'social life' (Marx 1844*b* pp. 90–3), that communist individuals would be 'social individuals' (Marx 1858 pp. 197, 705, 832), and that capitalism is a denial of our essentially social nature. But these statements are invariably sketchy, and should be interpreted carefully. My view is that Marx is not saying that there will be any necessary harmony or identity of interests and projects, nor that we should aim at creating such a harmony or identity of interests. Therefore, Marx must be adopting a different approach to the supersession of justice from the communitarian one.

Marx's comments on the social nature of communism are best approached through his critique of capitalism. Capitalism is a denial of our essentially social nature in three ways. Firstly, its social relations set 'man against man'. They are exploitative, not only in the specific sense of extracting surplus labour, but in the more general sense of using someone as a means, utilizing her to her detriment as a way of promoting one's own good (Marx and Engels 1846 p. 110; Marx 1844*a* pp. 121–2). This is true, we've seen, not only of the relations of production, but also of the relations of exchange. Secondly, it creates a variety of forms of social alienation, in which the social creations of an individual take on an alien independence, 'enslaving him instead of being controlled by him' (Marx and Engels 1846 p. 54). These include the imperatives of capitalist competition, role requirements of the division of labour, rigours of the labour market, and what Marx calls the 'fetishism' of money, capital, and commodities. These forms of alienation prevent us from recognizing our social products as our own. Thirdly, related to this second problem, capitalism alienates and separates the 'public' man from the 'private' man, the 'bourgeois' of civil society from the 'citizen' of the state. The state is supposed to be the arena where individuals consider and pursue the general interest, the common good. It's the arena where individuals act morally, accepting responsibility for their fellow citizens, in contrast to the pursuit of personal interest in competition with others in civil society. But this separation is not only sociologically impossible (the state, being superstructural, becomes an instrument of class rule), but psychologically alienating (we can't separate out our social concern from our everyday life without distorting and diminishing it). In all of these ways, capitalism tends to inhibit the expression of our social natures.

In contrast with these features of capitalism, communism will avowedly promote 'social life', conformity with our nature as a social animal (Marx 1844*b* pp. 92–3). It will witness the emergence of the 'social individual'. Different commentators have taken very different and often extravagant ways of interpreting such passages. But I think they have fairly limited and clear meanings, intended as contrasts to the three antisocial features of capitalism I mentioned above. I shall take them in reverse order.

In his response to the problem of the separation of state and society, Marx says that to be a 'species-being' leading a 'species-life',

The actual individual man must take the abstract citizen back into himself and, as an individual man in his empirical life, in his individual work and individual relationships become a species-being; man must recognize his own forces as social forces, organize them, and thus no longer separate social forces from himself in the form of political forces. (Marx 1843 p. 57)

Thus he envisions an end of the 'separation of man into a public and a private man' (Marx 1843 p. 47). 'Species-being' here means simply someone whose membership in a society (and consequent responsibility for its organization and direction) is given some concrete content in her everyday life, rather than being left to an alienated sphere with no real meaning for her. 'Species-life' here has nothing to do with altruism or any other affective tie.

The second problem was that of alienation and reification. Marx discusses how the development of capitalism means that 'social wealth confronts labour . . . as an alien and dominating power' (Marx 1858 p. 831), but goes on to say that

> with the positing of the activity of individuals as immediately general or *social* activity, the objective moments of production are stripped of this form of alienation; they are thereby posited as property, as the organic social body within which the individuals reproduce themselves as individuals, but as social individuals. (Marx 1858 p. 832)

Even more explicitly, he says that in communism

> it is neither the direct human labour he himself performs, nor the time during which he works, but rather the appropriation of his own general productive power, his understanding of nature and his mastery over it by virtue of his presence as a social body—it is, in a word, the development of the social individual which appears as the great foundation-stone of production and of wealth. (Marx 1858 p. 705)

These passages (and a similar one in Marx 1858 p. 197) are the only ones I know of where Marx uses the term 'social individual' to characterize post-capitalist individuals. He is discussing the changes that people go through in overcoming the alienation of capitalism, and he glosses these changes in terms of the emergence of social individuals. But notice that these changes are *cognitive* ones. That is, the social individual is one who has consciously 'appropriated' the powers of social production, who 'posits' the productive process as a social process, not one governed by alien and independent powers and forces. It is the overcoming of reification which restores the control we have over our own products. Again, it has nothing to do with affective ties between individuals.[5]

The first problem I mentioned was that social relations under the capitalist division of labour are exploitative. Marx says that 'the division of labour implies the contradiction between the interests of the separate individual or the individual family and the communal interest of all individuals who have intercourse with one another' (Marx and Engels 1846 p. 53). This in turn implies the absence of such contradictory interests in communism, which will abolish the division of labour. But the context of these and similar passages doesn't support the view that Marx is here predicting a complete harmony of individual interests in a communist community. He is referring only to conflicts that arise between people *independently of their choices*. Capitalism denies our social life by creating such conflicts, and communism will eliminate them. But that leaves entirely open the question of whether conflicts will arise *as a result of people's choices*. Marx does not say that conflicts of *this* kind, that reflect differences in our freely chosen projects, are denials of our social nature, or that communist society will seek to eliminate them.

Marx says that the division of labour is the cause of this contradiction in interests. The division of labour is an 'identical expression' for private property (ibid.). And private property, according to Marx, is a set of 'relations that are indispensable and independent of [the] will' of those who are in them (Marx 1859 p. 181). When this structure of social relations exists, 'activity is not voluntarily, but naturally, divided . . . each man has a particular, exclusive sphere of activity, which is forced upon him and from which he cannot escape' (Marx and Engels 1846 p. 53). It is this structure of social relations that Marx is referring to when he discusses the presence (or absence) of the contradiction between the individual's interest and the interest of other members of the community (ibid.). People are in relationships, unchosen by them, which inherently set their development against that of others, which inherently require that I utilize others as they utilize me. Communism will do away with this 'contradiction' in interest because the structure of communist relations won't inherently mean that others must be treated as means. People won't find themselves in conflict with others independently of their choices.

When Marx says that the contradiction between our interests will come to an end in communism, is he also claiming that there won't be any conflicts between individuals that arise from their choices? I see no reason to attribute this to him. As Elster notes, Marx never uses the term 'contradiction' to refer to mere conflict, only to *structurally generated* conflicts, conflicts generated by social relations which are independent of individual choice

(Elster pp. 43–4). The end of structurally generated contradictions doesn't imply anything at all about the rise of affective ties or the decline of conflicting individual choices.

In short, in the various places that Marx discusses the 'social' nature of communism, he has in mind either (*a*) the integration of political decision-making into everyday life; or (*b*) the cognition that the powers and forces of society are indeed the powers and forces of associated producers, not of some alien, natural thing; or (*c*) the absence of structurally generated conflicts of interest prior to and independent of individuals' choices. None of these claims suggest a harmony of concerns and projects. Indeed, none of them even discuss that question. To assume he meant anything more, or different, seems to me to be a gratuitous attribution.

In fact, in the 1859 *Preface* Marx makes explicit what I've been arguing—that he's not assuming the absence of individual conflicts in ends and goals. He says that 'The bourgeois relations of production are the last antagonistic form of the social process of production—antagonistic not in the sense of individual antagonism, but of one arising from the social conditions of life of the individuals' (Marx 1859 p. 182).

The fact that Marx's view of sociality is structural and cognitive, not affective, is suggested by some commentators. Elster, for example, suggests that Marx's ideal of social life under communism is akin to a community of scholars 'in which each member finds his satisfaction by offering *his* product to others, for criticism and appreciation. Identifiability then is of the essence' (Elster p. 454). We produce for the community, seeking the criticism and appreciation of others. We don't produce in order to prey upon their weaknesses, as in capitalist production, but nor do we produce in order to fulfil their purposes. But Elster goes on to say, without textual support, that communist man will produce 'for the sake of the community' (Elster p. 523). He then takes it as a paradox of Marx's view that the community of creators he envisions 'is also a domain in which altruism takes second place to emulation, competition and self-assertion' (Elster p. 524). But there's no paradox here, for Elster's attribution to Marx that people will produce altruistically is gratuitous. Elster was right the first time: sociality under communism is based on production for the community, 'for criticism and appreciation', and that is completely compatible with the individual self-assertion that Elster notes, and with the individual antagonisms that Marx explicitly allows may remain in communism.

But if Marx allows for conflicting goals and projects, how are the circumstances of justice overcome? Marx sees material scarcity as the crucial circumstance, and the one that can be eliminated.

In a higher phase of communist society, after the enslaving subordination of the individual to the division of labour . . . has vanished; after labour has become not only a means to life but life's prime want; after the productive forces have also increased with the all-round development of the individual, and all the springs of co-operative wealth flow more abundantly—only then can the narrow horizon of bourgeois right be crossed in its entirety and society inscribe on its banners: From each according to his ability, to each according to his needs! (Marx 1875 pp. 320–1)

Notice that Marx doesn't say that justice is superseded when individuals cease to have conflicting goals in life, or when a 'more developed form of altruism' arises (Elster p. 524). Justice is superseded because of abundance. The same thought is made even clearer in *The German Ideology*, where he says that the highest development of the productive forces 'is an absolutely necessary practical premise [of communism] because without it *want* is merely made general, and with *destitution* the struggle for necessities and all the old filthy business would necessarily be reproduced' (Marx and Engels 1846 p. 56). It was perhaps because he was so pessimistic about the social effects of scarcity that he became so optimistic about material abundance. Post-juridical life apparently is impossible without abundance, and is guaranteed by abundance. Affective ties and identity of interests don't seem to play much of a role in the account.

Now it might be thought that this can't be all of the story, for even if the *structure* of relations is non–exploitative, what prevents people from choosing to attempt to create exploitative relations on a limited, personal, and short-term scale? Why not form coalitions to exploit minorities in the workplace or community? Surely affective ties are needed to explain the absence of exploitation at the *individual*, not structural, level. If

Marx didn't embrace Elster's (or Gould's) idea of affective
'mutuality', why did he think that social interaction would be
'reciprocal' (Avineri p. 89; Gould pp. 175–6; Elster pp. 453–4)?
Why did he think that people would choose to treat each other
as equals? Because, I think, abundance ensures that people can
opt out of non-reciprocal relations, relations in which one party
is treated instrumentally, without fear of losing their means of
livelihood. As Avineri says, if one's relations and attachments
'are unilateral, they cease to be a relationship, degrading the
other person to the status of a mere object, rather than a co-equal
subject' (Avineri p. 89), and no one would accept that status
when they can opt out and get their resources from the stock
of social wealth (Elster p. 517).

   This seems to be Engels's solution at any rate. When discussing
the nature of sexual relations in communism, he says that the
old patriarchal relations will end, but

> what will there be new? That will be answered when a new generation
> has grown up: a generation of men who never in their lives have
> known what it is to buy a woman's surrender with money or any
> other social instrument of power, a generation of women who have
> never known what it is to give themselves to a man from any other
> considerations than real love or to refuse to give themselves to their
> lover from fear of the economic consequences. When these people are
> in the world, they will care precious little what anybody today thinks
> they ought to do; they will make their own practice and their
> corresponding public opinion about the practice of each individual—
> and that will be the end of it. (Engels in Jaggar pp. 227–8)

What seems to ensure that non-exploitative relations will develop
is that men lack any advantage in the social instruments of
power, and women lack any economic vulnerability. The extent
to which such relations involve a greater or lesser degree of
altruism, and the extent to which such relationships will have
different goals, are left open questions—there is no correct
socialist model of personal relations which is to be imposed on
people regardless of their affections or goals. The level of altruism
and harmony is left an open question, but the guarantee
of material well-being makes merely instrumental relations
untenable. Such unilateral relations are unavoidable in capitalism,
due to material scarcity, whether we have a theory of justice or

not; but they are unsustainable in communism, and justice isn't needed to prevent them.[6]

So Marx's defence of the overcoming of justice seems to rest more on abundance than on the harmony of interests that communitarians rely on. Of course the presence of abundance, as well as the other changes that Marx envisions (the end of reification, the integration of the political into everyday life, etc.), is sure to have a considerable effect on the kinds of choices that people make about what to do with their lives. As social scientists, we can try to predict what those changes will be, and Marx considered himself such a social scientist. His prediction was that these changes would lead people to choose more co-operative and productive life-styles (Marx 1844*a* p. 122). That is, rather than viewing labour as oppressive, and the privacy of their home as freedom, people in communism would see social labour as their prime want and most important project. That prediction follows from Marx's explanation of why people choose otherwise at present. According to Marx, the reification, alienation, and material insecurity of capitalism all serve to blind us to the value of co-operative life-styles, or indeed to their very possibility. If we assume, as Marx did, that such ways of life are really valuable, then while capitalism blinds us to their value, communism will let us see their value, and then people will freely choose such ways of life. But these predictions notwithstanding, Marx doesn't ever say, to my knowledge, that such changes are either the goal or the presupposition of socialist development. That is, Marx's prediction might turn out to be mistaken, but that wouldn't render communism untenable, nor would it warrant us using coercion or discrimination in trying to bring about such ways of life. While communism will obviously have effects on the kinds of choices people make, and the kind of altruism they display, I don't think that Marx *defined* communism in terms of any such pattern of choices or level of altruism: the level of altruism will be determined by the freely made choices of individuals once the structural and cognitive changes that define communism have been implemented. Nothing in these predictions warrants Pashukanis's claim that justice won't exist in communism because 'the social person of the future . . . submerges his ego in the collective and finds the greatest satisfaction and the meaning of life in this act' (quoted in Lukes p. 36).

So Marx did seem to have a different explanation of the supersession of justice from the one communitarians offer. However, neither explanation is plausible: the supersession of justice is not a plausible goal, for reasons well discussed elsewhere (Lukes pp. 63–6; Buchanan pp. 165–9). Certain kinds of potential conflicts and harms are inevitable even if we reduce egoism and create an abundance of certain resources. (One example that arises *because* of an ability and desire to help others is the potential conflicts and harms involved in paternalism.)

The difference in explanation is important, however, because if Marx does allow individual conflicts to remain in his higher community, then we still haven't got to the heart of why Marx feels that communism *is* a higher form of community. I said that it's a higher form of community because it has eliminated the need for justice. But that can't be the full story. It's true that most liberals have been sceptical of the possibility that abundance will render justice unnecessary. They point to certain resources (e.g. space, time) which seem to be inherently scarce. But nothing in liberalism excludes the possibility that abundance can be achieved in certain spheres, making justice unnecessary in them. And nothing in Marxism excludes the possibility that abundance is impossible in other spheres, making justice necessary in them. The question of the *necessity* of justice doesn't seem to capture the fundamental disagreement over the role of justice in a genuine community.

The real heart of the matter is that Marx thought that abundance renders justice not only unnecessary, but also *undesirable*. A liberal society, by contrast, even one of abundance, would still value justice. A liberal society is a juridical society, defined and governed by principles of justice. Liberalism has an inadequate account of community because it fails to see that justice is at best a necessary evil, under conditions of scarcity, and at worst, a barrier to a higher form of community, under conditions of abundance. Liberals have made a virtue out of necessity, and continue to cling to it when it is no longer necessary, and is in fact a positive liability.

But what is wrong with justice, and how is it a barrier to a higher form of community? Why should we *want* to go beyond justice? Nothing said yet explains this point. One argument seems to be that justice not only is not needed when conflicts aren't occurring, but in fact tends to create conflicts, or at any rate to decrease the natural expression of sympathy and sociability. It is better if people act spontaneously out of love for each other, rather than viewing themselves and others as bearers of rights, because a concern for justice displaces love.

But why are these two opposed, why must we choose one or the other?[7] The assumption can only be that if we give people rights they will automatically and always claim them, regardless of the effects on others, including the ones they love. But why can't I choose to waive my right whenever its exercise would harm the people I love? How does recognizing that someone is a bearer of rights prevent me from responding to them out of love? When Buchanan criticizes the juridical sphere for understanding human relations as interactions 'among right-holders *as right-holders*' (Buchanan p. 13, my emphasis), he implicitly, if unconsciously, accepts the possibility that right-holders could interact *as other than right-holders* (i.e. as friends, comrades, fellow members, etc.), without thereby ceasing to be right-holders. But he denies this possibility when he says: 'by casting the parties to conflict in the narrow and unyielding roles of rights-bearers we render the problems intractable' (Buchanan p. 178). A similar assumption about being 'cast' into an 'unyielding role' is needed to make sense of Sandel's otherwise incoherent discussion of the family (Sandel 1982 pp. 30–3), where he claims that rights displace love and concern. But no one 'cast' me into that role and no one will stop me if I choose to adopt a different one. Perhaps the suggestion is that, given human psychology, if I can claim something, I too often will. If I'm a right-bearer I will always confront others *as right-bearer* not because someone cast me into that role, but because, being human, I myself will always adopt it. It's hard to imagine a more deeply misguided and impoverished view of human nature. Do Buchanan and Sandel really believe that I'll only act out of love if I'm denied the opportunity to do otherwise?

Let's take their favourite example of the family. Does the fact that women in France now have the right to move to another town and work there without their spouse's permission mean that all of them will exercise that right rather than keep the family together? (Similarly, have men, who've always had that right, never forgone a career opportunity for the sake of the interests of their wives and children?) Buchanan says that 'for those who find the bonds of mutual respect among right-bearers too rigid and cold to capture some of what is best in human relationships, Marx's vision of genuine community—*rather than* a mere juridical association—will remain attractive' (Buchanan p. 178, emphasis added). But if the family is an example of what's best in human relationships, then the contrast is spurious. The family has always been a juridical association, the spouses and children all being right-bearers. Perhaps that means for the communitarians that marriage, for example, is after all not a sphere of mutuality and affection, but, as Kant put it, an agreement between two people for 'reciprocal use of each other's sexual organs' (quoted in Scruton p. 9). But if communitarians really believe that the juridical nature of marriage prevents loving relationships, that reflects the poverty of their view of human nature, not any feature of the real world.

But even if rights are *compatible* with affective ties, why should we view them as desirable, as liberals claim? Rights are desirable because they express an important form of respect and concern for people. It's often said that rights express the opposite—that they involve a self-understanding that is grounded in egoism and a concern to protect oneself against the likely antagonism of others in a zero-sum social world. Buchanan, for example, says that to think of oneself as a rights-bearer is to 'view oneself as a potential party to interpersonal conflicts in which it is *necessary* to assert claims' (Buchanan p. 76)—we value rights because we fear how others will respond to our requests. But Buchanan himself suggests other grounds for valuing the possession and recognition of rights. He says that for someone to think of himself as a rights-bearer is to think 'of himself as being able to demand what he has a right to as his due, rather than as something he may merely request as being desirable' (Buchanan pp. 75–6). This second self-understanding is about the *grounds* of our request. These are two very different self-understandings, despite the conflation by Buchanan and the communitarians. A person, absorbed in some communal practice, may not have the first conception, yet still value the second. The second self-understanding concerns not the probability of getting something I want or need, but the grounds on which I think of myself as properly (e.g. not selfishly) having it.

Just as justice can serve as a standard for determining what I am non-selfishly entitled to (even when others are prepared to give me more than my fair share), it can also serve as a standard for determining how to respond to the needs of others (even where the reason I want to help is love, not duty). Many of the people I love may be in need, and my desire to help is grounded in my love, unmediated by any thought that they are entitled to my help. But should their needs conflict, then how am I to act? As Rawls points out, it is no good to say I should act benevolently, rather than justly, since 'benevolence is at sea as long as its many loves are in opposition in the persons of its many objects' (Rawls 1971 p. 190). While love may be my motivation, justice may be the standard I appeal to, given that love yields conflicting imperatives. 'While friendship may render justice unnecessary as a *motive*, it may still require some aspects of justice as a *standard*. Friends do not automatically know what to do for one another' (Galston 1980 p. 289 n. 11). When making claims, I may wish to know what I am properly entitled to, even when others will respond to my claims without concern for my entitlements. When responding to the claims of others, I may wish to know what their entitlements are, even when the reason I respond to their claims is love. In neither case is my interest in the teachings of justice related to the necessity of 'standing up for my due'.

The public recognition of justice can be valuable in another way. A person may be sure of getting what she wants, spontaneously, from the love and admiration of others which she enjoys by virtue of her position within some highly respected social practice (e.g. as parent, or teacher). She has no need for rights, on the first conception of them. Yet she may want to know that she is owed something as a *person*, independently of her participation in the common good. She may want to know that her value as a human being isn't exhausted by that participation. And she may want to know this even if she has no desire or inclination to leave that role. She may want it socially recognized that her life has some value independently of her relationship to the common good, even if she never intends to leave that relationship, for such recognition shows that she herself is a source of value, not just she *qua* occupant of a social role. Justice does remedy defects in social co-ordination, and these defects are an ineradicable feature of social life, but it also expresses the respect individuals are owed as ends in themselves, not as means to someone's good, or even to the common good.[8]

But if justice is both ineradicable and desirable, what would communist justice look like? Lukes distinguishes a 'utilitarian', a 'Kantian', and a 'perfectionist' strain in Marx's account of the superiority of communism and says it is the 'teleological, Aristotelian, perfectionist Marx' (Lukes p. 87) which really underlies that moral judgement. If so, we might expect communist justice to specifically encourage the 'realization of distinctively human potentialities and excellences' (ibid.), such as our capacity for freely creative co-operative production, and to discourage those conceptions of the good life that value different goals. This is suggested by Elster, who considers whether 'communist society [would] exclude or stigmatize those who prefer the passive pleasures of consumption, be it in the contemplation of pushpin or of poetry' (Elster p. 522); and by Campbell, who says communist justice wouldn't be concerned with all needs, but would involve 'some selection of those forms of human interest and concerns which most fully express the ideal of co-operative, creative, and productive activities and enjoyments' (Campbell p. 138).

But this would, I think, be a mistake. Indeed, it would be a form of injustice, since it fails to treat everyone with equal concern and respect, and inconsistent with Marx's own emphasis on our freedom to question and go beyond the predetermined yardsticks of existing social roles and expectations. I think the Kantian strand in Marx is a more promising starting-point.[9] According to this premiss, individuals should be free to decide for themselves what is worth doing with their lives, within a community that is transparently intelligible, and that treats each individual as an equal. But of course that is the premiss that liberals start out from as well. The problem is that Marx gives us no clear idea of what it is to treat people as equals, or of how we go about answering that question. In what way (or ways) must individuals be treated equally if we are to be able to say they are treated as equals, i.e. with equal regard? This is the question which liberals like Rawls and Dworkin address. They attempt to give some concrete content to the vague but indispensable notion of 'being treated as equals', using such devices as the original position, or the hypothetical auction. It is a question to which Marx, and those following him, have made little or no theoretical contribution. Once we jettison the expectation of abundance, it is unclear what communist justice would look like, or whether it would provide a vision distinct from those given by theorists in other political traditions.

Therefore, liberal justice seems, for all that communists and communitarians have said against it, a viable political morality for the governing of our political institutions and practices. It expresses an attractive conception of community, recognizing our dependence on a cultural community for our self-development and for our context of choice, yet recognizing the independence we claim, as self-directed beings, from any of the specific roles and relationships that exist in the community. It recognizes the equal standing of the members of the community, through an account of justice, without forcing people to exercise their entitlements at the expense of the people or projects that they care about. The individualism that underlies liberalism isn't valued at the expense of our social nature, or of our shared community. Rather, it seeks to recognize the value of each person's life in the community, and promote that value in a way that the person involved can consciously endorse. It is an individualism that accords with, rather than opposes, the undeniable importance to us of our social world.

Many political institutions in liberal democracies have been shaped by a concern for the implementation of this conception of justice, and of the just community. Others would undoubtedly have to undergo substantial revision before they began to live up to their obligations under this conception (e.g. by attacking the entrenched inequalities of class and gender). While many people consider it a defence of the status quo, I've argued that nothing in this conception of justice warrants limiting its application to questions of income or non-discrimination, rather than to questions of ownership and power. I have accepted some of the criticisms directed at traditional liberal political practice, but as Dunn says, critics of liberalism 'are fundamentally undecided as to whether they have come to destroy liberalism or to fulfil it' (J. Dunn p. 28). The criticisms I have accepted are those which seek to better fulfil liberal ideals of justice and individual freedom. I don't think that communists or communitarians have given us any reason to reject (let alone destroy) those ideals.

Notes

1. Communism may not require the abolition of roles. At some points, Marx seems to have the more limited aim of abolishing those particular roles in the division of labour which embody the sharp distinction between mental and manual labour. Differentiation of roles may remain, but the individual no longer performs labour as an appendage to machinery and instead becomes its conscious master (Marx 1858 p. 705). But I think that he views this continuation of a role-defined division of labour as necessary under conditions of scarcity, rather than as a desirable or necessary feature of a good society. Under conditions of abundance, roles *per se* will disappear.

2. Marx emphasizes that there is a kind of equality, or at least impartiality, in the market. The market involves the exchange of equivalents, so that your money or service is as good as mine. But this is inadequate as an account of moral equality, since it makes the satisfaction of people's wants and needs dependent on their having something of value to others with which to bargain. In the market, people's needs have no inherent claim on social resources.

3. There is much more to be said for and against the view of Marx as an egalitarian. For a different critique of this view, see Miller pp. 15–97, and the response by Nielsen (1987).

4. More accurately, our concern should be with *control* of productive resources. If the state in a Soviet-bloc country is the legal owner of the capital goods, but control over them is exercised by managers, then the capital is, in an important sense, the property of the managers. The non-alienability of the enterprise—the fact that managers do not legally own the capital goods—does not seem to be the crucial point.

5. It is unclear what exactly this cognitive requirement comes to, or how it differs from the liberal aspiration to social transparency. For two interestingly different views, see Waldron pp. 147–9, and Gutmann 1980 pp. 115–16. Given the egalitarian content of most recent liberal theory, it may be that one of the central distinctions remaining between liberals and their left-wing critics concerns the

content and preconditions of this social understanding. Gutmann suggests that Marx desired not only that society be transparent to the individual, but also that the individual be transparent to society (whereas liberals might view this as an invasion of privacy). Waldron suggests that the difference concerns the possible role of the market: Marx sees the operation of the market as incompatible with social transparency, even if we have an adequate theoretical understanding of the workings of the market, and can ensure it operates within the constraints of a theory of equality of resources. Waldron suggests that Marxists are

> working with a more manipulative or technocratic conception of understanding: a process has not been made humanly intelligible unless there is a sense in which humanity can, as it were, take it over, not only representing it in thought but reproducing its workings in the concrete form of deliberate agency. (p. 149)

Waldron's suggestion is supported by the way Marx sometimes equates social transparency with planned control, as in his discussion of the way religion casts a veil over the real world:

> The religious reflections of the real world can, in any case, vanish only when the practical relations of everyday life between man and man, and man and nature, generally present themselves to him in a transparent and rational form. The veil is not removed from the countenance of the social life-process, i.e. the process of material production, until it becomes production by freely associated men, and stands under their conscious and planned control. (Marx 1867 p. 173)

6. What if people, even from a position of equality, choose shallow, possessive, materialistic life-styles, instead of the co-operative, creative, and productive lives Marx predicts they will choose? I don't believe Marx ever discusses the possibility. Perhaps he would have agreed, with Ackerman, that true equality

> would reveal the breadth and depth of human creativity in all its majesty—beyond the capacity of any single individual to survey, let alone evaluate. Yet, even if I were wrong, even if overwhelming numbers opted for lives that I consider mean and narrow, we should at last learn what human freedom amounts to. (Ackerman 1980 p. 375)

7. Marx thought so because he thought that all rights were essentially reducible to the right of private property (1843 p. 53), which inherently involved exploitative and egoistic relations. But that reduction was absurd in relation to the rights extant in Marx's

day, and is entirely misguided in relation to the concept of rights as such (Lukes pp. 63–6).

8. This leaves open the question of how best to recognize these rights institutionally. Liberals have historically failed to resist, or even encouraged, the pre-emption of public debate and decision-making by the courts or the bureaucracy. These bypass public deliberation about the kinds of injustices which exist in the community. If public recognition of principles of justice is as important as Rawls claims, and if people in the good community act not only from respect for existing rules, but from a respect for the principles underlying them, from a 'genuine and pervasive' concern for fellow citizens (Dworkin 1986 p. 213), then we should look first to decision procedures that encourage public input, debate, and consensus, rather than to closed adversarial procedures. It is a peculiarly American conceit to suppose that rights are internally connected to the idea of adversarial litigation.

On the other hand, proponents of consensual or informal decision procedures 'assume, often without sufficient evidence, that informal justice eliminates the adversary character of proceedings, results in mutually beneficial outcomes, or gives voice to fundamental values' (Rosenblum p. 167). I think that these questions are far from settled, and we need to think more flexibly about different forms of the public recognition of rights. Certain ways of institutionalizing rights can obviously lead to a distorted form of 'rights-consciousness' in which people perceive social relationships as necessarily adversarial. But when critics say that the very idea of rights creates such a perception, they 'commit the sin of false necessity in the very act of ascribing it to rights-consciousness' (Michelman p. 92).

So I don't agree that rights turn people into 'strangers' (Barber p. 71). But there may be another connection between rights and strangers. In a large diverse community, there will be 'distant strangers', quite independently of our legal system. And 'the practice of rights' is a good way of bringing distant strangers into the moral community, and ensuring fairness (Damico 1986*b* pp. 175–8). But while rights are particularly appropriate for relationships with distant strangers, it doesn't follow that they are inappropriate for relations with the members of more local communities.

9. I won't discuss the utilitarian strand that Lukes claims to find in Marx's thought, partly because I don't believe that there was such a strand. Marx was scathing about the tendency of utilitarians to reduce the value of all things to their lowest common denominator.

On the utilitarian view of the value of our relations of speech or love, 'these relations are supposed not to have the meaning *peculiar* to them but to be the expression and manifestation of some third relation introduced in their place, the *relation of utility*' (Marx and Engels 1846 p. 110). This 'verbal masquerade' reflects the tendency of bourgeois society to reduce all social relations 'to the one abstract monetary-commercial relation' (Marx and Engels 1846 p. 109). More importantly, he clearly rejected the idea that a person can be harmed just because that would increase the aggregate good. Speaking of the utilitarian justification of punishment as a way of deterring others, he asks: 'Now what right have you to punish me for the amelioration or intimidation of others?' He goes on to say that only the Kantian theory of punishment 'recognizes human dignity in the abstract', since it recognizes that society's right to punish is limited by the individual's right to autonomy ('Capital Punishment', *New York Daily Tribune*, 18 Feb. 1853; quoted and discussed in Murphy pp. 217–31).

LIBERALISM AND CULTURAL MEMBERSHIP

7

Liberalism in Culturally Plural Societies

So far, I have attempted to present the liberal conception of community, and explore some of its contours. But I have not made any explicit distinction between two different kinds, or different aspects, of community. On the one hand, there is the political community, within which individuals exercise the rights and responsibilities entailed by the framework of liberal justice. People who reside within the same political community are fellow citizens. On the other hand, there is the cultural community, within which individuals form and revise their aims and ambitions. People within the same cultural community share a culture, a language and history which defines their cultural membership.

Now clearly these two may simply be aspects of the same community: those people who have the same citizenship may also have the same cultural membership. A political community may be coextensive with one cultural community, as is envisaged in the 'nation-state', and this seems to be the situation implicitly assumed in most contemporary political theory. But the two forms of community may not coincide: the political community may contain two or more groups of people who have different cultures, speaking different languages, developing different cultural traditions. This is the situation in multinational, or culturally plural, states, and these form the vast majority of the world's states (Connor 1972 pp. 319–21; van den Berghe 1981*b* p. 62).

How should liberals respond to a situation of cultural plurality? Clearly the answer depends on the role cultural membership plays in liberal theory. But this is not a simple matter, and immediately raises a number of questions. What does it mean for people to 'belong' to a cultural community—to what extent are individuals' interests tied to, or their very sense of identity dependent on, a particular culture? And what follows from the fact that people belong to different cultures—do people have a legitimate interest in ensuring the continuation of their own culture, even if other cultures are available in the political community? If they do have such an interest, is it an interest which needs to be given independent recognition in a theory of justice?

These are all questions which arise most pressingly in a culturally plural state, but they go to the heart of the liberal conception of the relationship between self and community. And they give rise to an important political issue: the rights of minority cultures. In the remaining chapters, I use the question of minority rights, and in particular the rights of the aboriginal population in Canada and the United States, as a focal point for exploring these questions about the role of cultural membership in liberal theory.

Aboriginal rights are a part of political life in North America, and perhaps they are the most familiar example of minority rights to the Anglo-American world. Yet they are very much at odds with some of our common self-perceptions. While the United States is often viewed as a 'melting-pot', without permanently distinct minority cultures, this is clearly not true of the aboriginal population. There is a system of reservations for the American Indian population, within which the members of particular Indian communities have been able (to a greater or lesser degree) to protect their culture. But their ability to do so has rested on having, as a community, unusual rights and powers. The reservations form special political jurisdictions over which Indian communities have certain guaranteed powers, and within which non-Indian Americans have restricted mobility, property, and voting rights.

This scheme for the protection of a minority culture is often treated as an exception, an issue which arises prior to, or outside the bounds of, liberal theory. But it is far from unique in contemporary liberal democracies. It is similar to legislation which establishes special political and social rights for aboriginal peoples in Canada, New Zealand, and Australia as well. And these are similar to many of the special measures of political and cultural autonomy for minorities in the multicultural countries of Western Europe, such as Belgium and Switzerland. And if we look beyond Western liberal democracies to many African, or Eastern-bloc, countries, the story is very similar. On all continents, in countries of all ideological stripes, we find cultural minorities that have a distinct legal and political status. In these countries, individuals are incorporated into the state, not 'universally' (i.e. so that each individual citizen stands in the same direct relationship to the state), but 'consociationally' (i.e. through membership in one or other of the cultural communities). Under consociational modes of incorporation, the nature of people's rights, and the opportunities for exercising them, tend to vary with the particular cultural community into which they are incorporated. And the justification for these measures focuses on their role in allowing minority cultures to develop their distinct cultural life, an ability insufficiently protected by 'universal' modes of incorporation.

How should liberals respond to these kinds of measures for minority cultures? They may seem, at first glance, to be inconsistent with liberal theories of justice, and that indeed is the common presumption. But, if so, that is a serious matter, for these measures have been important to the political legitimacy, and very stability, of many multicultural countries. Wars have been fought in order to gain or protect these measures. Removing them would have a profound effect on the political culture of these countries, and on the lives of the members of the minority cultures.

It's surprising, then, that liberal theorists haven't explicitly defended, or even discussed, this implication of their theories. This is surprising even if we interpret writers like Rawls and Dworkin as writing only for the American market. Most of the conclusions they reach appeal to, or are consistent with, the provisions of the American Constitution. Removing the special constitutional status of Indians, on the other hand, is directly in conflict with the current political consensus in the United States. Yet it is never mentioned by either Rawls or Dworkin.

Why is it commonly supposed that liberals must oppose special status for minority cultures? Liberal opposition is often explained in terms of an alleged conflict between individual and collective rights. This is exhibited in recent debates concerning the constitutional definition of the special status of the aboriginal peoples of Canada (i.e. Indian, Inuit, and Métis). This special status was recognized, but left undefined, in Section 35 of the 1982 Constitution Act. Greater specification of this status was to be reached through a series of annual constitutional conferences between government and aboriginal leaders. There was a general consensus that aboriginal peoples should be self-governing, in contrast to the paternalistic legislation under which reservation life had been regulated in detail for decades. But aboriginal leaders said that the principle of aboriginal self-government must include the recognition of certain collective rights, rights which need to be weighed alongside and balanced against more traditional individual rights. For example, self-government would include the ability of aboriginal communities to restrict the mobility, property, and voting rights of non-aboriginal people. Many government officials, on the other hand, demanded that aboriginal self-government operate in a way that leaves intact the structure of individual rights guaranteed elsewhere in the constitution. So the initial agreement soon gave way to disagreement over the relationship between individual and collective rights. (These differences have, so far, proven too great to overcome, and the constitutional rights of aboriginal peoples in Canada remain undefined.)

The accepted wisdom is that liberals must oppose any proposals for self-government which would limit individual rights in the name of collective rights. I think that is a mistake, one that has caused serious harm to the aboriginal population of North America, and to the members of minority cultures in other liberal democracies. This chapter will explore some of the reasons why liberals have opposed collective rights for minority cultures.

But before I begin, a word about terminology. I have been describing a range of schemes through which multinational states have responded to the existence of distinct minority cultures, schemes which involve some variation in the standard liberal distribution of rights and resources so as to accommodate that distinct existence. Such measures have been described with different terms by different authors—'minority rights', 'special status', 'collective rights', 'group rights', 'consociational incorporation', 'minority protection'. The problem with using these as labels for the sorts of minority culture schemes I've been discussing is that each term is over-inclusive, and often under-inclusive as well. The term 'minority rights' is often used to refer to non-cultural minorities, or to rights of non-discrimination, rather than to special measures for distinct minority cultures. And many of the measures which are commonly described as 'group rights' (e.g. for the handicapped), or 'collective rights' (e.g. for unions), or 'consociationalism' (e.g. incorporating people into the state through membership in occupational groups), have nothing to do with cultural membership. If they are justifiable within a liberal perspective, the justification will involve different issues.

Conversely, some of the measures which might be justified in the name of the protection of minority cultures don't have all of the features which are said to define group, collective, or minority rights. For example, on many definitions of a 'collective right', a measure only counts as a collective right if it specifies that the community itself exercises certain powers. But some of the measures which define the special status of aboriginal peoples in Canada do not involve such collectively-exercised rights. Instead, they simply modify and differentially distribute the rights of individuals.

So terms like 'collective rights', as they are usually understood, do not quite capture the set of issues I am interested in. The policies I am interested in are defined not by any shared formal feature, but by a similar rationale. They are all said, by their defenders, to be appropriate responses to the fact that people belong to different cultural communities, a fact which is not given sufficient recognition or attention in universally incorporated liberal democracies. The measures claimed by minority cultures, as we shall see, typically involve both individual and collective rights, as those terms are commonly defined. So terms like 'collective rights' can obscure some of the issues involved in evaluating special measures for minority cultures.

Unfortunately, there seems no way to avoid these terms. I think that 'special status' and 'minority rights' are the least confusing terms, although I shall sometimes be employing the others as well. But I emphasize that these terms are simply labels for the sorts of measure just mentioned—they do not refer to some independently established theory of rights. The question I am discussing under the label 'minority rights' concerns the content and grounding of people's claims concerning cultural membership in culturally plural countries, and this question is both narrower and wider than standard debates over 'collective rights' or 'group rights'.[1]

What explains the common liberal opposition to such minority rights? It's not difficult to see why liberals have opposed them. Liberalism, as I've presented it, is characterized both by a certain kind of *individualism*—that is, individuals are viewed as the ultimate units of moral worth, as having moral standing as ends in themselves, as 'self-originating sources of valid claims' (Rawls 1980 p. 543); and by a certain kind of *egalitarianism*—that is, every individual has an equal moral status, and hence is to be treated as an equal by the government, with equal concern and respect (Dworkin 1983a p. 24; Rawls 1971 p. 511). Since individuals have ultimate moral status, and since each individual is to be respected as an equal by the government, liberals have demanded that each individual have equal rights and entitlements. Liberals have disagreed amongst themselves as to what these rights should be, because they have different views about what it is to treat people with equal concern and respect. But most would accept that these rights should include rights to mobility, to personal property, and to political participation in one's community. The new Canadian Charter of Rights and Freedoms embodies these liberal principles, guaranteeing such rights to every citizen, regardless of race or sex, ethnicity or language, etc. (Asch pp. 86–7; Schwartz ch. 1).

There seems to be no room within the moral ontology of liberalism for the idea of collective rights. The community, unlike the individual, is not a 'self-originating source of valid claims'. Once individuals have been treated as equals, with the respect and concern owed them as moral beings, there is no further obligation to treat the communities to which they belong as equals. The community has no moral existence or claims of its own. It is not that community is unimportant to the liberal, but simply that it is important for what it contributes to the lives of individuals, and so cannot ultimately conflict with the claims of individuals. Individual and collective rights cannot compete for the same moral space, in liberal theory, since the value of the collective derives from its contribution to the value of individual lives.

The constitutional embodiment of these liberal principles, in

Canada and elsewhere, has played an important role in many of liberalism's greatest achievements in fighting against unjust legislation. For example, in the *Brown v. Board of Education* case, ([1954] 347 US 483), the Fourteenth Amendment of the American Constitution, guaranteeing equal protection of the law to all its citizens, was used to strike down legislation that segregated blacks in the American South. The 'separate but equal' doctrine which had governed racial segregation in the United States for sixty years denied blacks the equal protection of the law. That case dealt solely with segregated school facilities, but it was a major impetus behind the removal of other segregationist legislation in the 1950s, the passage of the Civil Rights and Voting Rights Acts in the 1960s, and the development of mandatory busing, 'head start', and affirmative action programmes in the 1970s; which in turn were the catalyst for similar programmes to benefit other groups—Hispanics, women, the handicapped, etc. Indeed, 'its educative and moral impact in areas other than public education and, in fact, its whole thrust toward equality and opportunity for all men has been of immeasurable importance' (Kaplan p. 228). The 'thrust' of this movement was sufficiently powerful to shape non-discrimination and equal protection legislation in countries around the world, and it provided the model for various international covenants on human rights (especially the Convention on the Elimination of All Forms of Racial Discrimination, adopted by the UN General Assembly in 1965). It also underlies the prominent philosophical accounts of liberal equality.

The history of these developments is one of the high points of Western liberalism in the twentieth century, for there is a powerful ideal of equality at work here in the political morality of the community—the idea that every citizen has a right to full and equal participation in the political, economic, and cultural life of the country, without regard to race, sex, religion, physical handicap—without regard to any of the classifications which have traditionally kept people separate and behind.

The logical conclusion of these liberal principles seems to be a 'colour-blind' constitution—the removal of all legislation differentiating people in terms of their race or ethnicity (except for temporary measures, like affirmative action, which are believed necessary to reach a colour-blind society). Liberal equality requires the 'universal' mode of incorporating citizens into the state. And this indeed has often been the conclusion drawn by courts in Canada and the United States.

This movement exercised an enormous influence on Canadian Indian policy as well (Berger 1984 p. 94). The desirability of a colour-blind constitution was the explicit motivation behind the 1969 proposals for reforming the Indian Act in Canada. In 1968 Pierre Trudeau was elected Prime Minister of Canada on a platform of social justice that was clearly influenced by the American political movements. Canada didn't have a policy of segregating blacks, but it did have something which looked very similar. As in the United States, the native Indian population was predominantly living on segregated reserves, and was subject to a complex array of legislation which treated Indians and non-Indians differentially. While every Indian had the right to live on the land of her band, there were restrictions on her ability to use the land, or dispose of her estate as she saw fit, and there was a total prohibition on any alienation of the land. The reservation system also placed restrictions on the mobility, residence, and voting rights of non-Indians in the Indian territory; and in the case of voting rights, the restriction remained even when the non-Indian married into the Indian community. There were, in other words, two kinds of Canadian citizenship, Indian and non-Indian, with different rights and duties, differential access to public services, and different opportunities for participating in the various institutions of Canadian government.

Dismantling this system was one of the top priorities of Trudeau's 'Just Society' policy, and early in 1969 the government released a White Paper on Indian Policy which recommended an end to the special constitutional status of Indians (DIAND 1969). The government proposed that the reservation system, which had protected Indian communities from assimilation, be dismantled. Indians would not, of course, be compelled to disperse and assimilate. They would be free to choose to associate with one another, and co-ordinate the way they used their resources in the market, so as to preserve their way of life. Freedom of association is one of the individual rights to be universally guaranteed in a colour-blind constitution. But they would receive no legal or constitutional help in their efforts. Legislation discriminating against non-Indians in terms of property-rights, mobility rights, or political rights would not be allowed.

From its very conception to the choice of language in the final draft, the policy reflected the powerful influence of the ideal of racial equality which was developing in the United States and the United Nations. Paraphrasing UN human rights instruments, the authors said that the policy rested 'upon the fundamental right of Indian people to full and equal participation in the cultural, social, economic and political life of Canada', and this required that the legislative and constitutional bases of discrimination be removed (DIAND 1969 pp. 201–2). Echoing the *Brown* decision, the policy proposed that Indians no longer receive separate services from separate agencies, because 'separate but equal services do not provide truly equal treatment' (DIAND 1969 p. 204). Echoing Justice Harlan's famous dictum that the American Constitution should be colour-blind, the Canadian proposal said that 'The ultimate aim of removing the specific references to Indians from the constitution may take some time, but it is a goal to be kept constantly in view' (DIAND 1969 p. 202). Perhaps it was the weight of all this normative authority that gave the authors such a sense of righteousness. It is, they said, 'self-evident' that the constitution should be colour-blind, an 'undeniable part of equality' that Indians should have equal access to common services; 'There can be no argument . . . It is right' (DIAND 1969 pp. 202–3).

It is worth emphasizing that the issue was not about temporary measures to help Indians overcome their disadvantaged position in the broader society. While not all liberals are prepared to allow even temporary measures which differentiate on the basis of race or ethnicity, the government proposal followed the more common view that measures such as affirmative action are acceptable. But they are acceptable precisely because they are viewed as appropriate or necessary means to the pursuit of the ideal of a colour-blind constitution. Affirmative action of this sort appeals to the values embodied in that ideal, not to competing values. The issue posed by the special status of Canada's Indians, therefore, was not that of affirmative action, but 'whether the granting of permanent political rights to a special class of citizens (rather than special rights on a temporary basis) is possible within an ideology that maintains the principle of equality of consideration' (Asch p. 76). And for the liberal architects of the 1969 proposal, the answer was that liberal equality was incompatible with the permanent assigning of collective rights to a minority culture.

The proposal was immediately applauded by the media, even by opposition parties, as a triumph for liberal justice. Indians, on the other hand, were furious, and after six months of bitter and occasionally violent Indian protest, the policy was withdrawn. In the words of one commentator, the policy was a response 'to white liberal demands from the public, not to Indian demands' (Weaver 1981 p. 196). But liberals have only reluctantly retreated from that policy, despite the almost unanimous opposition it received from the Indians themselves. Liberals fear that any deviation from the strict principle of equal individual rights would be the first step down the road to apartheid, to a system where some individuals are viewed as first-class citizens and others only second-class, in virtue of their race or ethnic affiliation. These fears are strengthened when liberals see white South African leaders invoke minority rights in defence of their system of apartheid, and compare their system of tribal homelands to our system of Indian reservations and homelands (*International Herald Tribune* p. 2; *Toronto Star* p. B3). If we allow Indians to discriminate against non-Indians in the name of their collective rights, how can we criticize white South Africans for discriminating against blacks in the name of their collective rights?

So liberals have viewed the idea of collective rights for minority cultures as both theoretically incoherent and practically dangerous. Many commentators have argued that this liberal antipathy is the biggest stumbling-block to a satisfactory settlement of aboriginal claims in Canada (Weaver 1981 pp. 55–6, 196; 1985 pp. 141–2; Ponting and Gibbins 1980 pp. 327–31; Asch pp. 75–88, 100–4; Dacks pp. 63–79), and in the United States (Svensson pp. 430–3; Van Dyke 1982 pp. 28–30; Morgan p. 41; Barsh and Henderson 1980 pp. 241–8). And Schwartz's account of the recent constitutional conferences in Canada on aboriginal rights bears out the continued relevance of these liberal principles amongst government and court officials (Schwartz).

As I mentioned before, I believe that this is a mistaken understanding of the requirements of liberal equality, and my attempt to give a positive defence of minority rights will take up the next two chapters. But the first task is to take a closer look at the analogy between the segregation of blacks and aboriginal self-government. This analogy explains much of the liberal commitment to the idea of a colour-blind constitution. Breaking down the analogy won't remove that commitment, but I hope it will prepare the way for the more constructive arguments of the next two chapters.

The crucial difference between blacks and the aboriginal peoples of North America is, of course, that the latter value their separation from the mainstream life and culture of North America. Separation is not always perceived as a 'badge of inferiority'. Indeed, it is sometimes forgotten that the American Supreme Court recognized this in the *Brown* desegregation case. The Court did not reject the 'separate but equal' doctrine on any universal grounds. The Court ruled that, in the particular circumstances of contemporary American white–black relations, segregation was perceived as a 'badge of inferiority'. The lower motivation of black children in their segregated schools was a crucial factor in their decision. But in Canada, segregation has always been viewed as a defence of a highly valued cultural heritage. It is forced *integration* that is perceived as a badge of inferiority by Indians, damaging their motivation. While there are no special problems about motivation on segregated reserve schools, the drop-out rate for Indians in integrated high schools was over 90 per cent, and in most areas was 100 per cent for post-secondary education (Cardinal 1977 p. 194; Gross p. 238).

Michael Gross distinguishes the cases of blacks and Indians this way:

Where blacks have been forcibly *excluded* (segregated) from white society by law, Indians—aboriginal peoples with their own cultures, languages, religions and territories—have been forcibly *included* (integrated) into that society by law. That is what the [Senate Subcommittee on Indian Education] meant by coercive assimilation—the practice of compelling, through submersion, an ethnic, cultural and linguistic minority to shed its uniqueness and identity and mingle with the rest of society. (Gross p. 244)

Gross argues that the 'integration of Indian children in white-dominated schools had the same negative educational and emotional effects which segregation was held to have on blacks in *Brown*' (Gross p. 245). Therefore, the 'underlying principle' which struck down legislated segregation of blacks (i.e. that racial classifications harmful to a racial minority are unconstitutional) would also strike down legislated integration of Indians (Gross p. 248).[2] Assimilation for the Indians, like segregation for the blacks, is a badge of inferiority which, in the words of the Senate Subcommittee, fails 'to recognize the importance and validity of the Indian community' and which results in a 'dismal record' of 'negative self-image [and] low achievement' as the 'classroom and the school [become] a kind of battleground where the Indian child attempts to protect his integrity and identity as an individual by defeating the purposes of the school' (Gross p. 242). Similar situations arise when Indians have to assimilate later in life, e.g. at work.

But to say that segregation is preferred by the Indians is not to say it is, or even could be, the natural result of the interplay of preferences in the market. On the contrary, the viability of Indian communities depends on coercively restricting the mobility, residence, and political rights of both Indians and non-Indians. It is this which raises the need for the minority rights that are decried by many liberals, rights that go beyond non-discrimination and affirmative action.

These special needs are met, in Canada, by two different forms of aboriginal community arrangements (Asch ch. 7). In the reservations of southern Canada, where the population is high and land scarce, the stability of Indian communities is made possible by denying non-Indians the right to purchase or reside on Indian lands (unless given special permission). In the north, however, they are creating political arrangements for the Indian and Inuit population which would have none of these restrictions. Under these arrangements, non-aboriginal people will be free to take jobs, buy land, and reside as long as they want; the inhospitability of the environment ensures that aboriginal people are not likely to be outnumbered by non-aboriginal permanent residents. However, northern Canada is rich in resources, and development projects will often bring in huge influxes of temporary resident workers. While very few, if any, of these workers are likely to remain in the north for more than seven years, so that the aboriginal people will continue to constitute the majority of permanent residents, at any one time non-aboriginal people may well form the majority. If non-aboriginal transient workers were allowed to vote, they would probably decide to use public money to provide amenities for themselves—movie theatres, dish antennas for television reception, even a Las Vegas-styled resort. Since many aboriginal people in the north are dependent on short-term work projects due to the seasonal nature of most economic activity in the area, such a policy could force them to move into localities dominated by whites, and to work and live in another culture, in a different language. Transient residents might also use their voting power to demand that public services and education be provided in their own language, at the expense of the provision of services and education in aboriginal languages.[3]

To guard against this, aboriginal leaders have proposed a three-to-ten-year residency requirement before one becomes eligible to vote for, or hold, public office, and a guaranteed 30 per cent aboriginal representation in the regional government, with veto power over legislation affecting crucial aboriginal interests. If this scheme proved unable to protect aboriginal communities, they would have the power to impose even greater restrictions, most likely on immigration, and thereby move closer to the southern model, which avoids the necessity of restricting voting rights by simply denying non-aboriginal people a chance to gain residence. In other words, there is a continuum of possibilities, involving greater or lesser guarantees of power for aboriginal people, and greater or lesser restrictions on the mobility and political rights of non-aboriginal people (see Bartlett, and Lyon pp. 48–65, for some of the variants). Aboriginal groups have demanded the restrictions they believe to be necessary to protect their communities.

Historically, the evidence is that when the land on which aboriginal communities are based became desirable for white settlement and development, the only thing which prevented the undesired disintegration of the community was legally entrenched non-alienability of land. Indeed the most common way of breaking open stubbornly held Indian land for white settlement was to force the Indians to take individual title to alienable land, making the pressure on some individuals to sell almost unbearable, partly because Indians were financially deprived (and hence in need of money to meet the basic needs of the family), and also because they were culturally ill-equipped to understand the consequences of having (or selling) title to land (Sanders 1983*a* pp. 4–12; Kronowitz *et al.* pp. 530–1; MacMeekin p. 1239). Such measures to endow individual title are usually justified as giving Indians greater choice. The White Paper, for example, proclaimed that 'full and true equality calls for Indian control and ownership of reserve land . . . [this] carries with it the free choice of use, of retention, or of disposition' (DIAND 1969 p. 209). The Minister responsible for the policy said he was only trying to give Indians the same freedom to manage their own affairs as other Canadians (Bowles *et al.* p. 215). But Indians have as much free choice over the use of their land as the average renter has over her public-housing apartment. Indeed rather more, since the Indian bands are like co-operatively-managed apartment buildings. Moreover, unlike renters, Indians get a per capita share of the band's funds if they choose to leave the reservation. The reservation system can thus combine considerable freedom of individual choice over the use of one's resources with protection of the community from the disintegrating effects of the collective action problem that would result were the costs of maintaining the community borne individually (see Chapter 9). Whatever the motivation for the endowing of individual title, the effect has been to sacrifice the Indian community in order to protect the mobility rights of individual non-Indians.

But the reservation system causes a problem in the case of mixed marriages. Every member of an Indian band has the right to reside on the band reserve—not the right to buy land on the reserve, since that land can't be bought or sold, but the right to be allocated a plot of land to live on. If the band population grew at a natural rate from purely intra-band marriages, there wouldn't be a problem. But when there are a substantial number of marriages to people from outside the band, if the majority of such mixed couples prefer to live on the reserve (as they do), then there will soon be a problem of overcrowding. Unless there is the possibility of expanding the land-base, some mechanism is needed to control the membership.

In the United States, they use a blood criterion. Only those with a certain proportion of Indian blood can be full members of the band, so non-Indian spouses never acquire membership, nor do the children if they have less than the required proportion. Non-members never acquire the right to participate in band government, and should the Indian spouse die, they have no right to residence and so can be evicted; while non-member children must leave the reserve at the age of eighteen. In Canada, the obvious drawbacks of the blood criterion are replaced by a kinship system: everyone in a nuclear family has the same status. If one person in the family has membership, they all do, and so all have full non-contingent rights of residence and participation in band government. Clearly, however, not every mixed family can have membership—that would create the over-population. If some non-Indians gain membership for themselves and their children by marrying an Indian, there must also be some Indians who give up membership for themselves and their children by marrying a non-Indian. In Canada, until recently it has been Indian women who lose status upon entering into a mixed marriage.

There is an obvious trade-off here—sexual equality for family integrity. There are other models for regulating membership (Sanders 1972 pp. 83–7; Manyfingers) some of which are more equitable. But all options have this in common: if the land-base is fixed and over-population threatens, some Indians will not legally be able to marry a non-Indian and have him or her move in and become a full and equal member of the community. Again, there is a continuum of possibilities involved: some proposals allow non-Indian spouses to vote but not to hold office, others allow non-member spouses and children to remain after the death of the Indian spouse but not to vote, etc. (DIAND 1982). In all cases there are restrictions on the marriage and voting rights of both Indians and non-Indians: these are viewed as the concomitants of the reservation system needed to protect Indian cultural communities.

There are also controversial measures concerning language rights. The Charter of Rights and Freedoms guarantees to all Canadian citizens the right to a public education in either of the two official languages (English or French), and to deal with all levels of government in either of these languages, where numbers permit. Aboriginal leaders have sought exemption from this. Allowing new residents in the community to receive education and public services in English would weaken the long-term viability of the community. Not only will new residents not have to fully integrate into the minority culture, the establishment of an anglophone infrastructure will attract new anglophone arrivals who may have no interest in even partial integration into the aboriginal community. This is a concern shared by many French-Canadians in Quebec, who want to limit access to English-language schools for people moving into the province. On the other hand, parents will demand their right to a publicly funded education in English so that their children will not be at a disadvantage if they choose to enter the historically dominant and privileged social, political, and economic life in English Canada.

This is just a partial survey of some of the aspects of the aboriginal rights question in Canada. The arrangements are not uniform across the country, and they are all in a state of flux as a result of the unfinished constitutional negotiations. But we can at least get a sense of the basic issues raised for a liberal theory of justice. The common element in all these measures is that some of the recognized rights and liberties of liberal citizenship are limited, and unequally distributed, in order to preserve a minority culture. And we could tell similar stories about the goals and effects of minority rights schemes in other countries, notwithstanding their many variations.

As we've seen, many liberals treat these measures as obviously unjust, and as simple disguises for the perpetuation of ethnic or racial inequality. But once we recognize the differences between these measures and the segregation of blacks, judgements of fairness become more complex, and our intuitions concerning individual and collective rights may be divided.

What underlies this conflict of intuitions? At first glance, someone might suppose that the conflict is between 'respect for the individual' and 'respect for the group'. On this view, to endorse minority rights at the expense of individual rights would be to value the group over the individual. But there is another, and I believe more accurate, view of our intuitions. On this view, both sides of the dilemma concern respect for the individual. The problem is that there are two kinds of respect for individuals at stake here, both of which have intuitive force.

If we respect Indians as Indians, that is to say, as members of a distinct cultural community, then we must recognize the importance to them of their cultural heritage, and we must recognize the legitimacy of claims made by them for the protection of that culture. These claims deserve attention, even if they conflict with some of the requirements of the Charter of Rights. It may not seem right, for example, that aboriginal homelands in the north must be scrapped just because they require a few migrant workers to be temporarily disenfranchised at the local level. It doesn't seem fair for the Indian and Inuit population to be deprived of their cultural community just because a few whites wish to exercise their mobility rights fully throughout the country. If aboriginal peoples can preserve their cultural life by extending residency requirements for non-aboriginal people, or restricting the alienability of the land-base, doesn't that seem a fair and reasonable request? To give every Canadian equal citizenship rights without regard to race or ethnicity, given the vulnerability of aboriginal communities to the decisions of the non-aboriginal majority, does not seem to treat Indians and Inuit with equal respect. For it ignores a potentially devastating problem faced by aboriginal people, but not by English-Canadians—the loss of cultural membership. To insist that this problem be recognized and fairly dealt with hardly sounds like an insistence on racial or ethnic privilege.

Yet if we respect people as Canadians, that is to say as citizens of the common political community, then we must recognize the importance of being able to claim the rights of equal citizenship. Limitations on, and unequal distribution of, individual rights clearly impose burdens. One can readily understand the feeling of discrimination that occurs when an Indian woman is told she can't get a publicly funded education in English for her child (or when a white man is told that he can't vote in the community he resides in and contributes to).

There is, I think, a genuine conflict of intuitions here, and it is a conflict between two different considerations involved in showing respect for persons. People are owed respect as citizens and as members of cultural communities. In many situations, the two are perfectly compatible, and in fact may coincide. But in culturally plural societies, differential citizenship rights may be needed to protect a cultural community from unwanted disintegration. If so, then the demands of citizenship and cultural membership pull in different directions. Both matter, and neither seems reducible to the other. (Indeed, when Charles Taylor wanted to illustrate the ultimate plurality of moral value, he chose precisely this conflict between equality for Indians *qua* members of a cultural community and equality for Indians *qua* citizens of the political community: C. Taylor 1988 p. 25.)

The special status of aboriginal people can be viewed as an acceptable, if imperfect, resolution of this conflict. Such conflicts are, in fact, endemic to the day-to-day politics of culturally plural societies, and various schemes of minority rights can be understood and evaluated in this light.

Liberalism, as commonly interpreted, doesn't recognize the legitimacy of one half of this dilemma. It gives no independent weight to our cultural membership, and hence demands equal rights of citizenship, regardless of the consequences for the existence of minority cultures. As Taylor has said: 'The modern notion of equality will suffer no differences in the field of opportunity which individuals have before them. Before they choose, individuals must be interchangeable; or alternatively put, any differences must be chosen' (C. Taylor 1979 p. 132). This conception of equality gives no recognition to individuals' cultural membership, and if it operates in a culturally plural country, then it tends to produce a single culture for the whole of the political community, and the undesired assimilation of distinct minority cultural communities. The continued existence of such communities may require restrictions on choice and differentials in opportunity. If liberal equality requires equal citizenship rights, and equal access to a common 'field of opportunity', then some minority cultures are endangered. And this, I believe, does not respond to our intuitions about the importance of our cultural membership.

If we are troubled by this failure of liberal theories to do justice to our intuitions about the importance of cultural membership, two responses are possible. One response is to say that liberals have misinterpreted the role that cultural membership can or must play in their own theory. On this view, the correct interpretation of liberalism does not require universal incorporation or a colour-blind constitution, and liberals should accept the possible legitimacy of minority rights. The other response is to accept that liberalism accords no role to cultural membership, and precludes minority rights, but then say that liberalism is incomplete, or perhaps entirely inapplicable to the case of minority rights at stake. On this view, we should seek some other moral theory or set of values which will recognize the importance of cultural membership and the legitimacy of minority rights.

Supporters of aboriginal self-government in Canada have tended to adopt this second approach, defending aboriginal rights *against* liberalism. Liberalism is said to be incomplete or inapplicable for a number of reasons: some claim that the aboriginal population has special rights because their ancestors were here first (Cardinal 1969; Dene Nation; Robinson and Quinney); others claim that Indians and Inuit are properly viewed as 'peoples' under international law, and so have the right of self-determination (Sanders 1983*a* pp. 21–5; Robinson and Quinney pp. 141–2; L. C. Green p. 346); some claim that aboriginal peoples have a different value system, emphasizing the community rather than the individual, and hence group rights rather than individual rights (Ponting and Gibbins 1986 p. 216; Little Bear, Boldt, and Long p. xvi; Svensson pp. 451–2); yet others suggest that aboriginal communities *themselves* have certain rights, because groups as well as individuals have legitimate moral claims (Boldt and Long 1985*b* pp. 343–5). These are all common ways of defending aboriginal rights against liberalism, by locating our intuitions in favour of them in some non-liberal theory of rights or values.

However, I think that the first response—the attempt to reconcile minority rights and liberal equality—is worth considering, whether one's first commitment is to liberalism, or to minority rights. For proponents of minority rights, the second approach suffers from two weaknesses. Firstly, the various non-liberal arguments are quite controversial, legally and morally, although I shall not be delving into all the issues raised by them.[4] Secondly, they are not very strong *politically*, for they do not confront liberal fears about minority rights. They don't explain why minority rights aren't the first step on the road to apartheid, or what serves to prevent massive violations of individual rights in the name of the group. Opponents of liberalism may find them convincing, but they may not be the ones who need convincing on this point. For better or worse, it is predominantly non-aboriginal judges and politicians who have the ultimate power to protect and enforce aboriginal rights, and so it is important to find a justification of them that such people can recognize and understand. Aboriginal people have their own understanding of self-government, drawn from their own experience, and that is important. But it is also important, politically, to know how non-aboriginal Canadians—Supreme Court Justices, for example—will understand aboriginal rights and relate them to their own experiences and traditions. And, as we've seen, on the standard interpretation of liberalism, aboriginal rights are viewed as matters of discrimination and/or privilege, not of equality. They will always, therefore, be viewed with the kind of suspicion that led liberals like Trudeau to advocate their abolition. Aboriginal rights, at least in their robust form, will only be secure when they are viewed, not as competing with liberalism, but as an essential component of liberal political practice.

For liberals, the first approach offers two possible benefits. Firstly, it represents an opportunity to examine the question of cultural membership, and thereby flesh out a theory of individuality and community. The failure of liberals to appeal to our basic understanding of the importance of cultural membership has been cited by some communitarians in explaining their opposition to liberal individualism (as we'll see in Chapter 12). Secondly, there are important political reasons for liberals to find a defence of minority rights. In a political or legal conflict between minority rights and liberal equality, liberalism may lose out. For example, while the Canadian Supreme Court has doubted whether a liberal justification can be found for the special status of aboriginal communities, they have also been wary of dismantling the Indian Act, which has been a fundamental part of Canadian law. And this wariness has influenced their interpretation of the right to equality before the law.

Indeed, the most important historical cases for the right to equality before the law in Canada have been Indian Act cases (Polyviou p. 148; Morton pp. 73–7). Prior to the 1982 constitutional amendments, the Canadian Supreme Court wavered on whether that right was purely formal (i.e. guaranteeing impartial application of the law), or whether it gave a substantive guarantee against discrimination in the law itself. It was first interpreted in a substantive way in a 1970 case concerning liquor regulations that differentiated between Indian and non-Indian offenders (*Regina* v. *Drybones* [1970] SCR. 282). The law was struck down on the grounds that racial distinctions violated equality (citing *Brown* v. *Board of Education*). Some people viewed that judgement as beginning a new age in judicial activism, which would lead to the striking down of unjust and discriminatory laws (Morton p. 73).

But when another part of the Indian Act was challenged, the Court realized that the entire structure of the Indian Act, with its protected reservations and special political status for Indians, was threatened by this colour-blind interpretation of the equality guarantee. So the Court essentially reversed its position, and retreated from a substantive interpretation in order to protect Indian special status (*Attorney-General of Canada* v. *Lavell* [1974] SCR. 1349). As Morton says,

The Court's inability to reconcile the special status conferred through the Indian Act and authorized by the B.N.A. Act with a substantive definition of 'equality before the law' effectively undermined the potential for any American-style *Brown* v. *Board* equality jurisprudence under the 1960 Bill of Rights. Unwilling to adopt a definition of 'equality before the law' that would deny the validity of the Indian Act, the Court quickly abandoned the broad, substantive notion of 'equality before the law' articulated in *Drybones*, and returned to the procedural definition. (Morton p. 74)

This shift affected the judicial enforcement of the rights of all Canadians. Thus, a few years later, legislation which clearly discriminated against women was ruled not to violate the equality provision (*Attorney-General of Canada* v. *Bliss* [1979] 1 SCR. 183). Faced with a perceived choice between protecting Canada's tradition of minority rights and promoting liberal equality, the Court protected minority rights.

The equality section (Section 15) of the 1982 Constitution Act was rewritten to clearly provide substantive guarantees against discrimination. But the new section still needs to be interpreted, and this will still involve scrutiny of various aspects of Indian special status. If stronger interpretations of Section 15 are incompatible with the special status of aboriginal peoples and French-Canadians, then the section may be interpreted in a seriously weakened form. The fight for judicial protection against sexual and religious discrimination is, therefore, intimately linked to the question of minority rights.

So there are both political and philosophical reasons for trying to defend aboriginal rights within liberalism, not against liberalism. The current liberal hostility to minority rights is, I shall argue in the next two chapters, misguided. However, it is not the result of any simple or obvious mistake, and identifying the problem requires looking deep into the liberal view of the self and community. And even if we recognize the problem, there is no simple or obvious way to correct it within a liberal theory of justice. The issue for liberal theory is not as simple as Trudeau once suggested, in response to a question about his reasons for advancing and then withdrawing the 1969 proposal:

We had perhaps the prejudices of small 'l' liberals and white men at that who thought that equality meant the same law for everybody, and that's why as a result of this we said 'well let's abolish the Indian Act and make Indians citizens of Canada like everyone else. And let's let Indians dispose of their lands just like every other Canadian. And let's make sure that Indians can get their rights, education, health and so on, from the governments like every other Canadian'. But we learned in the process we were a bit too abstract, we were not perhaps pragmatic enough or understanding enough. (Quoted in Weaver 1981 p. 185.)

I shall argue that the problem isn't just one of pragmatism or prejudice. The idea of collective rights for minority cultures doesn't just conflict with the pre-reflective habits or prejudices of liberals. It seems in direct conflict with some of the most fundamental liberal principles, even in their most theoretically sophisticated formulations. And so the search for a liberal defence of minority rights will take us back into the heart of liberal theory. Hence the next few chapters will involve a rethinking, from a new perspective, of the liberal arguments which I defended in the first half of the book. The result will not, I hope, contradict those arguments, but will perhaps place them in a new light, and connect them to a broader and more adequate liberal theory of the relationship between the individual and the community.

Notes

1. One terminological point concerning the specific example of minority rights or special status that I am using: the issue of minority rights is raised in many countries by the presence of aboriginal peoples who have been conquered, colonized, or simply overrun by settlers from other countries and continents. The rights of Canada's aboriginal peoples are, therefore, representative of a major class of minority rights questions. However, the term 'aboriginal rights' is sometimes used in a more restricted sense, to refer solely to those rights which flow from original occupancy of the land. Hence some writers distinguish between the 'aboriginal rights' of aboriginal peoples (e.g. land claims) and their 'national rights', 'minority rights', or 'human rights' (e.g. to cultural freedom, self-determination, language rights, etc.)—e.g. Barsh and Henderson 1982 p. 76. But this restricted usage is uncommon, and I shall be using 'aboriginal rights' to refer to the rights of aboriginal peoples, not simply to those rights which aboriginal people have because they are the original occupants of the land.

    One of the most important aspects of minority rights claims concerns the ability of minority cultures to restrict the mobility or voting rights of non-members. In the context of Canada's aboriginal peoples, this is invariably phrased as a matter of whether aboriginal communities can restrict the rights of 'whites'. The historical basis for this usage is obvious, and it has become an unquestioned part of the political vocabulary of the debate over aboriginal rights. But it is important to note that 'whites' is not being used as a racial term—many people who are racially white have become members of aboriginal communities (by marriage or adoption), and Canadians who are not members of aboriginal communities have diverse racial ancestry (including aboriginal ancestry). The terms 'aboriginal' and 'white' refer to cultural membership, not race. 'White' has simply become a general label for those Canadians who are not members of aboriginal communities. Hence many of the aboriginal people who demand restrictions on the mobility of 'whites' have some white ancestry, and many of the people whose mobility is being restricted have some aboriginal (or black, or Asian, etc.) ancestry.

2. Similarly, the principles underlying the Supreme Court decisions which struck down legislation redrawing political boundaries so

as to *exclude* blacks from political subdivisions (e.g. *Gomillion* v. *Lightfoot* [1960] 364 US 339) would seem to argue against legislation to *include* Indians in political subdivisions which are unrepresentative and therefore harmful to their interests (Gross p. 250).

3. This is precisely what happened to the Métis in Manitoba, and to the Hispanic population in the American Southwest, during the second half of the nineteenth century. These groups formed a majority in their respective regions, and had rights to public services and education in their own languages. But once their regions became incorporated into the larger Canadian and American federations, these groups became outnumbered by anglophone settlers, who quickly proceeded to take away those rights (see J. Weinstein pp. 46–7 on the Métis; Glazer 1975 p. 25 and 1983 p. 277 on the Spanish-speaking population of the Southwest). Aboriginal self-government proposals have been designed with these dangers and historical precedents in mind (J. Weinstein p. 47; Purich p. 229).

4. I shall discuss the weakness of the last two arguments (about the different value systems of aboriginal peoples, and the moral standing of communities) in Ch. 12. I am unsure what to say about the first two, partly because they in fact have many variants, some of which contradict others. But I should say something about them, since they are important not only in Canada, but in the emerging international norms concerning aboriginal rights.

The fact of original occupancy is invoked to defend at least two different aboriginal claims. The first is 'aboriginal title' (i.e. ownership or usufructuary rights over land and natural resources), the second is sovereignty. I'll discuss sovereignty together with the self-determination argument, since they raise similar questions of international law.

The 'aboriginal title' claim, by itself, does not justify permanent special political status, unless it is further claimed that 'the ownership of the land is the fundamental concept on which other rights, including the right to self-government, are based' (Sanders 1983*b* pp. 328–9). This is in fact the argument amongst some aboriginal groups whose land-base is secure and legally recognized. However, the emphasis on aboriginal title raises a number of questions. Firstly, it is far from clear why it matters who first acquired a piece of land, unless one is inclined to a Nozick-like theory of justice (Lyons; McDonald 1976). Aboriginal communities were, of course, unjustly deprived of much of their land when whites settled, and those injustices have lingering effects which warrant some form of compensation. But that is not yet a reason why the ultimate goal shouldn't be some form of equality of resources for all the citizens of the country, rather than any permanent special status. Secondly, if self-government is supposed to flow from aboriginal title, then there may not be any grounds to demand that the federal government fund aboriginal self-government (Lyon pp. 13–14). Finally, it won't justify either land or self-government for some aboriginal groups, who for various (and often historically arbitrary) reasons lack recognizable title (Robinson and Quinney pp. 51, 86; Opekokew).

The sovereignty claim says that because aboriginal nations were here first, and have not officially relinquished their sovereignty, therefore, as a matter of international law, domestic Canadian law does not apply to aboriginal communities. Any relationship between the federal government and the aboriginal communities must be concluded by what are essentially state-to-state treaties. On the self-determination view, aboriginal peoples are entitled to the same right of self-determination that previously colonized peoples claim under Article 1 of the International Covenant on Civil and Political Rights. The two views often go hand in hand (e.g. Robinson and Quinney), but they are distinct, since aboriginal communities could have sovereignty even if they are not 'peoples' under international law, or they could be 'peoples' even if they do not have sovereignty under international law.

However, neither claim has heretofore been explicitly recognized in international law. Aboriginal rights have instead been viewed as coming under Article 27 of the Covenant, dealing with minority rights (see e.g. United Nations 1983 pp. 94–104), which is roughly how I have been treating them. Most aboriginal leaders have been concerned to change that pattern (see e.g. Sanders 1983*b* pp. 21–5; Barsh 1983 pp. 91–5, 1986 pp. 376–7; Kronowitz *et al.* pp. 598–600; L. C. Green p. 346; Robinson and Quinney pp. 141–2), although some people have thought Article 27 sufficient (e.g. Svensson p. 438). Aboriginal advocates rightly point out that international rulings have been quite arbitrary in limiting the recognition of sovereignty or peoplehood to overseas colonies (the 'Blue Water Thesis'), while denying it to internal groups who share many of the same historical and social features (e.g. Barsh 1983 pp. 84–91).

But since advocates of the self-determination and sovereignty views are not in fact seeking a sovereign state, it is not immediately clear what rests on the distinction between Article 1 and Article 27 rights. Article 27 has occasionally been interpreted as merely requiring non-discrimination against minorities. But the recent

Capotorti report on the international protection of minority rights decisively rejects that view, and insists that special measures for minority cultures are required for 'factual equality', and that such measures are as important as non-discrimination in 'defending fundamental human rights' (Capotorti pp. 40–1, 98–9). If the goal is not a sovereign state, then Article 27 may be as good as Article 1 in arguing for the right of minority cultures to freely develop and express their own culture. As Wirsing notes, recent changes in the interpretation of Article 27 go 'some distance towards closing the gap' between the expectations of minority cultures and the concessions of the international community (Wirsing 1980 p. 228). And while elimination of the 'Blue Water Thesis' in regard to the definition of 'peoples' would eliminate some arbitrariness, it would also essentially eliminate the category of 'minorities' (most groups which have sought special measures under Article 27 would constitute peoples, not minorities, according to the definitions offered by some aboriginal groups—e.g. the Mikmaq proposal quoted in Barsh 1983 p. 94).

One worry aboriginals have about Article 27, even on an expansive reading, concerns not the content of the rights it may accord to minorities, but the question of who *delegates* the rights. They are aware of the vulnerability created by the American system of aboriginal rights, in which self-government 'is a gift, not a right . . . a question of policy and politics' (Kronowitz *et al.* pp. 533, 535; cf. Barsh 1983 p. 103). Some aboriginal leaders believe that claims to sovereignty are needed to avoid this vulnerability (see e.g. Robinson and Quinney p. 123). But others say that such claims heighten misunderstanding and prevent the negotiation of adequate guarantees: 'The maximum height on the government side is generated by the word "sovereignty"; and on the Aboriginal side, by the word "delegated". Somewhere between the two lies an area of potential agreement' (M. Dunn p. 37).

Since Article 1 has not been applied to the aboriginal peoples of North America, and since Article 27 may still be too weak, some aboriginal groups have been pressing for the recognition of a specifically aboriginal category between those of 'peoples' and 'minorities', in which self-determination is neither sovereign nor delegated (see Moore pp. 27–8; Kronowitz *et al.* pp. 612–20; Barsh 1986 pp. 376–8; Sanders 1983*b* pp. 28–9). The question of whether self-government is delegated or not is clearly important, but it is somewhat distinct from the questions I am addressing. If aboriginal rights to self-determination are not delegated, or indeed if aboriginal communities retain their legal sovereignty, then aboriginals should be able to reject the substantive provisions of a Canadian government proposal for self-government, should they view them as unjust. My question is the prior one of evaluating the justice of the provisions. And it may be that the same substantive provisions would be just whether aboriginal groups are viewed as peoples, or as minorities, or as their own third category. The different categories would affect not the justice of their claims, but their domestic and international ability to negotiate for those just claims.

Even if aboriginal peoples have substantive claims which cannot be derived from Article 27, in virtue of aboriginal title or legal sovereignty, it is still important for liberals to determine what is owed minorities under that article. Even if aboriginal peoples have special rights beyond those owed them as a minority culture, liberals should ask what they (or other minorities) are owed just in virtue of plural cultural membership. In any event, it is doubtful whether all North American aboriginal groups could qualify as sovereign or self-determining peoples under international law. So a liberal defence of minority rights, if one can be found, would be a helpful argument for many aboriginal groups, and may be the only argument available for some of the groups.

8

The Value of Cultural Membership

HOW can we defend minority rights within liberalism, given that its moral ontology recognizes only individuals, each of whom is to be treated with equal consideration? We need to be able to show two things: (1) that cultural membership has a more important status in liberal thought than is explicitly recognized—that is, that the individuals who are an unquestionable part of the liberal moral ontology are viewed as individual members of a particular cultural community, for whom cultural membership is an important good; and (2) that the members of minority cultural communities may face particular kinds of disadvantages with respect to the good of cultural membership, disadvantages whose rectification requires and justifies the provision of minority rights. That is, we need to show that membership in a cultural community may be a relevant criterion for distributing the benefits and burdens which are the concern of a liberal theory of justice. I think that both of these steps can be made, but it will require a re-examination of some basic liberal premises about individualism and egalitarianism.

These two steps will form the basis of the next two chapters. In each case, I shall try to show that the same arguments that Rawls and Dworkin give for equal rights and resources within a nation-state can be used to defend special status for minority cultures in a culturally plural state.

So first I shall look at the liberal conception of the individual. Does the liberal account of the individual contain the resources to meet our intuitions about the importance of both citizenship and cultural membership? At first glance, Rawls's theory does not look promising. It seems that whatever interest individuals have in cultural membership, it is subordinated to their interest in securing what he calls the 'liberties of equal citizenship':

Each person possesses an inviolability founded on justice that even the welfare of society as a whole cannot override . . . Therefore in a just society the liberties of equal citizenship are taken as settled; the rights secured by justice are not subject to political bargaining or to the calculus of social interests. (Rawls 1971 pp. 3–4)

Individual liberty is so important that the only legitimate ground for restricting a particular basic liberty for everyone—like the right of political participation—is to secure a more extensive system of overall basic liberties for everyone. And the only legitimate ground for unequally distributing such a basic liberty is to secure for the less free person a greater system of basic liberty than she otherwise would have had. Other than that, 'the system of equal liberties is absolute' (Rawls 1971 p. 506 n.).

It is this insistence on the priority of the liberties of citizenship which makes Rawls's theory, as formulated in his two principles of justice, incompatible with minority rights. Neither of the two qualifications Rawls makes to the priority of liberty will support any of the measures for protecting cultural membership under consideration. Indeed, such measures violate both qualifications. They create unequal liberties in order to benefit not those with lesser basic liberty (e.g. the whites whose property and voting rights are restricted in aboriginal reserves or homelands), but those with the now greater liberty (the aboriginal inhabitants), and they restrict liberty in order not to enlarge liberty overall, but to protect cultural membership. They have an entirely negative effect on basic liberty, at least as Rawls defines it.[1]

But why are the liberties of citizenship so important? What gives individuals such an interest in preserving their liberties of citizenship, without any consideration of cultural membership? As I've already discussed, Rawls believes that the freedom to form and revise our beliefs about value is a crucial precondition for pursuing our essential interest in leading a good life. The individual is viewed by Rawls as a conscious and purposive agent—she acts so as to achieve certain goals or purposes, based on beliefs she has about what is worth having, doing, or achieving. These beliefs give meaning to our lives, they make sense of why we do what we do. But we may be wrong in these beliefs. We may come to question the value or worth of many of the things we do, from going to church to writing novels. These beliefs underlie the most important decisions we make in life, and we care whether these beliefs are true or false (no one wants to live a life based on a falsehood). Therefore Rawls claims that we should have the social conditions needed to intelligently decide for ourselves what is valuable in life. These conditions include the guarantees of personal independence (secured by the liberties of citizenship) needed to make such decisions freely. People should be free, not just to act in accordance with their current religious beliefs, for example, but also to question these beliefs, and to adopt other beliefs, without being deprived of their liberties or their resources, without being penalized or discriminated against by society (see Chapter 2 above).

The idea of seeing the value of our activities is very important. It's crucial to what Rawls calls self-respect, the 'sense that one's plan of life is worth carrying out'. Self-respect, as Rawls says, isn't so much a part of any rational plan of life, but rather a *precondition* of it. If we thought that our goals in life weren't worth pursuing, then there would be no point to our activities (Rawls 1971 p. 178). To ensure that we have this self-respect, we need the freedom to examine our beliefs, to confirm their worth. This is why liberty is so important to Rawls, and why he gives it precedence over material benefits and the prerogatives of office. Once material security is ensured, so that the conditions necessary for the effective exercise of liberty exist, it is irrational to trade off liberty for more wealth.

So far, that seems unobjectionable. But we need to look more closely at these beliefs about value which are said to give meaning and purpose to our lives. Where do they come from? Liberals say that we should be free to accept or reject particular options presented to us, so that, ultimately, the beliefs we continue to hold are the ones that we've chosen to accept. But the range of options can't be chosen. In deciding how to lead our lives, we do not start *de novo*, but rather we examine 'definite ideals and forms of life that have been developed and tested by innumerable individuals, sometimes for generations' (Rawls 1971 pp. 563–4). The decision about how to lead our lives must ultimately be ours alone, but this decision is always a matter of selecting what we believe to be most valuable from the various options available, selecting from a context of choice which provides us with different ways of life.

This is important because the range of options is determined by our cultural heritage. Different ways of life are not simply different patterns of physical movements. The physical movements only have meaning to us because they are identified as having significance by our *culture*, because they fit into some pattern of activities which is culturally recognized as a way of leading one's life. We learn about these patterns of activity through their presence in stories we've heard about the lives, real or imaginary, of others. They become potential models, and define potential roles, that we can adopt as our own. From childhood on, we become aware both that we are already participants in certain forms of life (familial, religious, sexual, educational, etc.), and that there are other ways of life which offer alternative models and roles that we may, in time, come to endorse. We decide how to lead our lives by situating ourselves in these cultural narratives, by adopting roles that have struck us as worthwhile ones, as ones worth living (which may, of course, include the roles we were brought up to occupy).

The processes by which options and choices become significant for us are linguistic and historical processes. Whether or not a course of action has any significance for us depends on whether, or how, our language renders vivid to us the point of that activity. And the way in which language renders vivid these activities is a matter of our cultural heritage (Sparham p. 335). Our language and history are the media through which we come to an awareness of the options available to us, and their significance; and this is a precondition of making intelligent judgements about how to lead our lives. In order to make such judgements, we do not explore a number of different patterns of physical movement, which might in principle be judged in abstraction from any cultural structure. Rather, we make these judgements precisely by examining the cultural structure, by coming to an awareness of the possibilities it has, the different activities it identifies as significant.

What follows from this? Liberals should be concerned with the fate of cultural structures, not because they have some moral status of their own, but because it's only through having a rich and secure cultural structure that people can become aware, in a vivid way, of the options available to them, and intelligently examine their value. Without such a cultural structure, children and adolescents lack adequate role-models, which leads to despondency and escapism, a condition poignantly described by Seltzer in a recent article on the adolescents in Inuit communities (Seltzer). The cultural structure they need and value is being undermined, and the Inuit have been unable to protect it.

But while culture is therefore a crucial component of Rawls's own argument for liberty, he never includes cultural membership as one of the primary goods with which justice is concerned. While he asks about the relative importance of liberty compared with other primary goods, he doesn't ask about its relation to the primary good of cultural membership. Perhaps, as I'll suggest later, he implicitly assumes that the political community is culturally homogeneous, and hence that no exercise of liberty within the basic structure of the community could affect cultural membership. But cultural membership is still a primary good, consideration of which is an important part of showing equal concern for individuals. This importance would have been recognized by the parties in Rawls's original position. The relationship between cultural membership and self-respect gives the parties to the original position a strong incentive to give cultural membership status as a primary good. As Rawls says, 'the parties in the original position would wish to avoid at almost any cost the social conditions that undermine self-respect' (Rawls 1971 p. 440); the loss of cultural membership is one such condition. Rawls's own argument for the importance of liberty as a primary good is also an argument for the importance of cultural membership as a primary good.

It is of sovereign importance to this argument that the cultural structure is being recognized *as a context of choice*. If we view cultural membership as a primary good within Rawls's scheme of justice, then it is important to remember that it is a good in its capacity of providing meaningful options for us, and aiding our ability to judge for ourselves the value of our life-plans. This affects the way that we should understand terms like 'cultural structure' or 'cultural community', which are notoriously difficult terms to define. In one common usage, culture refers to the *character* of a historical community. On this view, changes in the norms, values, and their attendant institutions in one's community (e.g. membership in churches, political parties, etc.) would amount to loss of one's culture. However, I use culture in a very different sense, to refer to the cultural community, or cultural structure, itself. On this view, the cultural community continues to exist even when its members are free to modify the character of the culture, should they find its traditional ways of life no longer worth while.

For example, the character of French-Canadian culture was radically transformed in the 1960s. It was the end of a 'culture' in the first sense. Very few of the institutions which traditionally characterized French-Canadian life (e.g. the Roman Catholic Church, parochial schools, the Union Nationale political party) could be secure in the knowledge that they had the continuing allegiance of the broad majority of the members of the culture. It was aptly called the 'Quiet Revolution' in French Canada, since French-Canadians began to make very different choices than they traditionally had done. But the existence of a French-Canadian cultural community itself was never in question, never threatened with unwanted extinction or assimilation as aboriginal communities are currently threatened. There was no danger to cultural membership in the sense I am concerned with—i.e. no danger to the existence of people's context of choice, no danger to their ability to examine the options that their cultural structure had made meaningful to them. It is cultural membership in this more fundamental second sense that should be viewed as a primary good in Rawls's theory, given its importance in Rawls's own argument for liberty. Protecting people from changes in the character of the culture can't be viewed as protecting their ability to choose. On the contrary, it would be a limitation on their ability to choose. Concern for the cultural structure as a context of choice, on the other hand, accords with, rather than conflicts with, the liberal concern for our ability and freedom to judge the value of our life-plans. The demise of a culture, in the first sense, occurred *because of* the choices that francophones themselves made from within their (stable) context of choice. The demise of culture, in the second sense, arises *in spite of* the choices of aboriginal people, and undermines their context of choice.

The notion of respect for persons *qua* members of cultures, based on the recognition of the importance of the primary good of cultural membership, is not, therefore, an illiberal one. It doesn't say that the community is more important than the individuals who compose it, or that the state should impose (what it views to be) the best conception of the good life on its citizens in order to preserve the purity of the culture, or any such thing. The argument simply says that cultural membership is important in pursuing our essential interest in leading a good life, and so consideration of that membership is an important part of having equal consideration for the interests of each member of the community.

But we must be on guard against abuses of the argument, since people often use similar arguments in order not to protect the community as such, but to protect their particular preferred vision of what sort of *character* the community should have. Thus we often hear Islamic fundamentalists claim that without restrictions on the freedom of speech, press, religion, sexual practices, etc. of its own members, their culture will disintegrate, thus undermining the self-respect individuals derive from cultural membership. Every society, it is said, has a public morality which is a seamless web, respect for which is necessary to the very stability of society, so that deviation in religious and sexual matters simply can't be tolerated without endangering the very structure of society. Of course we needn't invoke the Islamic fundamentalist to make the point. Lord Devlin has made a similar argument about English society (Devlin *passim*).

The problem with the argument, in either case, is that it suffers from a fatal ambiguity. On one interpretation, 'culture' is defined in terms of the norms currently characterizing it, so that, by definition, any significant change in people's religious affiliations thereby 'destroys' the old 'culture'. But that conclusion is entirely uninteresting, since it in no way suggests that the existence of the cultural community is threatened, and hence doesn't suggest that the primary good of cultural membership is threatened. On the other interpretation, 'culture' is defined, as I think it should be defined for these purposes, in terms of the existence of a viable community of individuals with a shared heritage (language, history, etc.).[2] But then it is wildly implausible to suppose that allowing individuals freedom of religion or sexual practices would lead to the breakdown of that community, be it England or Iran. Devlin later made it clear that he simply meant to say that one could never rule out the *possibility* that such freedoms could undermine the very existence of the community, for example by leading to massive increases in murders, suicides, and alcoholism and a crisis in public authority. The problem, as Dworkin notes, is that Devlin takes the preferences of those who dislike change as sufficient grounds for thinking that the survival of society is at stake (Dworkin 1977 ch. 10).

Dworkin's response to Devlin requires just the distinction I am drawing between the stability of a cultural community and its character at a particular moment (as does his response to Taylor discussed in Chapter 5 above). Liberalizing the homosexuality laws in England changed the character of the cultural structure, without jeopardizing its existence. This distinction is required whether we are discussing a country with one cultural community or a culturally plural country. To reject the possibility of making this distinction is not simply to give up the possibility of defending minority rights within liberalism, it is to give up the possibility of defending liberalism itself. Liberal values require both individual freedom of choice and a secure cultural context from which individuals can make their choices. Thus liberalism requires that we can identify, protect, and promote cultural membership, as a primary good, without accepting Devlin's claim that this requires protecting the character of a given cultural community. It is the existence of a cultural community viewed as a context of choice that is a primary good, and a legitimate concern of liberals. But the very reasons we have to value cultural contexts of choice argue against Devlin's claim that we should protect the character of a given cultural community. Protecting the homophobic character of England's cultural structure from the effects of allowing free choice of sexual life-style undermines the very reason we had to protect England's cultural structure—that it allows meaningful individual choice.

This is why a concern for the value of cultural membership is not illiberal. Perhaps certain cultural communities are less capable of liberalizing their practices than the English (the English have usually assumed they are more capable of it than other nations). But if the English can allow the character of their culture to change (by granting freedom of sexual life-style) without destroying their cultural community, why can't other cultures? In any event, it is important to notice that this potential problem has nothing in particular to do with minority cultures; it could equally well occur for majority cultures, or for nation-states. And however liberals respond to the problem in a nation-state, they can and should respond in the same way when the problem arises for a minority nation. Finding a way to liberalize a cultural community without destroying it is a task that liberals face in every country, once we recognize the importance of a secure cultural context of choice. That task may seem difficult in the case of some minority cultures. But if people respond to that difficulty by denying that we can distinguish the character of a cultural community from its very existence, then they have given up on the possibility of defending liberalism in any country, including Devlin's England.

Undoubtedly there are cases where the very survival of society does require some restrictions on the (otherwise legitimate) freedom of choice of its members. One occasionally hears of cases like that of an isolated tribe in Indonesia where a large number of children jumped off a cliff to their death in an attempt to emulate a Superman feat they had just seen on (recently introduced) television. The unregulated introduction of liquor to a society can have analagous effects on the adults. Our ability as individuals to make our way in the modern world of seemingly unlimited possibilities depends, in fact, on the existence of a structure of social understandings which point out the dangers and limits of the resources at our disposal. Where that structure is absent, the unregulated introduction, and free use, of such resources can have literally fatal consequences. If we refuse to let a cultural community have such temporary special restrictions on individual behaviour, knowing full well that without them the vast majority of its members will end up dead, or in jail, or on skid row, then that refusal isn't so much a victory for liberalism as a deliberate act of genocide. If certain liberties really would undermine the very existence of the community, then we should allow what would otherwise be illiberal measures. But these measures would only be justified as temporary measures, easing the shock which can result from too rapid change in the character of the culture (be it endogenously or exogenously caused), helping the culture to move carefully towards a fully liberal society. The ideal would still be a society where every individual is free to choose the life she thinks best for her from a rich array of possibilities offered by the cultural structure. Indeed, some Indian leaders in Canada defend their more restrictive special rights as precisely such temporary measures to ensure that the Indian community has sufficient strength and integrity to survive the (desirable) transition to a situation where its members have all the resources of the modern world at their disposal, should they choose to use them. Indian communities have been too weakened (and denigrated) by the white majority to currently allow every individual Indian to enjoy all the liberties she will enjoy once the cultural structure has recovered its normal healthy strength and flexibility.[3]

This short-term strategy of restricting liberties in order to promote the longer-term ideal of full liberal freedoms has its dangers. Measures that are initially defended as unavoidable temporary restrictions on individual liberty may come to be defended as inherently desirable. Should it be the case that temporary restrictions are likely to be seen as desirable in themselves, rather than as necessary measures to achieve the ideal state of affairs in which they are absent, then the strategy must be reassessed. We need to know more about how societies disintegrate, and about how we can reduce the birth-pangs of liberalization, before we can make any general statement about when illiberal measures can be justified on the grounds of respecting cultural membership. (I shall return to this question at the end of Chapter 9.)

In any event, this possibility—that in rare cases certain temporary illiberal measures can be justified by appeal to the importance of cultural membership—does nothing to warrant the pervasive liberal fear about recognizing that importance. It has no application to most cultures, and anyway does nothing to challenge the view that the long-term goal—the ideally just cultural community—is one in which every individual has the full range of civil and political liberties to pursue the life she sees fit. Undoubtedly there are many fundamentalists of all political and religious stripes who think that the best community is one in which all but their preferred religious, sexual, or aesthetic practices are outlawed. But the notion of cultural membership as a primary good will not provide them with any support. For so long as everyone has her fair share of resources and the freedom to live her life as she chooses within her cultural community, then the primary good of cultural membership is properly recognized. Promotion of fundamentalist politics in these circumstances, far from appealing to the primary good of cultural membership, conflicts with it, since it undermines the very reason we had for being concerned with cultural membership—that it allows for meaningful individual choice.

Fundamentalists can, of course, object at a much deeper level to the argument so far presented. They could assert that people's identity is bound up not merely with membership in a cultural community, viewed as a context of choice, but with participation in the shared ends of existing community practices. According to this objection, if some members of a culture work to change the character of the culture—e.g. by criticizing its traditional ways of life—this is as much an attack on members' self-respect as it is when the very existence of an aboriginal community is undermined by the actions of non-aboriginal people. Individuals' identities, it is said, are constituted by the shared ends which characterize the culture at the present moment, and so the secularization of Iranian society, or the liberalization of English laws on homosexuality, is an attack on the self-respect of the Iranians or English, even though, as individuals, they still have their fair share of resources and an equal ability to lead their lives in their own community.

One way of understanding the communitarian critique of liberalism is to see it as advancing this claim about the way individual identities are constituted by communal ends. But it is not, I think, a very plausible claim, as I've argued in Chapter 4. In any event, the potential illiberality of that view doesn't arise on my proposal, which claims that cultural community enters our self-understandings by providing a context of choice within which to choose and pursue our conception of the good life. This understanding of cultural membership doesn't involve any necessary connection with the shared ends which characterize the culture at any given moment. The primary good being recognized is the cultural community as a context of choice, not the character of the community or its traditional ways of life, which people are free to endorse or reject.

But an important issue for minority cultures remains. Even if cultural membership is a primary good, we haven't discussed whether it implies membership in any *particular* cultural community. People may require a cultural structure to make sense of their lives, but it doesn't follow that we ought to be concerned about their own culture. In the case of Canada's aboriginal peoples, why not just assist them in moving to English Canada and learning its language and culture? Why not let minority cultural communities disintegrate, and assist those who suffer that misfortune to assimilate to another culture?

This is a question that is raised by Schwartz's recent attempt to defend the rights of Canada's aboriginal peoples within liberal theory. He agrees that a cultural structure provides people with a context of choice. But he doesn't believe that people are bound, in a constitutive way, to any *particular* cultural community. He would perhaps agree with Ernest Renan's claim that 'Man is bound neither to his language nor to his race: he is bound only to himself, because he is a free agent, or in other words a moral being'.[4] As a result, aboriginal peoples have no particular claim to the protection of their own culture. We would be fulfilling our legitimate duties, in terms of respecting the primary good of cultural membership, if we facilitated their assimilation into another culture. Aboriginal rights can be justified, he thinks, but only on the grounds that they benefit *everyone*, by enriching and expanding the options available to all Canadians.

Now this is a peculiar way to defend aboriginal rights. Indeed, it's hard to see why we should continue using the term 'aboriginal rights' at all. For it is the usual implication of that term that aboriginal peoples (not Canadians generally) have rights to the protection of their culture. And what makes them *rights* is that they are claims to be respected even if some other policy would better serve the interests of the rest of the Canadian political community. Special rights are justified because aboriginal peoples have a legitimate claim to the protection of their cultural membership, whether or not the lives of non-aboriginal Canadians are thereby improved or enriched. (That is why constitutional entrenchment is desired.[5]) For Schwartz, on the other hand, protecting someone's cultural community is only one possible way of protecting her range of meaningful choices, to be considered alongside facilitating her assimilation into another culture. The strongest claim that Schwartz can make is that the special status of aboriginal peoples is consistent with, but not required by, liberal principles. But then in what sense do aboriginal people have a *right* to those special measures?

Schwartz recognizes that his defence of aboriginal rights does not fit the usual understanding of those rights. He recognizes that minority rights are usually grounded in appeals to the importance of membership in historical communities. But he considers these 'history-based groupist' claims to be illiberal, in conflict with the 'liberal individualist' picture of Canada as a 'community of equal individuals, whose rights are more or less independent of historical development'. That individuals belong to historical communities is not relevant to their just claims. As he says, 'it is better to view Canada as a political community of equal individuals, *rather than* as an agglomeration of historical communities' (Schwartz p. xvii, my emphasis). If we reject the history-based groupist conception of justice, then aboriginal rights can't be justified in terms of protecting cultural membership for a minority group. They can only be justified in terms of the benefits they provide for all citizens, regardless of their cultural membership.

Does Indian special status enrich everyone's range of choices? Undoubtedly, but so would a number of other cultural policies, many of which might do so in a more efficient way. Why not pay for the assimilation of Indians or the Inuit into English-Canadian culture, and then enrich the culture by sub-sidizing education about, and exchanges with, Ukrainian com-munities? This might well provide more options at less cost, since it would involve no restriction of the liberties of others, and the information would be easily accessible to the general population (unlike the segregated Indian reservations and geo-graphically remote Inuit communities).

Schwartz, to be fair, doesn't claim that aboriginal rights *are* the best way of enriching the choices of Canadians. He defends aboriginal rights, not because they are required, or even particularly appropriate, in terms of his liberal-individualist principles, but because minority groups will feel cheated if their history-based groupist claims are not met. As he puts it, 'we should work towards constitutional arrangements that advance the ideals of liberal individualism, but which satisfy, or do as little affront as possible to, those whose constitutional programmes are grounded in history-based groupism' (Schwartz p. 39). But if the 'affront' is grounded in a misguided theory of justice, why not work to change people's misguided views, rather than giving in to them?

Schwartz's response would probably be that history-based groupism is too deeply embedded in our political culture and institutions to be argued out of existence. I would agree. But Schwartz misses the kernel of truth in history-based groupism which explains why it is such a pervasive feature of our political culture (and that of many other Western democracies). People *are* bound, in an important way, to their own cultural community. We can't just transplant people from one culture to another, even if we provide the opportunity to learn the other language and culture. Someone's upbringing isn't something that can just be erased; it is, and will remain, a constitutive part of who that person is. Cultural membership affects our very sense of personal identity and capacity.

The connection between personal identity and cultural membership is suggested by a number of considerations. Sociologists of language note that our language is not just a neutral medium for identifying the content of certain activities, but 'itself *is* content, a reference for loyalties and animosities', a 'marker of the societal goals, the large-scale value-laden arenas of interaction that typify every speech community' (Fishman p. 4). Likewise cultural heritage, the sense of belonging to a cultural structure and history, is often cited as a source of emotional security and personal strength. It may affect our very sense of agency. This has been recognized not only by sociologists, but also by the leaders of racist and oppressive regimes around the world, who have tried to destroy and degrade the cultural heritage of the people they oppress in order to undermine their sense of personal efficacy. It is revealed in the following statement of F. Mkhwanazi, a black South African: 'The regime tried to make us believe that our people had no history . . . they wanted us to carry an image of ourselves as pathetic, utterly defeated, dependent, incapable and powerless' (Mkhwanazi p. 18). Harold Cardinal makes a similar point in discussing the way whites in Canada denigrated Indian heritage as a part of their 'pacification' programme (Cardinal 1969 p. 53). But this strategy only makes sense if one's sense of personal agency is tied to one's cultural heritage. Why else would telling an individual that her *people* had no history have the effect of giving the individual an image of *herself* as powerless? This suggests that cultural structure is crucial not just to the pursuit of our chosen ends, but also to the very sense that we are capable of pursuing them efficiently.

The same conclusion is suggested by the historical evidence that

human beings very reluctantly give up their [cultural associations], even in the face of negative costs of membership (such as discrimination). This is because the group functions as a mechanism for mobilizing the individual to act in general social situations, helps to define needs and desires and the ways to achieve them, and forms the locus of strong affective attachments which figure prominently in self-identity. It also has much to do with the pride and self-respect of individual members. (Svensson p. 436)

This tendency has been particularly clear in the history of the aboriginal peoples of North America, but it is evident throughout the world. Conversely, measures of enforced assimilation can have tragic results. While often designed with benevolent intentions, such measures—like the policy of terminating Indian special status adopted by the American government in the 1950s—have often been miserable failures (Kronowitz *et al.* pp. 533–4). Facilitating assimilation not only doesn't work as well as protecting cultural membership, it often doesn't work at all.

In these and other ways, cultural membership seems crucial to personal agency and development: when the individual is stripped of her cultural heritage, her development becomes stunted (Claydon pp. 134–6). And so respecting people's own cultural membership and facilitating their transition to another culture are not equally legitimate options. The affront minority groups feel at the latter proposal is grounded in the perception of real harm.

The constitutive nature of our cultural identity may be the result of contingent facts about existing forms of social life, rather than of universal features of human thought and development. But whether universal or not, this phenomenon exists in our world, and is manifested in both the benefits people draw from their cultural membership, and the harms of enforced assimilation. And the assumption that the importance of cultural identity would decline under modernizing conditions, a common assumption a few decades ago, has proved breath-takingly false (Gellner; Nicholls p. 58). So it seems that we should interpret the primary good of cultural membership as referring to the individuals' own cultural community.

But if cultural membership is an important part of the liberal concern for individual autonomy, why didn't Rawls make it clear that it was a primary good? Some people think that the reason Rawls fails to pay adequate attention to this question of the cultural context of people's voluntary actions is that he, like most liberals, is an 'atomist' who believes that individuals are self-sufficient outside of society and hence not in need of the cultural context of choice in order to exercise their moral powers.

But, as I argued in Chapter 5, Rawls isn't an atomist in that sense. Rawls talks about how we decide our life-plans not *de novo*, but rather by examining the models and ways of life of those who have preceded us (Rawls 1971 pp. 563–4). And he endorses Mill's argument for liberty, which relies heavily on the fact that we are dependent on the cultural structure around us for our personal development (Rawls 1971 pp. 209–10—see Chapter 2 above). Likewise Dworkin talks about the importance of one's cultural structure in providing the conditions necessary to make imaginative decisions about how to lead one's life. He says that 'the center of a community's cultural structure is its shared language', and that this language and structure can be enriched or diminished in the opportunities it provides. He concludes that 'We inherited a cultural structure, and we have some duty, out of simple justice, to leave that structure as least as rich as we found it' (Dworkin 1985 pp. 230, 233).

But if neither Rawls nor Dworkin ignores the importance of the cultural context of choice, it becomes even more of a puzzle why neither of them recognizes cultural membership as a primary good, or as a ground for legitimate claims. The answer, I think, lies not in any deep, foundational flaw in liberalism, but simply in the fact that Rawls and Dworkin, like most post-war political theorists, work with a very simplified model of the nation-state, where the political community is co-terminous with one and only one cultural community. Of course, cultural membership is still a primary good in a culturally homogeneous country. But it is a kind of public good, equally available to all, not the source of differential rights-claims. It isn't likely to be a source of unjust inequalities in such a country, since there is only one cultural structure for all citizens. It can essentially be taken for granted in identifying and remedying unjust inequalities within the community. But it isn't any less important to individual liberty because of that.

The assumption of cultural homogeneity can be seen in Dworkin's claim, quoted above, that 'we inherited *a* cultural structure' centred on *its* shared language. The 'we' in question in that passage is the American *political* community, but it by no means has one cultural structure or shared language. Rawls makes the same conflation of the political and cultural communities when he says 'the basic structure shapes the way the social system produces and reproduces over time a certain form of culture' (Rawls 1978 p. 55). The basic structure is an attribute of the political community, and nothing warrants Rawls's assumption that there will be only one cultural structure inside it.

So both Dworkin and Rawls require and invoke the notion of a cultural structure (the context of people's choices), which is distinguishable from the character of the culture at any moment (the product of people's choices). They both recognize the importance of protecting the cultural structure, since it provides the context of choice, yet both reject Devlin's claim that this requires protecting the particular character of the culture at any given time. They both implicitly recognize the primary good of cultural membership, in the sense I discussed above. The only reason that they don't explicitly give it status as a ground for legitimate claims is that they falsely assume there is only one such cultural structure in each political community. If we drop that assumption, then the primary good of cultural membership has to be explicitly recognized as a possible source of unjust inequalities. As I'll argue in the next chapter, this is a genuine possibility in many countries.

Notes

1. Rawls sometimes writes as if 'rights' and 'liberties' are interchangeable (1971 p. 239 n.), but while all basic liberties may be rights, it doesn't follow that all rights are liberties. The right not

to be libelled, for example, is a restriction 'not of liberty for liberty, but of liberty for protection from harm or loss of amenities or other elements of real utility' (Hart p. 548). Thus although one can say that there is a right to cultural membership, it won't thereby become a liberty that can be included within Rawls's liberty principle.

One could say that cultural membership helps secure the *worth* of liberty, but that won't make minority rights compatible with Rawls's liberty principle either. Rawls explicitly distinguishes between liberty and the worth of liberty (1971 p. 204) and denies that the liberty principle allows trade-offs of the former for the latter, as indeed he must if his claim that one can't trade liberty for material wealth is to make any sense. Wealth undoubtedly contributes to the worth of liberty, but if wealth counts as strengthening liberty since it strengthens the worth of liberty, then trade-offs between wealth and political liberty would be trade-offs *within* the primary good of liberty, not, as Rawls claims, trade-offs between liberty and another primary good. Therefore Rawls can't say that minority rights are justified in terms of their contribution to liberty as it's defined in the liberty principle. There's no way to include cultural protection measures within the priority of liberty, and still have a priority that is both meaningful and of liberty.

2. This raises the question of what defines a minority cultural community (or, as they are sometimes called in the social sciences or international law, 'ethno-cultural nations', 'national minorities', 'co-inhabiting nationalities'; see Capotorti pp. 95–6 for a discussion of the terminological variations). This is a vexed problem, and all attempts to stipulate necessary and sufficient conditions have been notoriously unsuccessful. Any definition will contain two components: (1) an objective component dealing with such things as a common heritage and language; (2) a subjective component dealing with self-identification with the group. But that by itself is much too vague, and one is inclined to agree with Seton-Watson that we are 'driven to the conclusion that no "scientific definition" of a nation can be devised; yet the phenomenon has existed and exists' (Seton-Watson p. 5).

We know that such communities exist, and we can all agree on some examples (like the French-Canadians, or the Inuit), however much we disagree about the proper definition of a minority nation or culture. And so, as a number of people suggest, 'the absence of a generally accepted definition should not constitute an obstacle to the application of Article 27 of the International Covenant on

Civil and Political Rights' (Capotorti p. 10). In fact, Capotorti claims that the real complication arises from the fact that many governments wish

> to restrict or refine the definition so that no minority is recognized as existing in their territory, and that consequently no international obligations arise for them in relation to the protection of minorities. If, however, the problem is examined without political prejudice and from a truly universal point of view, there can be no gainsaying that the essential elements of a minority are well-known. (Capotorti p. 96)

Likewise Wirsing claims that the key issue isn't finding a definition of 'minority', it is deciding who has the ultimate power to apply the definition (Wirsing 1980 pp. 222–6).

This may be a little over-optimistic, and we can always hope that conceptual clarification will be forthcoming. But it is the nearly universal conclusion of writers in the area that attempts to specify sufficient and necessary conditions are hopeless (for a representative discussion, see Sigler ch. 1). Therefore, in the words of Ernest Gellner, 'It is probably best to approach this problem [of defining cultural nations] by using this term without attempting too much in the way of formal definition, and looking at what culture *does*' (Gellner p. 7). I follow Gellner's suggestion since that is indeed the crucial issue in most disputes about minority rights. In the Canadian debate, for example, the issue is not over whether French-Canadians or the Inuit form minority cultures, but about what a culture *does* for its members.

3. See, for example, the Indian Association of Alberta spokesman quoted in Doerr (p. 54 n. 35); and the discussion by D. G. Poole in Bowles *et al.* (p. 195). The possibility that cultures can be liberalized is ignored by Raz in his discussion of minority cultures. Speaking, *inter alia*, of aboriginal communities which don't give their members the conditions of autonomous choice, Raz says we face the choice of 'taking action to assimilate the minority group' or of 'tolerating' their illiberality and allowing them 'to continue in their ways' (Raz 1986 p. 424). But why can't we endorse that an aboriginal community liberalize its institutions, while protecting it from undesired assimilation? Raz says that the 'break up' of aboriginal communities is the 'inevitable by-product' of an attempt to liberalize their institutions, like their separate schools (Raz 1986 p. 423). But if French-Canadians were able to liberalize their (distinct) school system in the Quiet Revolution, why not aboriginal Canadians? Raz gives no reason to suppose that aboriginal peoples

are incapable, or any less capable, of developing liberal institutions than any other cultural group.

4. This was, at one time, one of Trudeau's favourite quotes, which he invoked when attacking minority rights. See Gwyn p. 221.

5. As Berger puts it, entrenchment of aboriginal rights 'will limit the powers of Parliament and of the provinces. This is the whole point. These rights should never be subject to the will of the majority. They are *minority* rights' (Berger 1981 p. 261). It is unclear why Schwartz wouldn't endorse the American route, whereby Indian self-government is 'now a gift, not a right', and 'the powers of self-government and property-ownership allowed to the Indians are only a question of policy and politics' (Kronowitz *et al.* pp. 533, 535).

9

Equality for Minority Cultures

IF the arguments of the preceding chapter are correct, then liberals should accord cultural membership an important role in their theories of justice. But it is not obvious how this should affect the principles of justice they endorse, or the policies they recommend. Even if cultural membership needs to be secured, why does that require anything other than a colour-blind egalitarian distribution of resources and liberties? After all, liberal equality is meant to be able to accommodate the fact that different groups value different things, including, presumably, different cultural memberships. Each person is given an equal share of resources and liberties in order to pursue the things they value. Why should the members of minority cultures, such as the aboriginal peoples of Canada, have more than an equal share to protect the cultural heritage they value?

Part of the problem in the Canadian context is that aboriginal groups don't have an equal share of social resources. But that complaint, while certainly valid, is more about our failure to live up to the goal of a colour-blind society than about any flaw in that goal. Moreover, it would only justify temporary measures for aboriginal groups in order to raise them to an equitable level, not permanent constitutional differentiation. Liberals have no objection to such affirmative action programmes. Indeed, as we've seen, they were a part of the 1969 proposal which attempted to remove the special constitutional status of Canadian Indians.

Why then should aboriginal peoples have a special constitutional status that goes beyond equal rights and resources? A deeper examination of the liberal conception of equality is needed. The liberal view of justice that I discussed in Chapters 2 and 3 was founded upon the 'abstract egalitarian plateau'— the claim that the interests of each member of the community matter, and matter equally. Rawls's principles of justice, and

Dworkin's equality of resources scheme, are attempts to develop an attractive and persuasive spelling-out of the requirements of this notion of moral equality. And notwithstanding the differences between their theories, we can identify some important features they both take to be basic to a liberal conception of equality. For both, the interests of each citizen are given equal consideration in two social institutions or procedures: an economic market and a political process of majority government. Of course, neither of these institutions is perfect, and both can produce unjust results. But if they operate in a society with equal opportunity and equal political power, and if they are constrained by principles of justice, then they respect equality. And they do so because, in general, they make social outcomes the result of decision procedures in which each person's choices are given equal weight. Subject to various constraints about respecting individual rights and eliminating the corrupting effects of political inequality and social prejudice, these institutions fairly translate people's choices into social outcomes (see e.g. Dworkin 1978 pp. 128–36).

But remember the consequences of these institutions for the aboriginal population of northern Canada, discussed in Chapter 7; the effect of market and political decisions made by the majority may well be that aboriginal groups are outbid or outvoted on matters crucial to their survival as a cultural community. They may be outbid for important resources (e.g. the land or means of production on which their community depends), or outvoted on crucial policy decisions (e.g. on what language will be used, or whether public works programmes will support or conflict with aboriginal work patterns). It was in light of these possible threats that aboriginal leaders advocated restrictions on the mobility, property, and voting rights of non-aboriginal people.

This raises the conflict at the heart of minority rights claims. The proposed measures would set some people at a disadvantage in the economic and political procedures used to translate choices into outcomes. Yet this seemed to be necessary, in the case of transient workers and aboriginal communities in the Canadian North, to respect people's cultural membership. Since cultural membership is a primary good, special rights are needed to treat aboriginal people with the respect they are owed as members of a cultural community. But the effect of these special rights is to compromise the fairness of political and economic decision procedures.

Now it might be thought that I've simply accepted a bad model of majoritarian decision-making, and that colour-blind liberal equality will suffice when we have a better model. Perhaps the problem for Canada's aboriginal peoples isn't particularly one of cultural membership, but rather the general problem facing all persistent political minorities—the problem of getting their fair share. Such minorities might be based on regional identification (e.g. desiring government investment in one area when the majority always votes for subsidies in another), or leisure identification (e.g. desiring operas when the majority always votes for swimming-pools), or cultural identification (e.g. aboriginal people desiring to learn and work in their own language when the majority wants English-speaking schools and leisure-resorts). If these minorities constitute 40 per cent of the population they should win 40 per cent of the time. It isn't fair that they lose every vote 60–40. But we can prevent this without relying on any idea of protecting cultural membership. We could give everyone 100 votes which they can exercise as they please. They could spend one on every issue (and probably waste it), or save them all up for the few issues that really matter to them. Thus the aboriginal people could save up all their votes to defeat the legislation which proposed construction of a Las Vegas-style resort, or which proposed to make English the language of public-school instruction. Of course, they'd lose a few other issues they have an interest in, but why shouldn't they? Why should their preferences count for more than those of non-aboriginal people even after such cyclical majorities are prevented?[1]

Let me instead turn the question around. Why is it important that individuals *not* be at a disadvantage in these procedures? Why do such procedures enforce equal concern and respect in the first place? The answer may seem obvious, but deserves a more detailed account. There is a powerful view of equality at work in liberal accounts of the integrity of these decision procedures—the view, already mentioned in Chapter 3, that we are responsible for our ends, and hence for adjusting our aims and ambitions in the light of the legitimate interests of others.

The costs to others of the resources we claim should 'figure in each person's sense of what is rightly his and in each person's judgement of what life he should lead, given that command of justice' (Dworkin 1981 p. 289). We are responsible for forming our plans, including our associations and attachments, and hence

We are free to make such decisions [about our attachments] with respect to the resources that are properly assigned to us in the first instance, though not, of course, to dispose in this way of resources that have been assigned, or rather are properly assignable, to others. Equality enters our plans by teaching us what is available to us, to deploy in accordance with our attachments and other concerns. (Dworkin 1983*a* p. 31)

This emphasis on the responsibility for our ends helps explain the injustice of the segregation of blacks in America. Whites may wish to exclude blacks from their community. But they cannot do so, even though it would promote their chosen life-styles. Their claims are not informed by the teachings of equality. I don't mean that the shared ends of the racists get *outweighed* by the rights of blacks. That falsely suggests that we have a moral conflict here, that the claims of the racists have some legitimate weight, to be balanced against the rights of others. This might be the picture on a welfarist theory of equality. But in an equality of resources scheme, the claims of racists have no moral weight, since they don't respect the just claims of others. As Rawls puts it, 'The priority of justice is accounted for, in part, by holding that interests requiring the violation of justice have no value' (Rawls 1971 p. 31).

This picture of the relationship between responsibility and equality is central to the resource-based, as opposed to the welfare-based, view of equality. It is a distinctively liberal view, and I think it is an attractive one, and should play a part in any comprehensive theory of equality. This helps explain the liberal attraction to the market.[2] Given certain background conditions, the market assesses the cost to others of my choices. Under these conditions, an efficient market distribution of resources will be a fair one (Dworkin 1981 p. 305). Liberals value the market (or something that replicates the results of the market), not because maximizing wealth or preferences is a good in itself, but because markets provide a way of measuring what is in fact equitable.

However, this emphasis on fairness in the forming and aggregating of people's choices is only half of the liberal story. It presupposes some further account of those things which are unchosen, which are a matter of people's circumstances, not their choices. The distinction between choices and circumstances is in fact absolutely central to the liberal project. Differences between people in terms of their resources may legitimately arise as a result of their *choices*; such variations legitimately reflect different tastes and preferences, different 'beliefs and attitudes that define what a successful life would be like' (Dworkin 1981 p. 303). Differences that are due to people's choices are their own responsibility (assuming they are freely chosen, with adequate information about the costs and consequences of those choices etc.).[3]

But differences which arise from people's circumstances—their social environment or natural endowments—are clearly not their own responsibility. No one chooses which class or race they are born into, or which natural talents they are born with, and no one deserves to be disadvantaged by these facts. They are, as Rawls famously put it, arbitrary from the moral point of view. No one chooses to be born into a disadvantaged social group, or with natural disabilities, and so no one should have to pay for the costs imposed by those disadvantageous circumstances. Hence liberals favour compensating people who suffer from disadvantages in social environment or natural endowment. (This defines one of the background conditions on the fair operation of the market: Rawls 1971 pp. 74–102; Dworkin 1981 part 2.)

So a liberal needs to know whether a request for special rights or resources is grounded in differential choices or unequal circumstances. Someone who cultivates a taste for expensive wine has no legitimate claim to special public subsidy, since she is responsible for the costs of her choice. Someone who needs expensive medicine due to a natural disability has a legitimate claim to special public subsidy, since she is not responsible for the costs of her disadvantageous circumstances.

Now, as we've seen, aboriginal rights entail special costs for other people, by restricting the rights and resources of non-aboriginal people. Where should we locate these rights claims on the choices–circumstances divide? If aboriginal rights were defended as promoting their chosen projects, then they would, on a liberal view, be an unfair use of political power to insulate aboriginal choices from market pressure. We can legitimately ask that aboriginal people form their plans of life with a view to the costs imposed on others, as measured by the market. Assume that aboriginal people have chosen an expensive life-style by, say, choosing a way of life that requires a large section of land, valued by many groups in society, to be set apart and left undeveloped, even though the benefits of this only accrue to themselves. In such a case, aboriginal people should have to outbid those who plan to use the land more efficiently. They should have to pool their resources, or their votes, to secure the land they desire, which will quite properly leave them with little remaining for the pursuit of other preferences (e.g. with few dollars or votes left to express their preference for swimming-pools over operas). If the land aboriginal people wish to be left undeveloped is valuable to others, then their desire is costly to others, and it is only fair that they pay for this costly desire in a diminished ability to pursue other desires that have costs for society. The existence of special political rights would mean that they don't have to pay for the costs of their desires, or base their decision of what life they should lead on considerations of its cost to others.

However, we can defend aboriginal rights as a response, not to shared choices, but to unequal circumstances. Unlike the dominant French or English cultures, the very existence of aboriginal cultural communities is vulnerable to the decisions of the non-aboriginal majority around them. They could be outbid or outvoted on resources crucial to the survival of their communities, a possibility that members of the majority cultures simply do not face. As a result, they have to spend their resources on securing the cultural membership which makes sense of their lives, something which non-aboriginal people get for free. And this is true regardless of the costs of the particular choices aboriginal or non-aboriginal individuals make.

Let us look more closely at how this inequality arises, using Dworkin's equality of resources scheme (a similar result could be shown to hold for Rawls's difference principle). In Dworkin's scheme, we are to imagine that a vessel has shipwrecked on a deserted island, and the available social resources are to be auctioned amongst the passengers, who presumably are of the same culture. Each person begins with an equal amount of money (Dworkin imagines giving everyone 100 clam shells). The final prices of the goods will reflect the cost to others of the choices that individuals have made about how to lead their lives. And no one will prefer the bundle of resources held by any other person over their own, since each person had an equal ability to bid for the various resources (the 'envy test').

Contrast that with a case that is at once more fanciful and more realistic. Two ships, one very large and one quite small, shipwreck on the island, and to ensure a smooth auction, they proceed by entering bids into the ships' computers without ever leaving the ship (information about the nature of the resources was perhaps readily available in publications, or was gathered by a scouting party from one ship and communicated via the computer). The auction proceeds and it turns out that the passengers of the two ships are very similar in the distribution of different ways of life chosen—e.g. roughly 10 per cent from each ship bid for those resources that suit a contemplative life-style, 20 per cent bid for resources that suit an entrepreneurial life-style, and so on. Finally the resources are all bid for, but when they disembark from the ship they discover for the first time, what had been obscured by the use of a common computer language, that the two ships are of different nationalities. The members of the minority culture are now in a very undesirable position. Assuming, as is reasonable, that their resources are distributed evenly across the island, they will now be forced to try to execute their chosen life-styles in an alien culture—e.g. in their work, and, when the state superstructure is built, in the courts, schools, legislatures, etc.

Perhaps they would be allowed to demand a rerun of the auction, so as to revise their bids. But notice that the problem is not that minority members envy the bundle of social resources possessed by the majority members *qua* bundle of social resources. On the contrary, the bundle of resources they currently possess, *qua* resources, are the ones best suited to fulfilling their chosen life-style. What they envy is the fact that the majority members possess and utilize their resources within a certain context, i.e. within their own cultural community. In order to ensure that they can also live and work in their own culture, the minority members may decide, prior to the rerun of the auction, to buy resources in one area of the island, which would involve outbidding the present majority owners for resources which *qua* resources are less useful to their chosen way of life. They must incur this additional cost in order to secure the existence of their cultural community. This is a cost which the members of the majority culture do not incur, but which in no way reflects different choices about the good life (or about the importance of cultural membership within it).

In other words, rather than subsidizing or privileging their choices, the special measures demanded by aboriginal people serve to correct an advantage that non-aboriginal people have before anyone makes their choices. For the whites who wish to bid for resources in Northern Canada, the security of *their* cultural community is not in question. They are bidding solely on the basis of what is useful in pursuing the goals that they have chosen to pursue, secure in the knowledge that their context of choice is protected. For aboriginal people, on the other hand, it is necessary to outbid non-aboriginal people just to ensure that their cultural structure survives, leaving them few resources to pursue the particular goals they've chosen from within that structure.

This is an inequality that has nothing to do with the choices of aboriginal people. A two-year-old Inuit girl who has no projects faces this inequality. Without special political protection, like the restrictions on the rights of transient workers, by the time she is eighteen the existence of the cultural community in which she grew up is likely to be undermined by the decisions of people outside the community. That is true no matter what projects she decides to pursue. Conversely, an English-Canadian boy will not face that problem, no matter what choices he makes. The rectification of this inequality is the basis for a liberal defence of aboriginal rights, and of minority rights in general.

The argument here is the opposite of one of the non-liberal arguments for aboriginal rights that I mentioned at the end of Chapter 7. The point isn't that aboriginal people care more for their cultural community than others. We all care about the fate of our cultural community. French-Canadians have always been extremely sensitive to anything which threatens their existence as a distinct community, and many English-Canadians were paranoid that the bilingualism policy introduced by Trudeau would submerge their culture beneath that of French Canada. Aboriginal fears about the fate of their cultural structure, however, are not paranoia—there are real threats. The English and French in Canada rarely have to worry about the fate of their cultural structure. They get for free what aboriginal people have to pay for: secure cultural membership. This is an important inequality, and if it is ignored, it becomes an important injustice. Special political rights, however, can correct this inequality by ensuring that aboriginal communities are as secure as non-aboriginal ones. People should have to pay for their choices, but special political rights are needed to remove inequalities in the context of choice which arise before people even make their choices.

Contemporary theories of liberal equality seek, in Dworkin's terms, to be 'endowment-insensitive' and 'ambition-sensitive'; that is, they seek to ensure that no one is penalized or disadvantaged by their natural or social endowment, but allow that people's fates vary with their choices about how to lead their lives (Dworkin 1981 p. 311). But if that is the goal, then it must be recognized that the members of minority cultures can face inequalities which are the product of their circumstances or endowment, not their choices or ambitions.[4] And since this inequality would remain even if individual members of aboriginal communities no longer suffered from any deprivation of material resources, temporary affirmative action programmes are not sufficient to ensure genuine equality. Collective rights may be needed.

Hence minority rights can form an important part of a recognizably liberal theory of equality. If so, the section of the Canadian constitution guaranteeing aboriginal rights (Section 35) need not be viewed as conflicting with the Section 15.1 guarantee of equal protection of the law. The different sections can be seen as stemming from the same theory of equality. The relationship between Section 15.1 and Section 35 can be seen as analogous to the relationship between 15.1 and 15.2, which provides for affirmative action to promote the position of disadvantaged groups. Just as the provision for affirmative action can be seen as spelling out the basic right to equality guaranteed in 15.1, given the special circumstances of those disadvantaged groups (Tarnopolsky p. 259), so the guarantee of aboriginal rights can be seen as spelling out what it means to treat aboriginal people as equals, given their special circumstances. The requirement to compensate for unequal circumstances, through affirmative action and minority rights, is not in conflict with the demand that everyone have equal protection of the law. Rather, it helps instruct judges how to interpret that fundamental requirement.

Some commentators insist that minority rights claims cannot be reconciled with Section 15. Supreme Court Justices are said to face an 'impossible task', a 'philosophical contradiction', in reconciling the collective rights of French-Canadians and aboriginal peoples with the individual rights of Canadians under a 'single principle of equality' (Morton p. 81; cf. Knopff 1982 pp. 35–6; Penton; Weinfield p. 70). Indeed, minority rights are said to be a disguise for 'the traditional inegalitarian claim to rule on behalf of a particular way of life' (Knopff 1982 p. 29; cf. Knopff 1979 pp. 72–6). Minority rights are aspects of a pre-liberal politics in which 'the health of the soul' is a public concern, and government actively promotes some choices about the good life (Morton pp. 80–1). But this *need* not be so, and these various commentators do not explain why minority rights must be a tool for promoting particular choices, rather than a response to unequal circumstances.

In fact, most of the examples which Knopff and Morton cite are responses to circumstances, not to choices. Knopff does not show why French-Canadian concern for language rights 'prescribes the kind of life [people] must lead within that language' (Knopff 1979 p. 75). And Morton does not show why aboriginal concern over the control of group membership is based on a preference for 'a distinctive "way of life" ' (Morton p. 81). As I mentioned in Chapter 7, and as Morton seems to concede, aboriginal claims in this area are designed to avoid the danger of overpopulation on scarce reservation land (Morton p. 76). The minority rights for French-Canadians or aboriginal peoples which they discuss are not designed to favour one set of choices about the good life over another. They do not favour traditional practices over non-traditional life-styles, or religious over non-religious life-styles. They do not impose a particular conception of 'the health of the soul' on the members of minority cultures, or penalize dissenting conceptions. The inevitable conflict which Morton and Knopff find between liberal equality and pre-liberal minority rights is neither theoretically established nor exhibited in their examples. On the contrary, these minority rights help ensure that the members of minority cultures have access to a secure cultural structure from which to make such choices for themselves, and thereby promote liberal equality.

All this assumes that the appropriate response to the inequality in cultural membership is to try to prevent that inequality from arising. But this is not always the way we deal with inequalities in circumstance which corrupt the market. For example, physical and mental handicaps have to be fairly dealt with before the market operates equitably. It's unfair if people lose market power just because they are born with handicaps. The solution in this case is not to prevent the inequality from arising, but to compensate handicapped individuals according to some insurance scheme (one such scheme is described in Dworkin 1981 pp. 297–9). Likewise, we pay out insurance to the victims of natural disasters, to cover their unchosen displacement costs. We respond to unequal circumstances, not by preventing their occurrence, but by establishing some sort of insurance arrangement. Why not insure people against the costs of having to undergo cultural assimilation? We could employ a variant of the hypothetical insurance market envisaged by Dworkin, in which people, who do not yet know what cultural position they hold, decide how much insurance they would take out against the possibility that the operation of the political and economic processes of society will undermine their cultural community. We could then compensate those born into endangered minority cultures according to that insurance scheme.

But as I argued in Chapter 7, this compensation suggestion misunderstands the particular nature of the good of cultural membership. Monetary benefits are fair compensation for disadvantages due to natural handicap or natural disaster, since they compensate for undeserved limitations of the capacity to achieve one's ends through one set of means by extending one's capacity through another set of means. But cultural membership is not a means used in the pursuit of one's ends. It is rather the context within which we choose our ends, and come to see their value, and this is a precondition of self-respect, of the sense that one's ends are worth pursuing. And it affects our very sense of personal identity and capacity. When we take cultural identity seriously, we'll understand that asking someone to trade off her cultural identity for some amount of money is like expecting someone to trade off her self-respect for some amount of money. Having money for the pursuit of one's ends is of little help if the price involves giving up the context within which those ends are worth pursuing. It is irrational to expect people to accept that trade-off, and it is unjust to demand that people accept it. (It is worth noting that Indians in Canada have continually rejected offers to relinquish their land claims in return for large cash sums, offers which would be similar to the paying-out of such an insurance policy.)

So merely providing compensation for the loss of culture doesn't do justice to the importance of our membership in a particular cultural community. That doesn't mean that minority rights can't be viewed as a form of insurance. Insurance coverage can be aimed at preventing, as well as compensating for, hardship. In the case of natural handicaps, we get insurance to cover preventive measures, as well as compensation. We might similarly envisage an insurance scheme that enables aboriginal communities to outbid and thereby prevent community-undermining pro-posals for the use of their lands. But notice that it would have to be some form of collective insurance, since the insurance payments are useless to individuals by themselves. What matters is that the members of aboriginal communities as a group should have sufficient resources to outbid proposals that affect them as a community; that is what the insurance would be designed for. So any adequate insurance plan would presuppose a certain collective organization. Aboriginal people would need to receive and employ the insurance benefits collectively.

The gap between this collective insurance idea and the collective political rights currently existing in Canada is not large. Both forms of cultural protection share the same central feature: while the individual members of aboriginal communities do not have more resources at their disposal than other Canadians to pursue their individual life-plans, the community has the collective capacity to pre-empt majority decisions which un-dermine the community's existence.

Theoretically, one could implement some aspects of the collective insurance scheme without using collective *political* rights. Some of the insurance could be purely monetary, provided to a non-governmental aboriginal body, enabling aboriginal people to ensure that they are not outbid on important resources, without establishing any political constraints on the market. But there would still be a need for collective rights against being outvoted on important policy issues. And even in the case of market protection, the argument for political measures is very strong. Attempts to organize a community non-politically are impractical and inefficient, and run into collective action problems, especially where the population is widely dispersed. Moreover, special political status means that aboriginal land is protected from some of the non-market vulnerabilities that attach to privately held land (e.g. expropriation). Indeed, one of the main objections to the Canadian government's proposal to make Indian land alienable was not that individual Indians would sell the land to non-Indians, but rather that the land would now be subject to expropriation by provincial governments in a way that would destroy the community. The government would have to compensate for any expropriation, but the normal kind of compensation to individual title-holders would not ensure that the community could be relocated or re-established (Cardinal 1977 pp. 91–2, 127). To ensure that they could re-establish the community, aboriginal people would need a legal status different from that envisaged in any non-political insurance model.

So I believe that certain collective rights can be defended as appropriate measures for the rectification of an inequality in circumstances which affects aboriginal people collectively.[5] This defence has not, however, covered all of the measures discussed in Chapter 7. In particular, the denial of putative language rights is left undefended. In a society where the members of minority cultures (e.g. Indians, francophones) could get their fair share of resources within their own cultural community, it's not clear what would justify denying people access to publicly funded education in English. If some of the members of a minority culture choose to learn in that language, the notion of protecting the cultural context provides no grounds for denying them that opportunity. On the other hand it's not clear why there should be rights to publicly funded education in any given language other than that of the community. Why should the members of minority cultures have a right to a public education in English, but not, say, in Greek? They should of course be free to run a school system in whatever language they choose at their own expense, but why a right to it at public expense? There are good reasons of policy for having the teaching of English available, but that's a different matter, and anyway would only warrant teaching *of* English, not *in* English. People should have, as part of the respect owed them as members of a cultural community, the opportunity to have a public education in the language of their community; but whether they have the opportunity to have a publicly funded education in another language is perhaps a matter of policy (just as subsidizing cultural exchanges is), with people neither having a right to it nor a right to prevent it.[6]

The most troublesome aspect of the old Indian Act in Canada was the penalization of certain marriage choices, and the discriminatory way this was applied. But these problems arise unnecessarily, for they result from the fact that reservation lands are not just non-alienable, but non-expandable. An expanding population may need to occupy expanding territory, but Indians don't usually try to establish communities outside their present reserved lands, partly because they lack the resources to do so (since they lack their fair share), but also, and perhaps more importantly, because they'd have no way of protecting the new communities from plans to develop that and nearby land in such a way as would lead to unwanted assimilation. However, I see no reason why the government shouldn't, when overpopulation threatens existing reservations, aid in the establishing and protecting of new communities (Robinson and Quinney p. 147; M. Dunn).

One aspect of Indian policy in the United States (not present in Canada) which I haven't discussed is the denial of religious liberty on certain reservations. Some of the American Indian bands are essentially theocracies, with an official religion. Members of other religious denominations are limited in their freedom to worship, and are sometimes subject to discrimination in housing benefits etc. (Van Dyke 1985 pp. 72–4; Weston; Svennson pp. 431–3). Now this is usually defended in terms of the special semi-sovereign status of Indian nations in the United States—that is, whether or not the restriction on religious liberty is just, we have no right to interfere. It is a sovereign act of a quasi-independent nation. Indian bands have the right to reject certain constitutional rights if they feel justified in doing so. It might violate the right to equal treatment guaranteed by the American Constitution, but Indian members can't appeal to that right, since the actions of sovereign Indian bands are not fully subject to that guarantee (*Elk* v. *Wilkins* [1884] 112 US 94).[7]

This situation is, therefore, fundamentally different from the one I have been considering, in which special measures of cultural protection are defended as part of the best interpretation of political equality. Theocracies on American reserves are often defended as exemptions from, not interpretations of, the guarantee of equality. Still, it is worth examining why the restriction on religious liberty *couldn't* be defended by my account of minority rights. Quite simply, there is no inequality in cultural membership to which it could be viewed as a response. The ability of each member of the Pueblo reservation, for example, to live in that community is not threatened by allowing Protestant members to express their religious beliefs. Allowing religious freedom wouldn't make the Pueblo vulnerable to being outbid or outvoted on crucial issues by the non-Pueblo population (unlike allowing full voting rights for non-Inuit in the North); nor would it create internal disintegration (unlike the exposure of the Indonesian tribe to certain kinds of television).

It is true that, in the eyes of many of the Pueblo, 'violation of religious norms is viewed as literally threatening the survival of the entire community' (Svensson p. 434). But in fact the Pueblo 'would continue to exist with an organized Protestant minority as it now exists without one' (Weston p. 249). As with Devlin's claim that the acceptance of homosexuality would literally undermine the English community, the only evidence offered is the dislike the majority feels for the dissident practice. If the goal is to ensure that each person is equally able to lead their chosen life within their own cultural community, then restricting religion in no way promotes that. Were the theocracy ended, each majority member of the Pueblo would have as much ability to use and interpret their own cultural experiences as the dissident minority, or, indeed, as members of the non-Indian community. No one would be less able to lead their own lives in their own community than anyone else, and hence no one has grounds for saying that they are being treated as less than an equal with regard to cultural membership. On the contrary, as I argued in Chapter 8, supporting the intolerant character of a cultural community undermines the very reason we had to support cultural membership—that it allows for meaningful individual choice. To support the majority in an Indian reservation when it denies religious freedom to the minority is to support the imposition of gratuitous and unjust harm on others.

So nothing in my account of minority rights justifies the claim that a dominant group within a cultural minority has the right to decide how the rest of the community will use or interpret the community's culture. My theory supports, rather than compromises, the rights of individuals within the minority culture. This is not, of course, to say that the American Supreme Court should have the power to determine or enforce the religious rights of the Pueblo. Given the absolutely appalling record of the Supreme Court in respecting either the individual or collective rights of American Indians, the Pueblo might well wish to put their trust in tribal courts. If that is the consensus amongst the Pueblo, then surely it should be respected. (This was the position recently taken by the American Supreme Court in deciding that individual Indians must appeal to tribal courts for the interpretation and enforcement of the Indian Civil Rights Act (*Santa Clara Pueblo* v. *Martinez* [1978] 436 US 49).) If, on the other hand, those Pueblo most in need of court protection wish to have some form of external review, then the issue gets much cloudier. This seems to be the situation in Canada. Many of the aboriginal groups have argued against external review of aboriginal self-government. But some of the aboriginal women's groups have sought external review. It would be wrong to override a consensus on how best to entrench aboriginal rights, but there isn't a consensus, and so any solution will conflict with some aboriginal wishes. I don't see any obvious formula for dealing with this, except to encourage the development of a consensus. In any event, my concern is with what the principles being enforced ought to be—not with who ought to have the power to determine, interpret, and enforce those principles. And on a liberal theory of equality, the very reason to respect a principle affirming the importance of cultural membership to minority groups is also a reason to respect a principle affirming the rights of individual members of those groups.

So any liberal argument for the legitimacy of measures for the protection of minority cultures has built-in limits. Each person should be able to use and interpret her cultural experiences in her own chosen way. That ability requires that the cultural structure be secured from the disintegrating effects of the choices of people outside the culture, but also requires that each person within the community be free to choose what they see to be most valuable from the options provided (unless temporary restrictions are needed in exceptional circumstances of cultural vulnerability).

But what if the Pueblo community really would disintegrate without restricting religious liberty? Would that justify restricting religious liberty? If so, are there any limits on what can be done in the name of protecting cultural membership? These are difficult questions, although, as I argued in Chapter 8, they do not arise nearly as often as liberal critics of minority rights claim, nor are they unique to situations of minority cultures. There are a number of possible principles to apply in non-ideal, or 'partial compliance', situations, each of which is consistent with the argument given so far. The principle behind partial compliance measures can be to minimize violations of legitimate claims (what Nozick calls a 'utilitarianism of rights'), or to respect certain legitimate claims as inviolable even if the result is that overall claim-violations are increased (what Nozick calls 'side-constraints'). In between these, we might say that even if no individual claim is inviolable, one type of claim has absolute priority over other types: we might say that cultural membership has priority over the rights of individual members, since cultural membership provides the context of individual choice; or conversely that individual rights always have priority over cultural membership, since the value of cultural membership is in enabling individual choice. Or we could say that cultural membership sometimes takes priority over individual rights and sometimes not—depending not only on what would minimize claim-violations overall, but also on how severe, long-lasting, and equitably distributed the rights-violations would be, and what avenues exist for individual members to choose to assimilate to another culture.[8] People who agree on ideal theory can disagree on which partial compliance principle to use, and people who disagree on ideal theory can share the same partial compliance theory.

Settling these issues would require an investigation of difficult questions both about the particular sorts of sacrifices being asked and about the general question of the relationship between ideal theory and partial compliance theory. It seems unlikely in this case that any claim or set of claims has absolute priority over others, since the conflicting values really are interdependent. Assuming that there can be some legitimate restrictions on the internal activities of minority members, where those activities would literally threaten the existence of the community, to find the precise limits would be enormously difficult, and I doubt anything useful could be achieved without reasonably detailed knowledge of particular instances. These are complex issues in which our intuitions are pulled in different directions, and I don't see how any simple formula could cover all the relevant cases.

But while the view of minority rights I am advancing leaves this question open, that should not be taken as a reason to reject cultural membership as a liberal value. On the contrary, these questions would not pose such a conflict for liberals if cultural membership were not a primary value; for there would then be nothing of moral value to oppose the legitimate demands for individual rights. But there is a real problem here, and we need a theory which recognizes the genuine conflicts. Any theory which denies that there is a conflict has missed something of great importance.

In any event, it seems that some measures of cultural protection are justified, even if their precise application is subject to variation and their outermost boundaries are undefined. Once we recognize cultural membership as an important primary good which underlies our choices, then special political rights and status for minority cultures may be required. In a homogeneous society, this context of choice, being a kind of public good, is equally available to all (at least in a just and well-ordered society without large disparities in education etc.). Recognizing cultural membership as a primary good wouldn't change the conclusions Rawls or Dworkin reach concerning equality of resources in such societies. But it does make a difference in culturally plural societies. In such societies we must view the protection of that context of choice as a distinct source of political rights (or economic insurance). That is not to say that every culturally plural society will in fact need such rights; rather, vulnerability of the context of choice will always be a ground to which minorities can appeal in claiming rights. Whether their claim succeeds depends on many factors—e.g. whether the alleged inequality actually exists, and whether the putative rights actually serve to correct the inequality (see Chapter 13 below for a claim which doesn't succeed on either count). As Sigler notes, developing a theory of minority rights is not likely to demand radical changes in practice; it will simply affirm the already existing practice of many culturally plural countries, practice which has arisen in the absence of theory (Sigler p. 196).

This would require a modification in Dworkin's political morality, but he should not wish to resist the change. As I mentioned in Chapter 8, Dworkin emphasizes the importance of cultural structure, claiming that 'we have some duty, out of simple justice, to leave that [cultural] structure at least as rich as we found it' (Dworkin 1985 p. 233). If so, then surely it is important to protect minority cultural structures from dis-integration. And since the vulnerability of minority cultures is a matter of circumstances, not choice, Dworkin's own theory of equality requires that minority members shouldn't bear the costs of that protection. The system of aboriginal rights in Canada can be seen as an attempt to distribute fairly the costs that arise from our recognition of the value of cultural membership.[9]

Notes

1. The problem of permanent political minorities is often invoked as a reason for recognizing minority rights and consociational incorporation (e.g. Boulle; Sigler; McRae 1975; Lijphart; Van Dyke 1985). This raises important points about possible conflict between the democratic principle of political equality and the democratic procedure of majority rule. We have to think more imaginatively, in culturally plural countries, about forms of political representation; uncritical adoption of the Westminster or the American model of democratic rule could be inappropriate. But any sophisticated democratic theory recognizes the danger of permanent minorities. What consociationalists haven't adequately

defended, in their discussions of minority rights, is the view that minorities should have *special claims*, as opposed to special institutional protections for their usual claims.

2. This is not, of course, the only reason why liberals are attracted to the market. Also, and not unrelatedly, the market allows people to adjust their holdings so as to best fit their aims and ambitions (see the discussion of what Dworkin calls the 'principle of abstraction', and its relation to ideals of fairness, in Dworkin 1987). Both of these functions of the market could be replicated by state-run, non-market mechanisms, more or less efficiently. But a third reason for liberal support of the market is precisely that it serves as a block against such centralization of state power.

3. The claim that people are responsible for their choices has to be qualified. It is only plausible to assign beliefs and attitudes about the good life to the person, rather than to her circumstances, if she has the good fortune to have received a sufficiently broad education to be able to conceive the various options open to her, and moreover to live in a society which allows competing conceptions of the good life, and free debate amongst proponents of them. As Taylor says, the freedom 'by which men are capable of conceiving alternatives and arriving at a definition of what they really want, as well as discerning what commands their adherence or their allegiance . . . is unavailable to one whose sympathies and horizons are so narrow that he can conceive only one way of life' (C. Taylor 1985 p. 204). Therefore the claim that such beliefs and attitudes can be assigned to the person must be understood as part of ideal theory—as what we could hold people responsible for in an ideally just liberal society—and I follow that usage.

All sorts of interesting questions arise at the non-ideal level which I've left unaddressed. For example, in an ideally just liberal society, people who wanted to work in uneconomic coal mines would seem to have an expensive taste, no different from someone's desire to play tennis all day, and if either asked for the rest of society to subsidize them, to pay the costs of their choices, then we might legitimately decline to do so. But under existing conditions, we might believe that British coal-miners (including those just now leaving school in order to take up a mining job, who can't claim, unlike the older miners, that they didn't know it was a costly choice when they decided) lacked full and equal access to the sorts of education and careers that would involve fewer demands on the public purse. Someone could easily argue analogously for subsidization of the inefficient hunting and trapping occupations of the traditional Indian and Inuit economies in Canada.

These are interesting and important questions in partial-compliance theories of justice. However, like Rawls and Dworkin, I believe that these problems are best solved once we have a clear idea of what the ideal theory will look like.

4. Since the inequalities faced by members of minority cultures are unchosen, cultural membership clearly meets the criteria Rawls uses for selecting the viewpoints relevant to assessing social justice:

> The primary subject of justice . . . is the basic structure of society. The reason for this is that its effects are so profound and pervasive, and present from birth. This structure favours some starting places over others in the division of the benefits of social cooperation. It is these inequalities which the two principles are to regulate. Once these principles are satisfied, other inequalities are allowed to arise from men's voluntary actions in accordance with the principle of free association . . . the relevant representative men [for judging the social system], therefore, are the representative citizen and those who stand for the various levels of well-being. Since I assume that in general other positions are entered into voluntarily, we need not consider the point of view of men in these positions in judging the basic structure. (Rawls 1971 p. 96)

Rawls uses citizenship and socio-economic status as the positions from which he assesses the justice of the basic structure because these are *unchosen* positions. Other positions are not considered because they are voluntarily entered into. The relevant points of view represent the sites of unchosen inequalities, especially those that are 'profound and pervasive and present from birth', since these are the ones that require compensation or removal. But if this choices–circumstances distinction is the motivation for Rawls's choice of relevant points of view, then clearly he should have included cultural membership as one of the positions used in assessing justice, at least in culturally plural countries.

5. There are various ways of rectifying this inequality without legally granting 'permanent political rights to a special class of citizens' (Asch p. 76). The government could, for example, simply pass a law prohibiting a specific economic or political development whenever it endangers aboriginal cultural patterns. This would be the equivalent of an endangered species act. The problem is that aboriginal culture is evolving, as a result of the members' choices. So what endangers it changes over time, and to entrench a particular pattern of land use, for example, would prevent aboriginal peoples from adapting to new circumstances, from having a living culture. (It might also prevent them from voluntarily extinguishing

their culture and assimilating, which they should be able to do, if they so wish.) The result of such entrenchment in the case of the Salish Indians was that the special measures designed to protect traditional fishing practices 'isolated and fetishized only one element among many . . . as central to the task of guaranteeing cultural continuity'. The danger of this method is that it could 'hypostatize history and replace a living culture with a fossilized one' (Anderson p. 139). It could repeat 'The blatant paternalism of the U.S. Bureau of Indian Affairs, the Brazilian Indian Protection Service, and other similar agencies [which] made them functionally analogous to animal protection societies' (van den Berghe 1981a p. 343). Avoiding this danger would require adjusting the legislative measures so as to match the rights of minority cultures.

Somewhat differently, one can avoid naming a special class of citizens by 'indirect consociationalism'—i.e. redrawing the boundaries of political units, and redistributing powers between levels of government, so as to ensure that a minority culture controls a political unit which has sufficient powers to protect the community (Asch p. 79; van den Berghe 1981a p. 348). In federal regimes, giving rights to a provincial government which predominantly governs members of a minority culture can then be a way of ensuring minority protection (e.g. Berger 1981 p. 259). But as with the first solution, external circumstances and internal development might necessitate revising the boundaries and powers of regional units, in the light of the rights of minority cultures.

Both of these are possible ways of legally implementing minority rights. As Asch and Dacks say, 'What is important is not the details of particular models, but rather the logic which underlies all of them' (Asch and Dacks p. 51). Van den Berghe thinks that the indirect consociational solution, even if it is designed or revised for the explicit reason of protecting minority cultures, involves a 'fundamentally different' logic, since there is no legal recognition of minority groups (van den Berghe 1981a p. 348). It is one thing to define the powers and boundaries of a regional government so as to ensure the protection of a minority culture (indirect consociationalism), but quite another for the law to cite the existence of that minority as the reason for those arrangements (minority rights). But this is very peculiar. The 'fundamentally different logic' is not the distinction between intended and merely foreseen consequences, since he admits that in both cases the arrangements are designed in the light of the claims of minority cultures. Nor are there any differences in the powers being exercised by the regional government. The difference is simply whether the justification for the arrangements is made legally explicit or not, and it is difficult to see what moral or political significance attaches to that difference.

6. See the articles by Hanen, Braybrooke, and Davis in French 1979, all of which express scepticism about the sort of language 'rights' which would override legislation like Quebec's Bill 101 (the bill which ended publicly funded English education in Quebec for all but the children of English-Canadians).

7. American Indians are now partially covered by guarantees of equal protection in virtue of the 1968 Indian Civil Rights Act. There is a considerable amount of hypocrisy in the alleged federal government respect for Indian 'sovereignty'. The American state intervenes all the time in the affairs of the Indians. While 'sovereign', the Indian nations are also 'dependent' (*Cherokee Nation* v. *Georgia* [1831] 30 US 1). The American state appeals to the former status whenever it wishes to avoid responsibility for Indian affairs, and to the latter status whenever it wishes to control the Indian population. For a comprehensive review of the inconsistent and often unprincipled assertion and exercise of federal 'plenary power' over Indians, see Kronowitz *et al.* pp. 522–56 (federal encroachment on sovereignty), 561–83 (state encroachment).

8. Svensson ties the legitimacy of internal discrimination (as claimed in the Pueblo case) to the availability of exit for individuals. Individuals who are discriminated against in the name of cultural membership can, in the last resort, merge with the broader society to preserve their rights, whereas a community which is prevented from discriminating has nowhere to go to preserve cultural membership. Hence of these two possible injustices 'the former appears to be more acceptable than the latter, since it preserves the maximum openness of opportunity to members of both dominant and dependent communities. It also preserves at least some aspects of the equality formulation which underlies classical democratic theory' (Svensson p. 437). But I don't think the possibility of exit justifies any form of discrimination which might be needed to protect cultural membership. Surely justifiability also depends on other factors, such as the length, severity, and distribution of the burdens created by the discrimination.

9. My argument for minority rights has formal, as well as substantive, parallels to Dworkin's general framework for rights claims. Dworkin maintains that rights claims only make sense against a background framework of equality. For example, democratic decision-making and economic markets are background procedures

which are intended to model a conception of equality. Rights enter in when these background procedures fail, in various ways, to live up to that conception of equality. This is just the sort of argument I am giving. I have tried to show that liberal-democratic background procedures are intended to ensure an endowment-insensitive and ambition-sensitive distribution, but sometimes fail to deal fairly with the unequal circumstances of minority cultures. Collective rights can serve to correct that failing. So it is not that there is a collective right to cultural membership, the denial of which creates an inequality. Rather, members of cultural minorities may face an inequality, the rectification of which may require collective rights.

10

Minority Rights and the Liberal Tradition

THE claim that rights for minority cultures can be justified on liberal principles is likely to be met with scepticism by many critics and defenders of liberalism. For it is often said, by critics of liberalism, that what defines liberalism is its disregard for the context of choice, for the way that choices are situated in cultural communities. As Weaver says of the liberal response to Canada's Indian policy 'Because liberalism disregards the social *system* as the basis of society, the liberal concept of individual choice is frequently a fallacy. It fails to detect that choices are possible only under certain conditions' (Weaver 1981 p. 55). And as we've seen, Taylor thinks that liberal atomism implies that individuals are not in need of any cultural context in order to make sense of their options or exercise their capacity for choice (C. Taylor 1985 p. 197).

Indeed, advocates of liberalism seem to play down the importance of membership in a cultural community as a context of choice. Thus Rawls says that in a just society our self-respect is secured by our recognition as equal citizens, not, apparently, by membership in a cultural community (Rawls 1971 pp. 544–5). Porter says that 'the saliency of ethnic differences is a retreat from the liberal notions of the unity of mankind' (Porter p. 303). The 'egalitarianism' he sees underlying liberalism requires treating individuals as equal citizens, without regard to race or ethnicity. Speaking, *inter alia*, about Inuit claims for collective rights, he says that minority rights are not only 'regrettable', but 'regressive' (Porter p. 298).

So both critics and defenders of liberalism seem to say that the individualism and egalitarianism underlying liberalism require ignoring people's relationship to their cultural community. While Ponting and Gibbins criticize liberalism for being 'married' to the view that individuals ought to be incorporated into the state independently of cultural membership (Ponting and Gibbins 1980 p. 330), Schwartz considers it a virtue of liberalism that it refuses to see individuals as situated in any way in historical communities (Schwartz ch. 1).

In the face of this evidence, it would seem that an endorsement of minority rights must involve a rejection of liberal values, rather than an improved spelling-out of them. But it is important to note that all of these advocates and critics are post-war writers. If we look at the writings of earlier liberals, especially Mill, Green, Hobhouse, and Dewey, a different picture emerges. They emphasized the importance of cultural membership for individual autonomy, and so had a different view about the salience of cultural membership. For example, Dewey stressed the importance of belonging to 'communities', which involve not only the interactions and interdependencies of civil society, but a consciousness of commonality. This commonality is based on cultural membership, and so requires that the young 'be brought up within the traditions, outlook and interests which characterize a community' (Dewey pp. 153–4). Green says that an important part of the unity necessary to a good society derives 'from a common dwelling-place with its associations, from common memories, traditions and customs, and from the common ways of feeling and thinking which a common language and still more a common literature embodies' (T. H. Green pp. 130–1). Likewise Hobhouse praised those 'higher communities' which have 'a common sentiment and a common interest' (Hobhouse 1966 p. 41), best exemplified by 'the sentiment of nationality' which is

a composite effect of language, tradition, religion, and manners which makes certain people feel themselves at one with each other and apart from the rest of the world. Pride and self-respect are closely bound up with it, and to destroy a nationality is in a degree to wound the pride and lower the manhood of those who adhere to it. (Hobhouse 1928 p. 146)

Mill emphasized the importance of 'the feeling of nationality', a feeling which is generated by many causes, of which 'the strongest of all is identity of political antecedents: the possession of a national history, and consequent community of recollections;

collective pride and humiliation, pleasure and regret, connected with the same incidents in the past' (Mill 1972 p. 360). For these writers, human freedom was tied to the existence, and consciousness, of a common cultural membership.

Gerald Gaus believes that this emphasis on commonality of culture endangers their liberal project. He argues that the reconciliation of individuality and sociability was an important theme for these writers: in their works, liberalism was 'transformed from a doctrine of competitive individualism to a co-operative pursuit of individuality' (Gaus p. 270). But he thinks that this desired reconciliation is jeopardized by the concern these writers have with communal identification. The pursuit of individuality, he argues, is compatible with the social unity which arises from 'interlocking differences' (i.e. where each person developing her own individuality makes a unique contribution, especially through her vocation, which others can enjoy and benefit from), but is incompatible with the unity which arises from community built on commonality and similarity. The 'dynamics' of community and individuality are 'ultimately opposed' because the former 'draws its strength from commonality whereas individuality . . . is premised on diversity' (Gaus pp. 108–9).

But there needn't be any conflict here, for the *kind* of commonality involved—i.e. commonality of language and history, shared membership in a cultural community—doesn't constrain individuality. On the contrary, membership in a cultural structure is what enables individual freedom, what enables meaningful choices about how to lead one's life. Indeed, Hobhouse said that 'true freedom' was possible only in such 'higher communities' (Hobhouse 1966 p. 35), and Dewey said that 'fraternity, liberty and equality' were 'hopeless abstractions' outside of such communities (Dewey p. 149). Likewise Mill saw no conflict between his belief that individuals should be not only free but encouraged to experiment with unfamiliar life-styles, and his belief that communities should be united by a feeling of nationality based on common sentiment. Mill was so concerned with the freedom of individuals to express their individuality in unusual and unexpected ways that Dewey thought Mill equated individuality with quirky eccentricity (Gaus p. 16); yet Mill also believed that such free individuality was 'next to impossible' in a country without commonality of language and heritage (Mill 1972 p. 361). For Mill, as for the others, commonality of cultural membership wasn't in conflict with individual freedom, but rather was its precondition.

Mill, Green, Hobhouse, and Dewey were concerned with community, but were not thereby communitarians, not-withstanding Gaus's misgivings. They were as much concerned with the value of individual liberty as anyone before or since. Yet they recognized the importance of our cultural membership to the proper functioning of a well-ordered and just society, and hence they had a different view of the legitimacy of special measures for cultural minorities. Hobhouse, for example, believed that 'the problem of dealing with the minority nation is the hardest that statesmen have to solve' (Hobhouse 1928 p. 146), partly because it often leads to the demand for independence. It needn't do so, for if 'the claims of the people are satisfied by cultural equality, the distinctive problems of nationality [i.e. independence] do not arise. . . By the refusal of equality, however [their claims] may be forced into the national arena' (Hobhouse 1966 p. 297 n.). In dealing with the minority's claim to equality,

The more liberal statesmanship of modern times has maintained that any people that can be dealt with as a collective unity—whether as actually organized under a sovereign State, or as a dependency, or as a subject-group with recognisable nationality—should be treated as a Rechts-subjekt, on principles of equal right as determined by a common good without reference to force, just as the individual is treated by the State law. (Hobhouse 1966 p. 299)

There are different ways of meeting this legitimate claim of members of minority nations for cultural protection, but

Clearly it is not achieved by equality of franchise. The smaller nationality does not merely want equal rights with others. It stands out for a certain life of its own . . . [To] find the place for national rights within the unity of the state, to give scope to national differences without destroying the organization of a life which has somehow to be lived in common, is therefore the problem which the modern state has to solve if it is to maintain itself. It has not only to generalize the common rights of citizenship as applied to individuals, but to make room for diversity and give some scope for collective sentiments which in a measure conflict with one another. (Hobhouse 1928 pp. 146–7)

But what was clear to Hobhouse and to 'the more liberal statesmanship' of his day—i.e. that people are owed respect both as political citizens and as cultural members, and so equality of franchise may have to be qualified where cultural minorities exist—has become obscure to the liberal statesmen and theorists of our day.[1] Viewed in this light, Rawls's rather offhand comment that every state has the right to run its own affairs and protect itself from external interference (Rawls 1971 p. 378), while the nations within them apparently have no similar claim to the protection of their communal life and culture, reveals that an important question of justice and respect has been lost from the liberal agenda.[2]

Rawls's and Dworkin's failure to discuss this issue is part of a broader change in the post-war intellectual environment. Before World War II, questions of minority cultures and their protection were of paramount importance to the League of Nations. But attention has now shifted to 'human rights', which are to be ensured for every individual *qua* individual, regardless of her cultural membership (Thornberry; Robinson; Hauser; Kelly pp. 255–66; Kunz). Whereas before the war it was considered a victory and virtue of liberalism that the League managed to secure special political status for minority cultural groups in the multinational countries of Europe, now it is considered a defeat for liberalism, a betrayal of the liberal ideal, should anyone's treatment by government be affected by her ethnicity or race or group membership.[3]

Thus Milton Gordon says that the liberal ideal is characterized by

the absence, even prohibition, of any legal or governmental recognition of racial, religious, language or [ethno-national] groups as corporate entities with a standing in the legal or governmental process, and a prohibition of the use of ethnic criteria of any type for discriminatory purposes, or conversely for special or favored treatment. (M. Gordon p. 105)

Group-specific measures are said by Lijphart to be appropriate only if we are 'more concerned with the equal or proportional treatment of groups than with individual equality' (Lijphart p. 49), or, as Glazer puts it, only if 'the task of a just society [is] to make representation [of groups] equal, even if this means the individual is not treated as an individual, but must be considered as a member of a group' (Glazer 1978 p. 97).

When the alternative is expressed in this way it's not surprising that the liberal concern is with treating individuals as individuals and as equals, without regard to any group membership, rather than treating groups as equals. But these post-war liberal clichés need to be rethought, for they misrepresent the issue, and the liberal tradition itself. A government that gives special rights to members of a distinct cultural community may still be treating them *as individuals*; the provision of such rights just reflects a different view about how to treat them as individuals and as equals. As Glazer correctly says, whether the government should provide such rights depends on whether 'it sees the different groups as remaining permanent and distinct constituents of a federated society, or whether it sees these groups as ideally integrating into, eventually assimilating into, a common society' (Glazer 1978 p. 98). Glazer says that liberals should opt for the latter assimilationist view. This view presupposes that 'the state sets before itself the model that group membership is purely private, a shifting matter of personal choice and degree' (ibid.; cf. Ajzenstat 1984*a* p. 251). But accepting that 'model' isn't a decision to treat individuals, rather than groups, as equals. It's a decision to treat individuals as having a certain relationship to their cultural community, namely a relationship such that belonging to it is like belonging to a local club, i.e. a purely private matter of 'personal choice' (Svensson pp. 426, 433). But that isn't the only way to treat individuals. There are other, better ways, as earlier liberals recognized. Since Glazer's view misconstrues our relationship to our cultural community, it fails to treat individuals as equals, for it means that aboriginal peoples suffer an inequality not due to 'purely private personal choice'. If we decide that the inequality should be corrected, through the collective measures discussed above, we do so because that is what's needed to treat individuals as equals. Neither view is more concerned with treating individuals as equals than the other. They just reflect different views of what individuals are, and hence what it is to treat them as equals.

While advocates of minority rights are often accused of engaging in some kind of 'group-think', it is often critics who are unable to look beyond the group nature of minority rights to consider the individuals who are affected by them. Amidst the voluminous post-war liberal literature criticizing collective rights one is hard pressed to find anyone who actually looks at how collective rights affect individuals. These critics apparently believe that the mere fact of group incorporation into the state manifests illiberality, without considering the individual benefits and burdens it involves.

It would be interesting to have a more thorough study of the historical relationship between liberalism and minority rights. While World War II was clearly important in the development of liberal thought, that is not the whole of the story. Minority rights have often been thought to raise important issues of state security or civil peace, issues which pre-empt more subtle questions of social justice. In a culturally plural country, the development of a political consensus has often been thought to be impossible (e.g. Mill 1972 p. 361). Hence majoritarian democracy is thought to lead inevitably to the domination of one cultural group over another, and then to civil war and/or international intervention.

However, liberals have disagreed over how minority rights affect this alleged incapacity to develop a political consensus. Some nineteenth-century liberals felt that minority rights exacerbated the problem. Such rights could not prevent domination by the majority culture, and protecting the minority culture would just prolong the inevitable injustice by inhibiting the creation of a homogeneous culture. If a multinational country could have been stably governed by principles of justice, then minority rights might have played a valuable role. But since fair relations between different cultures are impossible, minority rights would simply have exacerbated the inevitable exploitation and oppression. Acton vehemently opposed this view, and criticized his liberal contemporaries for subordinating liberty to the demands of the nation-state (Acton; cf. Cameron ch. 5). But it was a very common view amongst nineteenth-century English liberals, and affected their thinking about the fate of the French minority in Canada. (Some recent commentators have attempted to read back into this view the quite different post-war liberal claim that minority rights are inherently unjust.[4])

On the other hand, many liberals before and after World War I believed that it was the refusal to meet the legitimate claims of minority cultures which created a danger to domestic and international peace. Considerations of peace and stability strengthened the fairness argument for minority rights. Mutual respect between cultures, based on respect for both the individual rights and the collective rights of minorities, would form the basis of international peace (Claude ch. 2).

This optimistic liberal view did not survive World War II. Abuse of the Minority Protection scheme by the Nazis led to widespread fears about the loyalty of minorities. And so demands for the recognition of minority rights by the United Nations were rejected as incompatible with international peace and stability. The Nazi manipulation of minority claims

created a general distrust of groups which were disposed to perpetuate their minority consciousness, and a strong reaction against the concept of international protection [of national minorities] . . . the hard fact was that statesmen, generally backed by a public opinion which was deeply impressed by the perfidy of irredentist and disloyal minorities, were disposed to curtail, rather than to expand, the rights of minorities. (Claude pp. 57, 69)

This insistence on curtailing minority rights was not based on arguments of fairness. The arguments against minority rights were made

by statesmen and publicists within whose frame of reference the interests of the national state ranked as supreme values. Minorities might raise anguished cries about their 'spiritual emasculation' and protest that sacred cultural values were being violated; but the welfare and security of the state were prior considerations . . . [The majority nationality] has an interest in making the national state secure, and its institutions stable, even at the cost of obliterating minority cultures and imposing enforced homogeneity upon the population. (Claude pp. 80–1)

This was the dominant motif in international rejection of minority rights—one which implicitly and often explicitly subordinated fairness to questions of 'the interest of the international community in the stabilization and pacification of political relationships' (Claude p. 83). This consideration was dominant in domestic American thinking as well (Claude pp. 81–2).

Out of this mixture of domestic and international factors the current liberal hostility to minority rights was born. None of these factors are entirely lacking in significance, but neither do they imply that minority rights are inherently unjust. If anything, these post-war arguments conceded that universal incorporation involves unfairness to minorities. However, within ten years or so of the founding of the United Nations, the ideology of 'colour-blind' legislation was evolving, according to which the refusal of minority rights was done for reasons of principle, out of respect for the individuals of all races and cultures. This ideology proved so successful in the United States that by the 1970s many commentators could claim that it defined the liberal tradition, from which demands for minority rights are a recent and illiberal deviation.

In fact, however, the colour-blind ideology has only a contingent relationship to the Western liberal tradition. Its post-war popularity is really due to the state of black–white race relations in the United States in the 1950s and 1960s. The development of this ideology was not based on a reinterpretation of the liberal tradition, or a comprehensive review of the situation of minority cultures. It was based on the struggle against the segregation of blacks in the South (to which the idea of a colour-blind constitution provided a useful rallying-point). Yet the prohibition on special status for ethnic groups is now taken to be definitive of classical liberalism and is applied to situations far removed from black–white race issues, like that of American Indians (Svensson pp. 430–3; Sigler p. 77; Van Dyke 1985 p. 93—see ch. 14 below).

If we look beyond this current (mis)interpretation of the history of minority rights, we find that there has not been anything like a consistent principle underlying liberal policy concerning minority cultures, domestically or internationally. As Kunz puts it, 'At the end of the first World War, "international protection of minorities" was the great fashion . . . Recently this fashion has become nearly obsolete. Today the well-dressed international lawyer wears "human rights" ' (Kunz p. 282; cf. van den Berghe 1981*b* p. 4). Rather than reflecting benign shifts in fashion, however, these theoretical changes 'reflect shifts in dominance in world affairs between different states, who have put their weight behind versions suiting their own foreign policy requirements' (Dench p. 204). Minority policy has been determined not by any clear and simple rule against group incorporation, but by a myriad of changing domestic and international factors, of which respect for the legitimate claims of minorities has played a varying role. The current liberal orthodoxy obscures all this beneath its deceptively simple and familiar formula.[5]

There are very few challenges to the hegemony of this colour-blind model within contemporary liberalism. One notable exception involves some writers within the consociational school of democratic theory. They have attempted to bring out the ways in which minority rights and group incorporation can promote liberal-democratic values in a culturally plural society (e.g. McRae 1975; Asch and Dacks pp. 37–41; Boulle ch. 1–3). But from the point of view of a comprehensive theory of liberal equality, the consociationalists have a similar tendency to subordinate considerations of fairness to considerations of *realpolitik*. Minority rights are still viewed essentially in terms of protecting domestic and international peace. Unlike the founders of the United Nations, however, consociationalists do not think it is the mere existence of cultural minorities which endangers stability. Rather, it is the equation of the state with the majority nationality. Attempts to create a 'nation-state' out of a culturally plural society threaten minorities, who then must seek to change their relationship to the state. Minority rights prevent, rather than create, threats to the state (Sigler pp. 188–92; C. Young pp. 523–5; McRae 1979 p. 688; Maybury-Lewis 1984*b*). Given that their main concern is with preventing political instability, consociationalists do not try to develop a broader liberal theory which would justify deviations from a colour-blind regime. Consociationalists treat minority rights as a response to the lack of a moral consensus, a way of preventing the lack of consensus from deteriorating into political instability, rather than as an independently justified requirement of liberal theory.

While minority rights may indeed prevent instability in some circumstances,[6] this provides a very limited argument for them. It leaves those who need minority rights the most—the minorities which are most powerless *vis-à-vis* the state—with the weakest argument. And it presents the acquisition of minority rights, where minorities have had the power to insist on them, as merely the consequence of power politics. If we are to challenge the hegemony of the colour-blind model of liberal equality, we need to show how minority rights can be grounded in a liberal theory which recognizes the value of cultural membership and the fairness of the special claims of minorities.[7]

Notes

1. This sometimes leads to misinterpretations of earlier liberals. Dworkin, for example, misconstrues Mill's position on the importance of a shared cultural heritage for a free community. Mill said that there are three preconditions of a free community: education, a sense of nationality, and a common respect for a public political morality. Dworkin says that, for Mill, the second would only continue to survive in respect for principles of 'individual freedom and social equality' (Dworkin 1977 p. 264, quoting Mill 1962 pp. 122–3). But Mill in fact said that the *third* precondition would only survive in that form. He does not say, either here or elsewhere, that the second precondition, a shared cultural structure, would cease to be important in its own right (Mill 1962 pp. 124–5). Shared cultural context has an importance for individual freedom beyond the shared recognition of principles of justice. Mill, like Hobhouse, felt that freedom required not only the interdependencies of civil society (governed by principles of justice), but also the consciousness of commonality based on cultural identity.

    The failure of liberals to emphasize the importance of a shared public culture for a free community is discussed by Raz (Raz 1986 p. 251). His explanation of this failure is that our shared culture is such a natural background that we too often fail to notice its contribution to the exercise of individual freedom. But I don't think that one *naturally* fails to notice this. The playing down of the importance of culture amongst liberals has a much more contingent and historical explanation. Liberals stopped emphasizing the cultural context only after they saw what horrors could be done in the name of one's culture.

2. See Van Dyke (1975 p. 614) for a discussion of the arbitrariness involved in Rawls's claim that nations only get such rights when they become states.

3. Compare recent characterizations of the liberal ideal (e.g. Porter p. 295; Ajzenstat 1984*a* pp. 251–2; Knopff 1979 pp. 68–70; van den Berghe 1981*a* p. 347; 1981*b* p. 81), with Thornberry's account of the goals and ideals of pre-WWII liberal statesmen (Thornberry pp. 428–33).

4. For example, Ajzenstat claims that Lord Durham rejected minority rights for French-Canadians because such rights opposed 'the founding principle of liberal philosophy', which prohibits official recognition of cultural identities. These rights are based on ascription, not achievement, and hence are inherently unjust (Ajzenstat 1984a pp. 251, 243). But she conflates this modern view with two different arguments that Durham and other liberals made. Firstly, they believed that members of disadvantaged minorities would choose to assimilate, and thus minority rights protect an option which is likely to disappear (Ajzenstat 1984b pp. 105–6; 1984a p. 251). Secondly, they believed that minority cultures are inevitably driven into subordinate economic roles, and are thereby made subject to exploitation (1984a pp. 243, 252; 1984b p. 106). Neither of these arguments involves the claim that group incorporation is inherently unjust, and both are compatible with the claim that it would be best, from the point of view of justice, if measures could be taken so that members of minority cultures were not forced to choose between their cultural membership and acquiring a fair share of resources. Durham argued that injustice was endemic to the relationship between majority and minority cultures. Minority rights could not solve the injustice, but nor were they the cause of it.

5. It is worth noting that the Marxist tradition has gone through similar transformations, although not in the same order. Marx and Engels began by denying that nationalities had rights to self-government, and indeed felt that many of the European minorities should be assimilated into one or other of the great nations, even if it required 'iron unscrupulousness'. But the Soviet Union, especially since World War II, has argued for the international protection of minority rights, often against liberal resistance (Sigler pp. 186–8). As with liberal states, the Communist stand on domestic and international questions of minority rights has fluctuated with the perception of political interests and necessities (Connor 1984 ch. 1).

6. Critics of consociationalism reject this claim about domestic peace and stability. Like nineteenth-century liberals, some writers assert that majority dominance is inevitable, even if there are guarantees of minority rights (e.g. M. G. Smith 1969; Rabushka and Shepsle pp. 62–92; van den Berghe 1981b ch. 2). Hence the best, and ultimately the only, solution is the assimilation of minorities through the 'benign neglect' of the state (van den Berghe 1981a p. 354), or the formation of client relationships between dependent minorities and the dominant nationality (Dench pp. 259–60). It

seems unlikely that any single theory about the effects of minority rights on state stability will apply to all cases, even though that seems to be the operative assumption amongst both advocates and critics of consociationalism.

These questions of how national majorities will respond to the legitimate claims of minorities are clearly important in evaluating the prospects for minority rights in any particular country. My immediate concern, however, is with the prior question of what the legitimate claims of minorities are.

7. In addition to the consociationalists, Van Dyke and Berger have discussed the relationship between minority rights and liberal values, and I want to say a word about each. It is hard to describe exactly what the differences are between my theory and Van Dyke's. He sometimes seems to accept that minority rights are a matter of equal consideration for individuals (e.g. 'It is perhaps an odd way to put it, but those who believe in the dignity and the equal worth of individuals may in some circumstances need to endorse status and rights for groups'—Van Dyke 1985 pp. 219, 221). But elsewhere he is prepared to consider that groups have *sui generis* interests that are not reducible to the interests of individuals (Van Dyke 1982 p. 24), interests which need to be weighed against the demands of equality for individuals. Thus he describes a minority right as an 'ambivalent' balancing of two principles, communalism and individualism, with the former constraining the latter (e.g. Van Dyke 1985 pp. 89–90). But what he takes to be an ambivalent balancing of two distinct principles seems to me to be the consistent working-out of a single principle: respect for the freedom of individuals to develop within their cultural community, and to use and interpret its cultural heritage. Communalism, if it is to play a legitimate role, does not compete with individualism, but rather is an interpretation of it, specifying a relevant feature of the respect owed to individuals.

These are perhaps merely verbal differences. The main difference concerns the extent to which minority rights can be determined independently of the structure of individual rights. While Van Dyke's discussions of particular examples of minority rights often show how these rights correct inequalities left by the structure of individual rights, his theoretical discussion implies that we can determine the rights of groups without knowing whether the distribution of individual rights and resources leaves legitimate interests unsatisfied. The criteria he provides for identifying when a group is entitled to collective rights do not require that it be disadvantaged relative to other groups, so that a majority culture seems equally entitled to special rights as a minority culture (Van Dyke 1982 pp. 32–4; 1985 pp. 213–15). On my view, minority rights are only justified if some inequality in circumstances is present.

Berger defends minority rights in terms of dissent:

> we have many linguistic, racial, cultural, and ethnic minorities. Each of them has a claim to collective as well as to individual guarantees under the new Constitution and the Charter of Rights and Freedoms, and each of them has a claim on the goodwill of the majority. For all of these minorities the right to dissent is the mainstay of their freedom. (Berger 1981 p. xiv)

But a claim on the goodwill of the majority is not the same as a claim to restrict the political power or social resources of others, as is required for the implementation of many collective rights. The right to toleration of dissent is a negative right, even if we take it 'not as mere indifference, but in its most positive light, as the expression of a profound belief in the virtues of diversity and in the right to dissent' (Berger 1981 p. xvii). Even in its most positive light, it doesn't tell us why any group needs more than the individual rights and resources allotted to its members, or why some groups need special measures where others don't.

11

Walzer and Minority Rights

I HOPE to have shown that liberalism can accommodate respect for cultural membership, although I doubt this will satisfy every defender of minority rights. To some, the liberal defence I have given may seem unduly abstract, grounding the claims of minorities in a theory of equality which pays little attention to the particularity of the community in question. Two minority cultures with very different shared meanings or shared practices might well have similar collective rights, if they face a similar inequality in circumstances. The liberal recognition of cultural membership may seem rather 'thin', ignoring the 'thick' pattern of communal valuations and practices. Now this is not, of course, a merely contingent or accidental feature of the theory. Any liberal theory will prefer, and indeed demand, that each of the goals and values which have historically characterized a community's cultural life be subject to the evaluation of individuals, who should be free to affirm or reject any particular value without thereby suffering a loss of rights or resources.

Critics may feel that liberalism pays insufficient attention to the historical values of a particular culture, as embodied in the shared meanings and practices that characterize the community's cultural life. On the communitarian view, cultural membership should be understood to carry with it a commitment to, or an embeddedness in, these communal practices and valuations. And so the rights of minority cultures should be tied more closely to those membership-defining communal values. This enlarged conception of cultural membership offers an argument for a 'thicker' set of minority rights. And since cultural membership has this enlarged meaning, it would seem to be all the more important to ensure that minorities have the rights needed to protect their membership.

In the next two chapters, I shall argue that the communitarian emphasis on particular shared meanings and practices weakens the argument for minority rights. In Chapter 12, I shall look at two communitarian attempts to go beyond a liberal view of minority rights by tying these rights to the promotion of particular shared practices within the community. In this chapter, I want to examine the way that Michael Walzer employs shared meanings in his discussion of minority rights. In both chapters, I shall argue that the distinctive emphasis which communitarians put on ideas of shared meanings and practices, while seeming to add to the importance of cultural membership, in fact weakens the argument for minority rights.

This contrast between the demand for an enlarged notion of cultural membership on the one hand, and yet an inability to protect such membership on the other, is very clear in Michael Walzer's *Spheres of Justice*. The theoretical framework Walzer employs seems to make cultural membership the foundational value. He says that his theory of justice is grounded in respect for people's cultural membership. We are one another's equals by virtue of 'one characteristic above all . . . we are (all of us) culture-producing creatures; we make and inhabit meaningful worlds' (Walzer 1983 p. 314). We fail to treat people as equals if we fail to notice that they 'make and inhabit' a different 'meaningful world' from our own. And respecting people as culture-producing creatures, for Walzer, requires deriving principles of justice from the 'shared understanding' of social goods in a given culture. 'Since there is no way to rank and order these worlds with respect to their understanding of social goods, we do justice to men and women by respecting their particular creations . . . to override those understandings is (always) to act unjustly' (Walzer 1983 p. 314). Walzer contrasts this approach to determining what is owed people as culture-producing creatures with the liberal egalitarian framework of Rawls and Dworkin, which seeks to determine principles of justice from a viewpoint which abstracts from the particular values or life-styles which characterize any given culture (e.g. Walzer 1983 p. xiv).

Hence Walzer seems to be giving cultural membership a larger role to play within political theory. But this apparent emphasis on cultural membership does not yield a justification for the measures that are needed to protect cultural membership. Walzer is in fact quite hostile to rights for minority cultures, and I shall argue that this is the predictable result of his abandonment of the liberal egalitarian framework employed by Rawls and Dworkin. Walzer's claim that respecting individuals' cultural membership requires respecting their shared meanings precludes the development of an adequate theory of minority rights.

The problems for minority cultures arise as soon as Walzer begins the elaboration of his theory of respect for people as culture-producing creatures. If it is always unjust to violate a culture's shared meanings, it becomes very important to identify the community which is the bearer of this culture. Walzer says the *political* community is the appropriate setting for distinguishing meanings and marking out distributive spheres:

The political community is probably the closest we can come to a world of common meanings. Language, history, and culture come together (come more closely together than anywhere else) to produce a collective consciousness . . . the sharing of sensibilities and intuitions among the members of a historical community is a fact of life. (Walzer 1983 p. 28)

But this is simply untrue: less than 10 per cent of the countries of the world have the kind of cultural homogeneity Walzer claims for them. In all the rest there is a plurality of 'historical communities'. Walzer recognizes that

Sometimes political and historical communities don't coincide, and there may well be a growing number of states in the world today where sensibilities and intuitions aren't readily shared; the sharing takes place in smaller units. And then, perhaps, we should look for some way to adjust distributive decisions to the requirements of those units. (Walzer 1983 pp. 28–9)

One would expect, then, that where historical and political communities do not coincide, justice requires that we respect the meanings shared in the historical community, for that is the real world of common meanings, the place where language, history, and culture have produced a collective consciousness. However, Walzer continues in a different direction:

But this adjustment [of distributive decisions to the requirements of historical communities] must itself be worked out politically, and its precise character will depend upon understandings shared among the citizens about the value of cultural diversity, local autonomy, and so on. It is to these understandings that we must appeal when we make our arguments. (Walzer 1983 p. 29)

But this is very confusing: if, on his own terms, sensibilities are not readily shared between the different historical communities in a country, then there's no reason to think there will be any shared meanings over the value of local autonomy and cultural diversity. And if these adjustments must be settled by appeal to the (non-existent) shared meanings of all citizens, then they will in fact reflect, by default, the meanings of the majority culture, which could, in the relevant respects, violate the shared meanings of minority cultural communities—a result in fundamental conflict with Walzer's first principles.

The quoted passage provides one argument why decisions should be based on the shared meanings of the citizens of the political community—namely, that that is where decisions must be worked out. But this is inconclusive. It leaves entirely unanswered the question of whose understandings are held to be authoritative in making that decision. Should political decision-makers treat Indians' understandings as authoritative for decisions concerning their historical community, or as only part of the understandings extant in the political community and so defeasible by the understandings of larger cultural groups? If Canada were still a colony of Britain, or a protectorate of the UN, would decision-makers in London or New York be justified in taking into account the understandings of local autonomy throughout Britain, or the whole world? The fact that a decision must be worked out at the level of a particular political community is no argument for letting the understandings of that community take precedence over the understandings of a historical community.

Walzer has a second argument for treating the (non-shared) understandings of citizens as authoritative, even when they conflict with the genuine collective consciousness of historical communities. He says that 'Politics, moreover, establishes its own bonds of commonality' (Walzer 1983 p. 29). Now there is considerable truth to this claim. Politics does establish bonds of commonality. Integration into national political structures is as important to assimilating minority cultures as is integration into national economic and educational structures. That is, in fact, why Indians in Canada have consistently rejected proposals to give them special representation in federal political institutions. It would indeed bind them in bonds of commonality with other citizens and increase their vulnerability to the decisions of the dominant culture. But that is precisely why, on Walzer's own terms, appealing to the understandings of all citizens is unjust. The shared meanings of a historical community are violated, their requirements subordinated, in order to create a commonality unrelated to the particular creations of the minority culture.

There may be other reasons for wanting to establish bonds of commonality politically. Machiavelli, for example, advised his prince to eliminate cultural differences in the population, and submerge cultural groups into a homogeneous polity, because national unity was crucial to the defence of the republic in a predatory international environment (Machiavelli p. xxxiv). National defence trumps cultural respect. The fear of apathy, if not outright disloyalty, has been the excuse used for the often brutal suppression of cultural minorities ever since the rise of the (misnamed) 'nation-state' (Claydon p. 138; Claude pp. 43–7). This was particularly in evidence in Europe after World War II, because of the abuse of the minorities protection scheme of the League of Nations by the Nazis, and continues in Latin America and black Africa today (Maybury-Lewis pp. 222–7; W. Weinstein). But Machiavelli and his heirs would perhaps be surprised to learn that their 'nation-building' policies could be justified not only on the usual *realpolitik* grounds, but also on Walzer's grounds of respect for people as cultural creators.

That Walzer is indeed prepared to contemplate the sacrifice of historical communities in the pursuit of common citizenship is evident in his discussion of immigration and mobility. Membership in a political community, he says, is itself a good, and this requires that there be a community capable of making decisions about admission and exclusion. Somebody must put restrictions on mobility because a world of complete mobility unlimited by any state or local restrictions would be

a world of radically deracinated men and women. Neighbourhoods might maintain some cohesive culture for a generation or two on a voluntary basis, but people would move in, people would move out; soon the cohesion would be gone. The distinctiveness of cultures and groups depends upon closure and, without it, cannot be conceived as a stable feature of human life. If this distinctiveness is a value, as most people (though some of them are global pluralists and others only local loyalists) seem to believe, then closure must be permitted somewhere. At some level of political organization, something like the sovereign state must take shape and claim the authority to make its own admissions policy, to control and sometimes restrain the flow of immigrants. (Walzer 1983 p. 39)

Now Walzer is clearly right about the need for an admissions policy. But whose understandings should be authoritative in making these decisions? Should the understandings of the Indian, Inuit, and French-Canadian communities be authoritative in deciding migration and mobility rights where they are affected? As we've seen, this is a volatile issue in Canada, where Quebec demands the right to restrict immigration into the province, and where aboriginal peoples demand the right to restrict the entry not only of immigrants but also of non-aboriginal Canadians. They demand these rights precisely because the larger Canadian political community favours much greater mobility. If the value at stake in an admissions policy is the preservation of distinct cultural groups, then one would expect cultural communities to have the final word on admissions.

Walzer admits that it need hardly be anything like a sovereign state which restrains the flow of immigration. On the contrary, members of distinctive groups within a country 'will organize to defend the local politics and culture against strangers'. Indeed he admits it is only 'nationalization of culture and politics that opens the neighbourhood communities to whoever chooses to come in' (Walzer 1983 p. 38). In other words, the sovereign state is not the natural response to protecting distinct cultural groups, but on the contrary it becomes the acceptable ultimate authority over admissions only when all but one of the distinct cultural groups has been assimilated, when culture has been 'nationalized'.

But far from opposing this process of nationalizing culture, Walzer obviously thinks it is a reasonable price to pay for greater mobility. For only when the state is the ultimate authority on admissions

can local communities take shape as 'indifferent' associations, determined solely by personal preference and market capacity. Since individual choice is most dependent upon local mobility, this would seem to be the preferred arrangement in a society like our own. The politics and the culture of a modern democracy probably require the kind of largeness, and also the kind of boundedness, that states provide. I don't mean to deny the value of sectional cultures and ethnic communities; I mean only to suggest the rigidities that would be forced upon both in the absence of inclusive and protective states. To tear down the walls of the state is not, as Sidgwick worriedly suggested, to create a world without walls, but rather to create a thousand petty fortresses. (Walzer 1983 p. 39)

Walzer here recognizes what I argued above against Rawls and Dworkin—that if patterns of mobility are 'determined solely by personal preference and market capacity', then the culture must be (or must be in the process of becoming) nationalized. Having recognized the problem, however, he says that the desire for mobility by members of the dominant ('modern') culture trumps the desire of minority (backward?) cultures to set up 'petty' communities where their culture is protected.

It is hard to make sense of Walzer's position here. State immigration policies are justified for Walzer on the grounds of preserving distinct cultural groups. But it turns out that this only applies to the dominant culture whose desire for a peripatetic life-style outweighs any claims to protection minority cultures might make. The nationalizing of culture is, evidently, a reasonable price to pay for the mobility of the members of the dominant (and soon to be homogeneous) culture. Whatever reasons there might be for such an assessment of the overriding importance of mobility, I fail to see how it can be said to reflect a concern for preserving distinct cultural groups, or a respect for people as cultural agents. Despite Walzer's avowed concern and respect, these considerations just don't appear to have any weight against the goal of maximizing individual mobility within a nationalized culture, at least for our modern democratic societies.

The same contradiction between initial premises and ultimate conclusions appears in Walzer's discussion of the rights conferred by naturalization. He begins by saying that

Admission and exclusion are at the core of communal independence . . . Without them, there could not be *communities of character*, historically stable, ongoing associations of men and women with some special commitment to one another and some special sense of their common life. (Walzer 1983 p. 62)

He thus begins by presenting and defending our intuition that members of historical communities should be free to protect the continuity of their common life. He goes on, however, to draw a very different conclusion—one in which historical communities have no moral claim at all to such protection:

these rights [of admission and exclusion] are to be exercised only by the community as a whole (*even if, in practice, some national majority dominates the decision making*) and only with regard to foreigners, not by some members with regard to others. No community can be half-metic, half-citizen and claim that its admissions policies are acts of self-determination or that its politics is democratic. (Walzer 1983 p. 62, my emphasis)

In other words, once Canada chooses to accept someone as a citizen, the French-Canadians or Indians cannot refuse her admittance, or restrict her political rights, or exclude her from consideration for the holding of offices (Walzer 1983 p. 148), even if it is necessary to preserve their culture. These restrictions would be violations of the rights of citizenship which are conferred on her, in full and once and for all, by the 'community as a whole'.

The result of this shift from cultural to political community is that the desired equality of individuals as members and co-creators of a culture is replaced by the fictitious equality of individuals as citizens of a self-determining state. The equality of citizenship is fictitious because, as Walzer readily admits in the italicized passage, the equal rights of citizenship mask the dominance of the majority culture. Hence a policy justified in terms of protecting a historical community ends up legitimizing decisions by the majority culture which undermine minority cultures. The conclusion Walzer reaches contradicts his initial premiss.

Walzer recognizes one exception to all this. One group in a culturally plural society can restrict the mobility and candidate rights of other citizens if and only if it achieves or accepts the status of a 'foreign' political community. In the case of mobility rights, minority communities must become fully independent states: 'If the community is so radically divided that a single citizenship is impossible, then its territory must be divided, too, before the rights of admission and exclusion can be exercised' (Walzer 1983 p. 62). In the case of candidate rights, their denial 'might be acceptable in a bi-national state, where the members of the two nations stand, in fact, as foreigners to one another. What is required between them is mutual accommodation, not justice in any positive sense' (Walzer 1983 p. 149). He doesn't stick consistently to the idea that questions of justice don't arise in such societies, for he says that if the United States became a 'federation of groups rather than a community of citizens', a principle of equal consideration would still apply within and between federated groups, but not across them (Walzer 1983 p. 150).

While he considers this a possibility, he rejects it for the United States because it is 'inconsistent with our historical traditions and shared understandings—inconsistent, too, with contemporary living patterns, deeply and bitterly divisive' (Walzer 1983 p. 151). In other words, minorities must either play by the rules of the majority culture, without any special protection, or get out entirely and play their own game. This is, I believe, a multiply perverse view.

(1) It is perverse to think that the right of minorities to protect their culture depends on their ability to secure and support an independent or federated state. On Walzer's scheme, minorities only have claims if they are sufficiently large in number and geographically concentrated to be a viable economic state (as Canadian Indians and Inuit aren't), or if they have sufficient economic or political clout to make common citizenship impossible and thereby force mutual accommodation instead. These are morally arbitrary factors. It can't be right that a minority only has the right to protect itself if it has the power to fend off the assimilationist drive of the majority's 'historical tradition' of nationalizing culture. That is mere *realpolitik*, not moral argument. I do not see any moral reason to connect the legitimate exercise of minority rights with the possession of an independent or federated state.

(2) It is perverse to make such a fetish out of citizenship rights. Walzer refuses to let Indian and Inuit communities restrict the mobility and candidate rights of other Canadians unless they separate and 'stand, in fact, as foreigners' to the rest of Canada.

This has the virtue, from Walzer's point of view, of preserving his theory that people are treated equally (in our society) in virtue of being common citizens. It has no virtue from anyone else's point of view. It's second-best from the point of view of the aboriginal peoples, who would prefer to exercise their right to the protection of their cultural community within Canada and thereby have the rights of Canadian citizens in non-aboriginal lands. It is sub-optimal from the point of view of non-aboriginal Canadians, who would prefer to have at least some citizenship rights in aboriginal lands. Neither side gains in the move from having partial citizenship rights in the others' territory to having no rights at all. Walzer saves his theory at the expense of the values the theory was supposed to secure (Van Dyke 1985 pp. 207–11).

The theory begins to make sense, from the point of view of the majority, if we know that the choice between common citizenship and independent/federated status is not a genuine one. If we know that minorities are incapable of a viable independence, then forcing them to 'choose' between common citizenship and independence would secure a value for the majority—indeed, their preferred solution. It would force minorities to relinquish their claims to the protection of their cultural membership, and hence secure unrestricted mobility for the majority. Whatever virtues that tactic would have, justice isn't one of them.

(3) It is perverse to say that the relationship between cultural communities, once they've become established as permanent components of a binational or multinational state, is not a subject of a theory of justice. That relationship need not (and should not) be governed only by 'mutual accommodation', rather than 'positive justice'. Canadians do not view it as just a question of mutual accommodation whether an English-Canadian child has the right to an English education when in Quebec, or whether non-aboriginal residents will have full voting rights in the proposed aboriginal homelands of northern Canada. People in Canada agree that justice sets limits on the extent to which the citizenship rights of members of one national group can be limited when in the territory of the other national group (although they certainly disagree over what those limits are).

Despite Walzer's claim that in binational countries 'the

members of the two nations stand, in fact, as foreigners to one another', there are many binational or multinational societies where that is not true. People do not feel themselves bound by ties of 'mutual accommodation' rather than the demands of 'positive justice'; they do not view themselves as 'a federation of groups *rather than* a community of citizens'; they do not see themselves as concerned with 'equal standing for races and religions; communal integrity, self-respect for the members as members', *rather than* 'equal consideration for individuals' (Walzer 1983 p. 150, my emphasis). On the contrary, 'self-respect for members as members' is an aspect of 'equal consideration for individuals'. It's *because* people are citizens of the same country—and recognize that justice between citizens requires, amongst other things, respect for members as members—that they decide to accommodate the enforcement of citizenship rights to the needs of membership in the federated groups. And this raises questions, not faced by Walzer, about how equality of citizenship is to be fairly balanced against equal respect for members as members. These questions arise continually in culturally plural societies, and it is simply perverse to say that they don't, or shouldn't, arise.

Walzer fails to confront these questions because he assumes that people are citizens of homogeneous states; where cultural minorities exist, his theory envisages assimilation to the dominant culture; where that is impossible, his theory envisages only a federation of national groups whose members are not connected by any common citizenship. As a result, Walzer never allows people's citizenship rights to extend beyond their own (or what is soon to be their own) culture, and hence never allows that the individual citizenship rights of members of one group could (permanently) conflict with the rights of members of another group to the protection of their cultural membership. He thereby removes from his theory a problem that is properly and unavoidably faced every day by politicians and jurists in many countries of the world.

Why would Walzer deny the reality and legitimacy of these questions? Perhaps because his theory could never make sense of how politicians and judges deal with these conflicts. His insistence on appealing to locally shared meanings leaves no room for the standards that public officials would be appealing to. Citizenship rights must be limited to a culture because, for Walzer, *morality* is limited to a culture, limited to its shared meanings. Social meanings are the 'necessary structure' for any moral debate: 'there are no external or universal principles that can replace it. Every substantive account of distributive justice is a local account' (Walzer 1983 p. 314). Since sensibilities and intuitions about justice are not shared in multinational states, relations between groups cannot be based on justice. Minority relations must, therefore, be decided on grounds of 'mutual accommodation' (i.e. co-operation based on rational self-interest), or by the simple exercise of majority power (as Walzer concedes will occur).

Minority relations can't be based on justice, because Walzer has no room for intercultural arguments about the justice of such relations. If understandings of justice are not shared, and there are no principles external to the cultures to which they could jointly appeal (and whose decision they could jointly accept as binding), then there is no point arguing. Yet such arguments go on every day in culturally plural societies. People do think there are standards independent of their own shared meanings which are authoritative for the different cultural groups.

And this reveals a fundamental ambiguity in Walzer's notion of a culture's 'shared meaning'. In one sense of the term, we could determine a community's shared understanding of, say, economic justice by drawing up a questionnaire asking everyone what sorts of trade-offs are considered legitimate under what conditions and then working on the data to come up with some combination or function of the competing views. The community may think that justice in distribution means distribution by merit and need, although people disagree about their relative weighting. We might even be able, on inspection, to find some deeper unity amongst the initially divergent answers. But the shared meanings, on this view, always remain tied to existing beliefs.

But there's a second aspect to our 'shared understanding' of morality and justice. We recognize that we could, in principle, be mistaken in our beliefs about justice, and about the justice of institutions we currently believe to be legitimate. As Dworkin notes, Walzer's theory ignores the 'social meaning' of a tradition much more fundamental than the discrete traditions it asks us to respect. For it is part of our common political life, if anything is, that justice is our critic, not our mirror, that any decision about the distribution of any good . . . may be reopened, no matter how firm the traditions that are then challenged, that we may always ask of some settled institutional scheme whether it is fair. (Dworkin 1985 p. 219)

We don't think that however a community understands the nature of its social goods (and hence how to distribute them), the resulting shared meanings legitimately determine the framework of justice for that community. The real demands of justice are not determined by our present understanding of them; nor would we agree, for instance, that should our future shared understandings come to favour it, the reimplementation of a caste society would, just for that reason, be not only consistent with but demanded by justice.

The fact that we currently believe some distributions are just or unjust is not, therefore, conclusive. Justice means to us something that is independent of what we (currently) think it to be. To paraphrase Dworkin, justice isn't some function or combination of the competing claims about justice being made, it is rather what each of the competing claims claims to be (Dworkin 1977 pp. 128–9). The shared meaning of justice, on the first view, is some combination or interpretation of existing claims about justice. The shared meaning of justice on the second view is what each of the existing claims claims to be.

It is the shared meaning of justice in this second sense that grounds political argument. Since our present beliefs about justice do not determine the nature of justice, and since we are prepared to reconsider our reasons for accepting those present beliefs, the fact that two cultures don't share the same beliefs about justice (in the first sense) is no obstacle to political argument. Differences in the meaning of justice in the first sense invite rather than undermine debate, because both cultures share the same meaning of justice in the fundamental second sense. Both share the view that justice is what each of their competing claims claims to be.[1]

Walzer's claim that arguments must appeal to the shared meanings of a local community rests, therefore, on an unwarranted scepticism about our ability to rationally debate and criticize different understandings of social goods. And while the demand that we appeal to local shared meanings may have seemed like a promising way of strengthening the importance of cultural membership, we can now see that it in fact undermines the likelihood of gaining justice for minority cultures.

Defending minority rights requires that we find an adequate account of the value of cultural membership, an account which can justify minority claims to both the goodwill and the social resources of people outside the culture. Walzer's theory is of no help here. He does say that cultural membership is important, that we are one another's equals by virtue of 'one characteristic above all . . . we are (all of us) culture-producing creatures' (Walzer 1983 p. 314). But he goes on to defend this claim in a way that, from the point of view of minority cultures, is inadequate. The reason why cultural membership is important, for Walzer, is that 'Since there is no way to rank and order these worlds with regard to their understanding of social goods, we do justice to actual men and women by respecting their particular creations . . . to override these understandings is (always) to act unjustly' (ibid.). This way of grounding a concern for cultural membership is politically unhelpful. Despite the avowed commitment to the importance of cultural membership, it in fact leaves the defence of minority cultural membership to the vagaries of majority sentiment about the value of such goods as diversity and cultural autonomy. If the majority community has an understanding of social goods which ignores or plays down the role of cultural membership, Walzer offers the minority no ground on which to demand protection of their cultural structure (other than forcing the majority group into mutual accommodation).

In an earlier work, Walzer says that his arguments are based on the right 'of contemporary men and women to live as members of a historic community' (Walzer 1980 p. 211). But as we've seen, Walzer's scepticism, far from grounding that right, is in fact a threat to it.[2] It leaves the protection of minority cultures to the vagaries of power politics and mutual accommodation. If it's important to treat people as equals in virtue of their equal status as members of cultures, it should be because cultural membership is an important part of a correct understanding of social goods, not because we have no way to criticize any culture's shared understanding of morality. Cultural membership is important because it fits into that understanding of social goods which we've ranked and ordered as the most defensible one, not because we have no way to rank and order different cultural understandings.

Walzer's emphasis on the social understandings of historical communities may seem like a useful corrective to recent liberal inattention to questions of cultural membership. But in fact it provides no cogent account of *why* cultural membership matters to us, or how it helps our lives go better or worse. And it provides even less of a defence of measures that might be needed to protect that cultural membership in culturally plural countries. Walzer's account of the importance of cultural membership is therefore, theoretically weak, and politically disastrous.

Notes

1. This points to an ambiguity that plagues a lot of discussions, communitarian or otherwise, about 'social meanings' and their relationship to 'forms of life'. The term 'meanings' is often ambiguous in this way between 'opinions/beliefs' and a more general 'understandings'. When Nozick says that justice is 'From each as they choose, to each as they are chosen' (Nozick 1974 p. 160), and Marx says 'From each according to his ability, to each according to his needs' (Marx 1875 p. 321), they can plausibly be said to disagree on the meaning of justice. But at another level they both might fully agree about what justice 'means'—it is the system of entitlements on the basis of which people can demand social recognition of their legitimate claims (e.g. for resources, freedoms, etc.). They may well share this same 'concept' of justice, yet have very different 'conceptions' of what justice requires (see Dworkin 1977 p. 134).

   Saying that meanings are shared in a form of life is therefore ambiguous. The *concept* of justice is shared by many people who do not share the same *conception* of justice. This ambiguity often does no harm, since the claim that meanings are shared in forms of life is sometimes only meant to deny the contrary claim that meanings are free-floating, or part of the furniture of the universe, or whatever. That denial can be made without specifying what exactly the appropriate context is, without specifying the boundaries of the relevant form of life.

   But Walzer claims something much more specific. He claims that social meanings, in the sense which is fundamental for political argument, are shared within, and only within, discrete historical communities. But once we've made clear what that sense of shared meanings is, and what sorts of communities we have in mind, it becomes very doubtful whether there will be either shared understandings within, or distinct understandings across, these communities. Understood as beliefs, attitudes, and opinions, 'meanings' are shared in units much smaller than historical communities. Understood at a more general level, 'meanings' are quite possibly shared in units much larger than a single culture—Western democracies, say, share the same concept of justice. Of course one can cover up this problem by using 'forms of life' in such a broad way as to include, on the one hand, a predominantly working-class immigrant neighbourhood in Brooklyn, and, on the other hand, the modern Western world. As Rosenblum says, 'Among romantic sensibilities [the context] is more likely to be a society of friends or a counterculture. Or shared meanings can be so general that the relevant community is nothing less than the western European intellectual tradition' (Rosenblum p. 172).

If we leave both 'meanings' and 'forms of life' unspecified in this way, and allow ourselves to broaden or restrict their range as needed, then there may be a sense in which meanings are shared, and only shared, within a form of life. But that sort of claim won't support Walzer's belief that moral argument has to appeal to local standards. Political philosophers would do best by forgoing such vague claims about 'shared meanings' and 'forms of life' and sticking closer to the actual terrain of moral beliefs—i.e. to the disagreements people actually have and the arguments they give in defence of their positions. If we did so, Walzer's claim that justice is determined by the shared meanings of a political community might never be able to get off the ground. The opportunities for, and also the limitations on, meaningful argument do not coincide in any interesting way with discrete communities, and are not specifiable in advance anyway.

2. In other contexts, Walzer has been more willing to accept the rights of minority cultures. In an article on ethnic pluralism, he argues against the recognition of minority rights only in immigrant countries like the United States, where the population was formed by the addition of individuals who had voluntarily left their old culture to enter a new nation. 'The Old World call for self-determination had no resonance here: the immigrants (except for black slaves) had come voluntarily' (Walzer 1982 pp. 6–7). Immigrant groups, therefore, do not have the same claims as minority nations; they are not cohesive historical communities

whose homeland has been incorporated into a larger political entity, and whose members reject emigration or assimilation. Where minority nations do exist, Walzer accepts that they may be entitled to political status. He sees this as a legitimate approach to minority cultures in the Old World, but argues that it does not apply to New World countries whose populations are based on voluntary emigration and assimilation. (Obviously American Indians, Puerto Ricans, and others offer important exceptions to the claim that the United States lacks minority nations, and Walzer seems somewhat embarrassed in discussing them—Walzer 1982 pp. 18, 27–8.)

So according to Walzer's ethnic pluralism article, the justice of rights claims by minority ethnic groups depends on whether they are minorities by choice or not, and whether their members have voluntarily relinquished their cultural membership or not. This approach implies that minority rights are a question of positive justice, not just mutual accommodation. Involuntary minority cultures have legitimate claims whether or not they have the power to insist on those claims. The 'shared meanings' framework Walzer uses in *Spheres of Justice*, however, requires that minority rights be a matter of mutual accommodation, not positive justice. Hence Walzer shifts from distinguishing between voluntary immigrants and minority nations to distinguishing between ethnic groups which can force mutual accommodation (even if they are voluntary immigrant groups) and those which cannot (even if they are minority nations by conquest). The latter approach may be needed to make minority rights questions fit into Walzer's relativist framework, but it has no other attractions.

12

Communitarianism and Minority Rights

FOR those who find the liberal defence of minority rights insufficiently sensitive to the particularity of the community in question, the communitarian picture of the self may seem like a more appropriate starting-point. In this chapter, I shall look at two communitarian attempts to move beyond a liberal view of minority rights by emphasizing the way that individuals are embedded in the shared practices which characterize a cultural community. I've already argued (in Chapter 4) that the communitarian account of the self conflicts with our self-understandings, and mislocates the importance that cultural membership has for us. My concern in this chapter is to show how that flawed account of the self weakens the communitarian defence of the measures needed to protect cultural membership. I shall argue that defences of minority rights which abandon the framework of liberal equality conflict with, rather than strengthen, our intuitions about minority rights. They do not support claims which are legitimate, and fail to defend against claims which are not legitimate. The special emphasis communitarians place on shared practices, while seeming to strengthen the argument for cultural membership, in fact weakens it.

The first communitarian argument I shall consider is advanced by Michael McDonald. It begins by emphasizing the importance of cultural membership in providing our sense of self. McDonald follows Sandel's claim that

to have character is to know that I move in a history I neither summon nor command, which carries consequences nonetheless for my choices and conduct . . . As a self-interpreting being, I am able to reflect on my history and in this sense to distance myself from it, but the distance is always precarious and provisional, the point of reflection never finally secured outside the history itself. (Sandel 1984*a* pp. 90–1)

This is a common theme of communitarians. MacIntyre similarly emphasizes the way membership in a historical community partially defines our identity, supplying a part which is 'found', not chosen, and which sets the context for those things which are chosen (MacIntyre pp. 204–6). For communitarians, to be cut off from this membership in a historical community is to be cut off from part of one's self, part of one's character.

Working from this picture of the role of cultural membership, McDonald develops a defence of the idea of minority rights. Because cultural membership is constitutive of who people are, therefore protection of that membership is an essential part of showing respect for people. McDonald approvingly quotes MacCormick's claim that 'the Kantian ideal of respect for persons implies . . . an obligation in each of us to respect that which in others constitutes any part of their sense of their own identity' (McDonald 1987 pp. 37–8). Under certain circumstances, this respect for persons justifies respecting minority rights. Their cultural membership is part of who aboriginal people are, and respect for that part of them requires, under certain circumstances, special political status. Minority rights are part of what it is to treat people as equals, once we view them as 'complete', not 'truncated' (McDonald 1987 p. 38).

Now this, so far, parallels the defence I gave of minority rights in Chapters 8 and 9. But the crucial question remains: under what circumstances are minority rights justified? McDonald's answer is that people must share an identification with a 'form of life' (ibid.). Now that is a very vague term, needing specification. McDonald supplies two criteria for identifying a form of life, one that is common to the liberal defence, one that is distinctly communitarian.

The first criterion is that an identification with a form of life is an identification that is 'recognized or found, not chosen or created' (McDonald 1987 p. 36). This fact, he says, defines 'a crucial juncture in the argument'. It is an identification that we take as a given in choosing and creating our other identifications. But McDonald goes on to say that he wants to give a 'communitarian reading' of this idea of a form of life: forms of life should be considered as defined by shared projects and ends and conceptions of the good (McDonald 1987 p. 38).

McDonald is here following Sandel and MacIntyre in saying

that particular social roles and projects are part of our unchosen social context. In finding myself in a certain historical community, I also find myself in 'this or that guild or profession' (MacIntyre p. 204). In being tied to a particular historical community, my identity is also 'tied to the aims and interests' which govern particular social practices (Sandel 1984a p. 86). In other words, I have certain constitutive projects or ends which are found and recognized, as a part of my cultural membership. Hence collective rights should be tied to the protection and promotion of these existing practices. (The collective right of the Pueblo to protect religious homogeneity by penalizing religious dissent might be an example, although McDonald does not discuss it.)

Now, as I argued in Chapter 4, this communitarian picture of personal reflection is wrong. Two people who share cultural membership may share no ends or projects at all—one French-Canadian may be committed to serving God, another may be committed to dispelling all religious mysticism. Their life-plans conflict, yet they share a common identity as French-Canadians. A Catholic French-Canadian may, on reflection, become an atheist without thereby having to find a 'point of reflection . . . outside history itself' (Sandel 1984a p. 91), without having to be (or become) 'deracinated' (McDonald 1987 p. 31 n. 24). Such decisions do not require rejecting one's membership in the cultural community. The same is true about decisions to revise our professional, sexual, artistic, or family practices. These are reflections and judgements that occur *within* a historical community, judgements made about the various options provided by the cultural structure. Our reflections are reflections about the plans and projects that are present in our cultural structure, but no particular plans or projects are exempt from possible rejection on the basis of that reflection. Being a French-Canadian is an unchosen identity, but French-Canadians still have to choose, and may want to revise, the religious, sexual, professional, and recreational practices they identify with.

As I argued in Chapter 9, the fact that our ends are matters of individual choice means that shared practices and projects provide weak grounds for a defence of minority rights. In making choices about our ends, including choices about which practices and associations to join or create, we should respect the legitimate claims of others. Thus racial supremacists who wish to deny the rights of blacks and Jews in their community cannot do so, even though it would promote their shared projects. Their claims are not informed by the teachings of equality. And if the defence of the special status of aboriginal peoples were similarly based on the existence of certain shared projects, then we'd find it similarly unpersuasive. In each case, we can legitimately expect people to form their plans of life with a view to the proper claims of others. Neither group should consider themselves as having any legitimate claim over the resources or liberties of others, since it is unfair to expect others to pay for the costs of one's own choices.[1]

Yet most people feel very differently about the two cases. Any satisfactory defence of aboriginal rights will have to identify features of the aboriginal case that do not apply to the racists. The main difference, I've argued, is that the aboriginal peoples of Canada, unlike the racists, face unequal *circumstances* even before they make their choices about which projects to pursue. Unlike English-Canadians, the very existence of their cultural communities is vulnerable to the decisions of the non-aboriginal majority around them. And that is true no matter what projects they end up pursuing. Two Inuit children may end up sharing no projects at all—like the French-Canadians, one may serve God while the other fights religious false consciousness. But all Inuit people face the same inequality in circumstances, and rectification of that inequality provides the basis for a liberal defence of minority rights.

The liberal defence, therefore, accords with our intuitions about the difference between choices and circumstances. McDonald's defence also appeals to that difference. But he wrongly includes our ends and roles on the unchosen side of that line, with the result that people's choices are no longer informed by the teachings of equality. This weakens the defence of aboriginal rights in two ways. If the collective rights of cultural groups are grounded in projects that are in fact chosen, then aboriginal rights appear to be unfair subsidies of aboriginal people's choices. But if we none the less accept that shared projects are a legitimate ground for collective rights, we have no way to distinguish the situation of aboriginal peoples from that of other groups (including non-minority groups) whose claims have no moral weight at all because they are grounded in choices which violate the teachings of equality. Only if we ground collective rights in unequal circumstances can we distinguish the legitimacy of aboriginal rights from the illegitimacy of attempts by assorted racial, religious, class, or gender groups to gain special status for their preferred goals and practices.

Charles Taylor, in a brief discussion of aboriginal rights, attempts to avoid grounding minority rights in people's choices. He discusses the apparent conflict between the requirements of individual equality and the survival of historical communities, and notes that measures intended to protect the communities might appear as 'giving these people more than their share, pandering to one of their inexplicable tastes' (C. Taylor 1988 p. 24). Taylor rejects this appearance of unfairness. One would expect Taylor to make a distinction here between people's choices and their circumstances, such that cultural protection serves to correct an inequality in circumstances. But like McDonald, Taylor wants to include people's 'understandings of the good' in his definition of membership in the historical community. Yet unlike McDonald, he doesn't want to say that the members of the community merely find these projects, unchosen.

So Taylor is confronted with the problem of defending the fairness of special measures to protect the shared projects of members of a historical community, without wanting to claim that those projects are an unchosen part of people's circumstances. Why don't these measures simply constitute unfair subsidies of some individuals' tastes? His solution is to say that the question isn't about *individual* equality at all. The defensibility of these measures depends on whether the target equality we are pursuing is equality 'amongst *individuals* living in these provinces. Or, are we trying to equalize well-being between these historic communities?' (C. Taylor 1988 p. 24). Taylor says that we face a dilemma that arises 'from the demands of different kinds of goods: equality of needs versus the health of historic communities' (C. Taylor 1988 p. 25). Special protection of the historical community, including the shared choices of its members, may not be justified on the grounds of treating individuals as equals. But there is some independent claim by the community itself to equal treatment.[2]

Now if this is meant literally, I find it incoherent. Groups have no moral claim to well-being independently of their members—groups just aren't the right sort of beings to have moral status. They don't feel pain or pleasure. It is individual, sentient beings whose lives go better or worse, who suffer or flourish, and so it is their welfare that is the subject-matter of morality. It seems peculiar to suppose that individuals can legitimately be sacrificed to further the 'health' of something that is incapable of ever suffering or flourishing in a sense that raises claims of justice. If we accept that every individual matters equally, and deny that historical communities have any independent moral status, then any acceptable and intelligible defence of the rights of cultural groups must show how they play a role in treating people as equals. Talking about the claims of the community, underived from any account of individual equality, may help get around the charge that minority rights based on shared ends allow individuals to make unfair claims. But it gets around the charge that *individuals* are making unfair claims only by making it completely obscure who *is* making the claims.[3]

Communitarians like to emphasize the importance of cultural membership, the importance of the fact that we move in a history and language not of our own choosing. This is supposed to be an insight beyond the ken of liberalism. And indeed they have stressed the importance of cultural membership in a way that contemporary liberals like Rawls and Dworkin haven't. But their attempt to pin the blame at the foundational level in liberalism, rather than on the complex of historical factors I discussed in Chapters 7 and 10, mislocates the problem. And their misplaced fears about the 'abstract' and 'atomistic' nature of liberal equality lead them to conflate individuals' cultural membership with embeddedness in particular communal relations, or with the shared meanings of social goods in the community. Each of these can justify some minority rights, but they can also justify a politics that denies cultural freedom to some people, and allows cultural extinction for others. While claiming to affirm the importance of cultural membership, they fail to provide the grounds on which to protect it safely.

Notes

1. This bears on one of the non-liberal arguments for aboriginal rights mentioned in Ch. 7. It is often said that because the aboriginal 'form of life' places more emphasis on the communal and the spiritual than does the individualistic and materialistic English-Canadian culture, therefore they are entitled to collective rights. In the words of the Métis and Non-Status Indian Constitutional Review Committee,

   The value system of the dominant socio-cultural system in Canada is liberalism which places emphasis on the individual, individual rights and private property. This is in contrast to the value system of Native peoples which places a far higher value on the collectivity or upon the community. (Ponting and Gibbins 1986 p. 216)

   Liberalism, with its individualism, ignores the value that community has to aboriginal people; collective rights would be more appropriate than individual rights for the members of such a collective-minded form of life (Little Bear, Boldt, and Long p. xvi; Van Dyke 1985 p. 83; Svennson pp. 431–2).

   This differs from McDonald's claim, I think, in saying that collective rights are justified not for any form of life that has shared ends, but only for those forms of life with specific kinds of shared ends. But it suffers from the same flaw as McDonald's argument. Why should aboriginal people have more resources to pursue their communal ends than non-aboriginal people have to pursue their less communal ends? Collective rights for aboriginal peoples, if defended on the grounds of different value-systems, seem to amount to unfair privileges, just as it would be unfair to give self-styled aristocrats an unequal share of the resources to pursue their expensive ideals, or to give racists unequal voting rights to pursue their shared ideals. In each case, equality should enter into their decisions about what sorts of projects to pursue, and hence into the resources and liberties they claim in pursuing them.

2. Again, this bears on one of the non-liberal arguments cited in support of aboriginal rights. Unlike the argument discussed in n. 1, the claim is not that community matters more to aboriginal people than to non-aboriginal people, but that community matters independently of how much it matters to individuals. Historical cultures have a moral status beyond the value they have for their members, and hence have legitimate moral claims in their own

right to be weighed against the claims of individual equality. Thus some commentators talk about the conflict between individual equality and the group 'need' for survival (Ponting and Gibbins 1980 p. 27) or for self-determination (Dacks p. 78). See also Boldt and Long 1985c pp. 343–5.

3. Perhaps Taylor only meant to emphasize the way that community is important to individuals *intrinsically* as well as instrumentally. Since individuals are constituted by and through interaction with others in a network of cultural practices, there is no such thing as an individual prior to society. The value that society has to individuals is a non-contingent one.

All of that is true. But it doesn't warrant Taylor's abandonment of the plateau of individual equality. For the claim that individuals, not communities, are the ultimate bearers of moral value is simply a recognition of the separateness of consciousness. It may well be that membership in a community partially defines my identity, and hence defines the conditions of my flourishing. But it is still *me* who suffers or flourishes, and it is *my* (and other individuals') suffering or flourishing that gives community its moral status. As Galston says, 'While the formative power of society is surely decisive, it is nevertheless *individuals* that are being shaped. I may share everything with others. But it is *I* that shares them—an independent consciousness, a separate locus of pleasure and pain, a demarcated being with interests to be advanced or suppressed' (Galston 1986a p. 91). Acceptance of this fact of the separateness of consciousness does not foreclose the question of the ways in which community forms our interests and identity. If Taylor's concern was with the importance of community to individual welfare, then he has no reason to abandon the egalitarian plateau.

13

Apartheid in South Africa

OVER the course of the last six chapters, I have tried to set out the contours of a liberal theory of minority rights, and to show how it differs from other approaches to conditions of cultural pluralism. I have concentrated on the philosophical challenge of recognizing and reconciling the legitimate claims of political citizenship and cultural membership, and have tried to locate the suggested reconciliation within the liberal philosophical tradition. But as we've seen in Chapter 10, perceptions of fairness are sometimes shaped to fit pre-existing fears about the possible consequences of minority rights. And contemporary perceptions of fairness are strongly influenced by our horror of apartheid in South Africa. Apartheid is the most common illustration used by people who argue against the legitimacy of minority rights. Indeed, once the analogy with apartheid is made, many people view the injustice of aboriginal special status as 'self-evident' (see Chapter 7 above).

Any argument for minority rights needs to confront apartheid. For if cultural protection justifies limiting citizenship rights, what grounds do we have for criticizing South Africa's whites? Botha has recently said: 'if other population groups have rights and a rightful claim to humanitarian treatment, then I say that the whites, who have their own minorities, are also entitled to justice and to live' (*International Herald Tribune* p. 2). And he has often stressed that the justification of apartheid is a cultural one, not a racial one—the need to protect the 'First World culture' of the whites from being submerged into the Third World cultures of the other peoples of South Africa.

The possibility that Afrikaners would use the idea of minority cultural protection to defend their policies has exercised lawyers and jurists who have sought to institute protective measures in other countries, and they have often looked for a clear principle that would deny the whites in South Africa a legitimate claim to cultural protection (Thornberry p. 423; Van Dyke 1975 p. 613). But they have looked, I think, in vain. We can't deny the prima-facie applicability of minority rights to white South Africans.

However, the perspective of cultural membership will be of no help in justifying their actual policies. In the first place, nothing in that perspective could ever justify the system of 'petty apartheid', i.e. the segregation of washrooms, swimming-pools, restaurants, trains, the refusal to transport blacks in 'white' ambulances, etc. There are no questions of cultural security here, as the South African government has begun to admit. I don't mean to suggest that the existence of petty apartheid is irrelevant to our evaluation of the larger system. On the contrary, its existence shows, what was obvious anyway, that South African apartheid isn't based on any notion of equal respect for cultural groups, but on blatant racism. I just mean that protection of cultural membership could never justify petty apartheid.

Secondly, while the South Africans have indeed invoked the example of Indian reservations, they have done so in a most peculiar way. I quote Botha again: 'we are dealing with a hypocritical Western world. In the United States, President Ronald Reagan who has much to say in his mispronouncing way about apartheid, is shoving Indians into reservations' (*International Herald Tribune* p. 2). But of course the Indians aren't being 'shoved' into reservations—on the contrary, 'the dominant policy of the [American] government has been one of coercive assimilation' (Senate Subcommittee on Indian Education, quoted in Gross p. 242). Since 1880, the trend has been to encourage the Indians to assimilate into the mainstream and give up their reserved lands (MacMeekin pp. 1239–40). The analogy is misconceived in another way. The whites in the United States are both dominant and numerically in the majority and hence would have no right to shove anybody anywhere on the grounds of cultural security. Surely if Botha wanted to defend apartheid while criticizing our moral hypocrisy, the relevant point would be exactly the opposite: while we recognize the right of Indians to voluntarily segregate themselves from an alien majority culture and keep others out, we refuse to recognize the right of white South Africans to do the same. But of course this would hardly serve Botha's purpose: Indians have demanded the right to voluntarily segregated cultural communities, but they, unlike South African whites, have not demanded 87 per cent of the land mass of the country, nor the right to force the remaining 84 per cent of the population into discrete homelands against their will according to racial classifications that bear no resemblance to people's self-understandings.[1] Botha does indeed need an analogy which justifies him 'shoving' people around; but the special status of Indians could never provide that.

Thus the notion of cultural membership, and the principle of equalizing cultural circumstances, provides no ammunition for those who would defend the current practices of South Africa. The groups that are incorporated into the South African state are defined by imposed racial classifications which contradict cultural membership. And the method of incorporation is designed to protect a system of racial privilege which contradicts the requirement to equalize circumstances. Far from respecting cultural membership as part of a theory of justice, apartheid violates cultural membership so as to protect injustice.

However, the notion of cultural membership does require a revision of some of the arguments we've directed against apartheid. Given the extreme and multiple injustices in South Africa, there is no reason or excuse for missing the real target. Yet I think the UN General Assembly, and the international community in general, has done just that, on more than one occasion. I shall consider one example where neglect of the question of cultural membership has led opponents of apartheid to misidentify, and indeed to obscure, its real horrors.[2]

Much of the international criticism of South Africa is phrased in terms of the right to self-determination. The UN General Assembly has passed resolutions affirming the right of South African blacks to be free from alien subjugation (and hence the right to self-determination in that sense), and condemning the policy of homelands (formerly known as 'Bantustans') as a violation of that right. These claims are beyond dispute. But the international community has operated on the assumption that the blacks are a *single people* entitled to this self-determination. Therefore, in passing those resolutions, the United Nations said that the reason the homelands policy violates the right to self-determination is that they deny the right of blacks as a single people 'to take control of a natural patrimony the territorial integrity of which has been preserved' (Richardson p. 198). In concrete terms, this means that granting independence to the Transkei homeland was held to violate the 'authoritative expectations of the international community about the behaviour of the immediately preceding sovereign of the territory before its lawful and expected delivery to the people whose rights to self-determination are then in the process of being exercised' (Richardson p. 199). In other words, the problem with the homelands policy is that the international community has the 'authoritative' expectation that the government must hand over the territory of South Africa, as a single bundle, to the blacks, as a single people. But these expectations, authoritative or not, have not been adequately defended, and this account of the problem with the homelands is bizarre.

Why should the blacks be viewed as a single people, when they in fact are members of different nations, each with its own language and political traditions? What if one of the nations freely desired separate development, and hence an independent homeland? How would that deny anyone their right of self-determination? Of course, this is the way that the South African regime defends its system of black homelands. The Xhosa, for example are said to have chosen independence for their Transkei homeland in a free election. That is absurd, and the United Nations has rightly condemned the elections as fraudulent (Richardson p. 212). There is no way in which the homelands policy can be seen as respecting the right of black nations like the Xhosa to self-determination. The homelands are not freely chosen, but are forcibly imposed, and allegedly independent governments are completely subject to political, economic, and military pressure from Pretoria (Richardson pp. 204–13). The whole policy was designed not out of respect for the equal standing of black nations, but precisely out of racist contempt for those nations. They were a way of ensuring a cheap supply of black labour, without having to provide the labourers, or their families (categorized as 'superfluous appendages'), with any of the benefits which come with citizenship, or even permanent residence, in the South African political community (Richardson p. 187).

The United Nations is quite right to say that the homelands policy denies the right of blacks to self-determination. But it seems peculiar to say that it does so because it violates the right of self-determination of blacks *as a single people*, a right that includes the right to inherit the land as a single bundle, and then distribute it in accordance with the views of the blacks, taken as a single group. That both trivializes the problem with the homelands, and denies the distinct black nations their proper standing. Apparently, the Transkei homeland violates self-determination, not because (or not only because) it prevents the Xhosa from freely deciding how to dispose of their land, but because it prevents members of *other* black nations from deciding what to do with the Xhosa's land. The UN objection implies that if a black nation, like the Xhosa, had freely chosen to accept genuine self-government, that would *still* count as a denial of the right of self-determination of blacks.

But why should the Xhosa, in these imaginary circumstances, need the approval of the other nine tribal groups (assuming, of course, that the land being granted to the Xhosa didn't legitimately belong to another tribe)? If China invaded Western Europe, unified it in a single province, then decided to grant what is now Denmark independence, would anyone say that that violated the right of the 'white people' of Western Europe to self-determination? Would anyone demand that the Danish get the approval of a majority of that single 'white people'? I don't think so; the Danish are a single people, a cultural nation, and hence have their own right to self-determination, not simply as one component of the right of the 'white people' to self-determination. The Xhosa, too, should be considered to have their own right of self-determination, a right which, I repeat, the current homelands policy violates, rather than respects. If white South Africans are defending that policy on the grounds that it respects the self-determination of separate black nations, the response should be to call the bluff, not to deny that black nations have a right to self-determination. The United Nations' response is wrong in principle and politically inopportune, since it gives apologists for apartheid a completely undeserved opportunity to claim that they take Xhosa self-determination more seriously than the United Nations does.

The United Nations is undoubtedly right to have the expectation that South African blacks will only acquire self-determination if they acquire it together. There is no way, in the current circumstances, in which one of the black nations can exercise that right of self-determination without all of them doing so. The power of the South African regime, and its determination to preserve the essentials of apartheid, means that no one group is in the position to assert or defend its independence. The protection of apartheid requires that the homelands be viewed as appendages of the South African state and economy, and the South African regime will not grant powers to the homelands that are inconsistent with that function. So long as the commitment to apartheid remains, the homelands, like the Group Areas Act, will be mechanisms for the control and exploitation of blacks, mechanisms which prevent blacks from exercising their rights of self-determination. (Indeed, existing homelands would be exploitative even if apartheid control over them were abolished, because the land comprising each homeland is of such poor quality, is fragmented into dozens of pieces, and is too small relative to the population.[3])

But it is a mistake, I think, to say that the reason the homelands deny black self-determination is that they involve carving up the country. There is nothing in principle wrong with a system of distinct homelands in a single country. To isolate that as the evil in South Africa is to miss the real horrors of apartheid—the brutal coercion with which the system is forced on the black (and other non-white) population, the massive disparity in the health and educational resources that are allocated to members of the different races, the suppression of basic civil and political liberties. None of these have anything to do with segregation *as such*. They have to do with the racism that underlies South African policy—the belief that blacks and other non-whites are less human, less worthy of consideration. They are viewed as means to the ends of the white minority. The system of homelands in South Africa reflects and perpetuates that racism. That is why apartheid is unjust.

A just constitution in South Africa would eliminate that system. But whether it would contain some other system of distinct communities is a question that can't be answered in advance. A system of equal rights and common citizenship within an integrated political community is no more prima facie just than a system of plural citizenships and special rights within a federation of distinct national communities. Either system can enforce equal respect just as either system can violate it. It depends on what choices the distinct communities make, and whether any find themselves in circumstances of cultural vulnerability.

To know whether any particular system of cultural self-government does in fact enforce equal respect, we must look at more than equality of citizenship. We must complement our emphasis on citizenship with a view of cultural membership as an important focal point for the political expression of respect for individuals. A proper balancing of these two perspectives helps define the limits of a fair and just constitution in culturally plural countries, whether it is in Canada today, or in the South Africa of the future.

Notes

1. As Adam points out, 'In all plural or divided societies, with the sole exception of South Africa, members of subgroups voluntarily identify with their ethnic unit. It is indeed their *self*-concept' (Adam p. 288). White South Africans defend their policies

    in the name of preserving group identities as the 'most important dimension of human rights'. However, these 'cultural identities, life-styles and basic social institutions of historically established groups' as far as blacks are concerned exist in South Africa mainly by definition of the ruling group. (Ibid.)

    This is manifested in the totally artificial category of 'Coloureds', and in the fact that urban blacks had no choice but to relinquish South African citizenship:

    Had they been given the choice, the concept of *self*-determination would have been credible . . . ethnicity will always be considered a form of racialism by those affected, as long as it is imposed and does not correspond with the self-concept of ethnic group members. (Adam p. 289)

    For discussions of the differences between apartheid and legitimate consociationalism, see Adam pp. 288–97; Van Dyke 1985 ch. 7; Asch and Dacks pp. 40–1; Boulle pp. 36–8, 64–6; Degenaar 1978 pp. 239–41; Purich pp. 223–4; Simkins pp. 28–9. For discussions of the more general contrast between 'pluralist' and 'hegemonic' incorporation of groups (sometimes called 'equivalent' versus 'differential' incorporation, or 'consociation' versus 'control'), see M. G. Smith 1969 pp. 434–6; Worsley pp. 188–92; Lustic.

2. For another example, see Van Dyke's discussion of an American counsel's argument before the International Court of Justice in the 1966 South West Africa Cases (Van Dyke 1985 p. 194).

3. See Adam p. 295 and Erkens pp. 28–9 for the necessity of ensuring justice in resource distribution before cultural groups are incorporated into the state with special political status.

14

Conclusion

IN much of the recent literature on liberalism, we are offered a choice between liberal theories which are essentially 'individualistic' and opposing theories which are essentially 'social'. Liberalism is said to be individualistic because it concentrates on the individual at the expense of the social conditions and relations within which individuals develop and exercise their truly human capacities. Whereas liberals view communal and cultural associations as (sometimes unavoidable) constraints which limit the natural freedom of individuals, those theories which recognize our social nature understand that community and culture are the preconditions of genuine freedom. Expounded in this way, it is hard to understand how liberalism ever managed to gain any more than a handful of adherents, let alone define the political morality of a number of modern democracies.

But the real disagreements between liberals and their critics cannot be understood as a contrast between 'individualistic' and 'social' theories. Even in its least satisfactory forms, liberalism has always included some account of our essential dependence on our social context, some account of the forms of human community and culture which provide the context for individual development, and which shape our goals and our capacity to pursue them. The question is *which* forms of community and culture should we seek to create or maintain?

Throughout this book, I have tried to show that liberalism, in its most attractive form, offers a very plausible and compelling account of community and culture. It recognizes the way that communal and cultural aspects of social life provide the possibility for, and locus of, the pursuit of human values. But it also insists that these values, like most important values, ultimately depend on the way that each individual understands and evaluates them. The value of the communal and cultural aspects of our existence depends, to a large degree, on the way that individuals form and revise attachments and projects around those features of our social life. Hence the value of the 'social' depends on, rather than conflicts with, the 'individualistic' picture of people forming and pursuing their own understandings of the good.

Liberal individualism, on this view, is not about believing in self-interest rather than love, or presocial interests rather than culturally formed interests. Nor is it about valuing individual choice and detachment over social commitments and attachments. None of these could ground the distinctive liberal mixture of rights to public expression and association on the one hand, and to personal liberty and property on the other. Liberal individualism is rather an insistence on respect for each individual's capacity to understand and evaluate her own actions, to make judgements about the value of the communal and cultural circumstances she finds herself in. Indeed, individuals have not only the capacity but also the responsibility for making such judgements; respect for the legitimate claims of others should enter into the very formation of our aims and ambitions. Liberal individualism is grounded in this irreducible commitment to the role of individual self-direction and responsibility in a just community, and to the principle of moral equality which underlies both.

Liberal individualism of this sort does not conflict with the ideal of community, but rather provides an interpretation of it. The result of this conception of individual responsibility is not to set people against each other, but to tie all citizens in bonds of mutual respect. And the result of this conception of individual self-direction is not to distance people from each other, but to enable various groups of people to freely pursue and advance their shared communal and cultural ends, without penalizing or marginalizing those groups who have different and perhaps conflicting goals. These are the best conditions under which all members of society, individually and in community with others, can intelligently form and successfully pursue their understandings of the good.

In these areas, the resources available to a liberal theory of community and culture have simply been underestimated by its critics. But in other areas, contemporary liberals have failed to work through the implications of their own views. While liberal theory implicitly or explicitly refers to the importance of cultural membership in defining the context in which individuals lead their lives, a variety of factors have kept liberals ι.om drawing out the implications concerning the relevance of cultural membership to their political theory.

I think that the question of cultural membership provides both a philosophical opportunity and a political challenge for liberals. The philosophical opportunity is to refute those critics who explain the neglect of cultural membership by attributing various unattractive features to liberalism. Some explain it in terms of a liberal hostility to group attachments (e.g. Worsley p. 188), or at least a desire to transcend them (e.g. Adam pp. 265–6); others in terms of a liberal belief that individuals can develop outside of relationships (e.g. Degenaar 1978 p. 241), or that humans act only from material self-interest (e.g. Rich 1976 pp. 239–40; Svennson p. 425), or that humans are purely rational and unfeeling creatures (e.g. Adam pp. 266–7). These proposed explanations all derive from the same mistakes that inform recent communitarian critiques of liberalism, and the question of cultural membership provides an excellent opportunity for liberals to respond to both sets of complaints.

But the question of cultural membership also creates political challenges for liberalism. It requires a reinterpretation of one of the fundamental features of liberal political practice in many countries—constitutional guarantees of equal protection under the law. As currently interpreted, minority rights are often seen as violating equal protection guarantees, and it is for this reason that aboriginal peoples and French-Canadians have sometimes sought exemption from equality provisions of the Canadian Charter. As I discussed at the end of Chapter 7, this perceived conflict between minority rights and liberal equality has weakened the judicial enforcement of both. The political task, then, is to devise constitutional provisions (or new interpretations of existing provisions) which will be flexible enough to allow for the legitimate claims of cultural membership, but which are not so flexible as to allow systems of racial or cultural oppression.

It is interesting to compare the development of Canadian and American jurisprudence in this area. It is commonly noted that desegregation cases were the most important ones for recent changes in the interpretation of equality guarantees in America (e.g. Polyviou chs. 6, 7), whereas Indian Act cases were the most important in Canada (Polyviou ch. 4). When commentators compare the two developments, Canadian Justices are usually criticized for not having worked out an interpretation as rigorous or expansive as the American Supreme Court. But it is less commonly noted that the development of American juris-prudence in this area was often accompanied by a neglect of, and an insensitivity to, the situation of aboriginal people, whose claims and aspirations could not be accommodated within the new jurisprudence.

For example, when Thurgood Marshall was arguing the case for desegregation in *Brown* v. *Board of Education*, as counsel for the NAACP, he was asked whether his demand for a colour-blind constitution would apply to the segregated education facilities for American Indians. His reply was 'I do not think that they stand in any special category . . . But I think that the biggest trouble with the Indians is that they just have not had the judgement or the wherewithal to bring lawsuits' (quoted in Friedman p. 50). It is fortunate that the Supreme Court's judgement in the *Brown* case didn't depend on Marshall's answer here. American Indians have brought lawsuits, and, like Canada's aboriginal population, they have brought them to protect their special status from state and federal government incursion. Having adopted the principle of a colour-blind constitution, however, Marshall had to defend it by ignoring and mis-representing the special circumstances and aspirations of American Indians.

The American Supreme Court did not accept Marshall's views about the illegitimacy of Indian special status. But nor, on the other hand, has it made any attempt to reconcile that special status with the existing interpretations of the equal protection clause. American Justices have been under no obligation to consider how their equality provisions affect Indian community life, since Indians aren't guaranteed the protection of the Fourteenth Amendment (*Elk* v. *Wilkins* [1884] 112 US 94). And while the 1968 Indian Civil Rights Act does extend some guarantees of equal rights to Indians, the Supreme Court has left their interpretation and enforcement to tribal courts. That may well be a progressive move, but it also saves the Court from having to reconcile its pronouncements about equal protection with Indian special status. The American Supreme

Court has loudly proclaimed that there are rights which attach to all persons regardless of race or ethnicity, while quietly refusing to extend them to Indians. In contrast, the Canadian Supreme Court has operated on the assumption that guarantees which are said to belong to all persons regardless of race or ethnicity should belong to all persons regardless of race or ethnicity. We don't know how the American Supreme Court would have responded had it faced the task of reconciling the special status of Indians with the desegregation of blacks under a single principle of equality. But if Canadian Justices have had more difficulty enunciating a consistent principle of equality it is at least in part because they have set themselves this more difficult task.

The refusal to consider the distinct situation of Indians is a common affliction of modern American liberal thought. Thus Nathan Glazer begins his discussion of the 'protection of minorities' in the United States by saying: 'While our primary focus here on blacks obviously simplifies a very complex development, their experience does provide the basic protective machinery for other ethnic and racial minorities' (Glazer 1981 p. 23). This is false, of course, in the context of American Indian policy. The situation of American Indians also contradicts his claim that there is in America a traditional 'clear and simple understanding, that rights attach to the individual, not the group, and that public policy must be exercised without distinction of race, color, or national origin' (Glazer 1975 p. 5). Like Marshall, Glazer builds his argument for colour-blind law by treating the case of American Indians (when he considers it at all), as a mere anomaly, of no real interest (e.g. Glazer 1975 p. 28). And as Van Dyke says, perhaps the special status of Indians has little interest when viewed from an ethnocentric perspective. But 'It is much more difficult to dismiss the treatment of the indigenous as an exception, and thus without any intellectual significance or consequence, when the situation and practices of other countries are considered' (Van Dyke 1985 p. 108). In fact, it is the situation of Indians, not blacks, in America which is most relevant for understanding questions of the protection of minorities (Van Dyke 1985 p. 93). It is the special circumstances of American blacks that are anomalous in the international arena. Far more of the world's minorities are in a similar position to

American Indians (i.e. as a stable and geographically distinct historical community with separate language and cu .ure rendered a minority by conquest or immigration or the redrawing of political boundaries).

American liberals rightly take pride in their role in the struggle for the civil rights of blacks. It was a remarkable victory, both for blacks and for all the other marginalized and disadvantaged groups who have been aided and inspired by their example. But it detracts from the quality of that victory when the principles relevant to blacks are thoughtlessly and insensitively applied to the situation of American Indians, or the members of any other minority culture. It would not have taken much investigation for Marshall or Glazer to discover that Indians suffer the same harms and feel the same humiliation when they are denied the freedom to live fully in their own community, as a result of forced integration, that blacks felt when they were denied the freedom to live fully in their community, as a result of forced segregation. And it would not have taken much investigation for them to realize that the situation of Indians, far from being anomalous, is in fact quite common. Or that the issues about individual and collective rights raised by Indian status are confronted daily in countries all over the world.

Considering the nature and value of cultural membership not only takes us down into the deepest reaches of a liberal theory of the self, but also outward to some of the most pressing questions of justice and injustice in the modern world.

Bibliography

Ackerman, B. (1980). *Social Justice in the Liberal State*. Yale University Press, New Haven.

—— (1983). 'On Getting what we Don't Deserve.' *Social Philosophy and Policy*. Vol. 1.

Acton, J. (1922). 'Nationalism.' In *The History of Freedom and Other Essays*. Ed. J. Figgis and R. Laurence. Macmillan, London.

Adam, H. (1979). 'The Failure of Political Liberalism.' In *Ethnic Power Mobilized: Can South Africa Change?* Ed. H. Adam and H. Giliomee. Yale University Press, New Haven.

Ajzenstat, J. (1984*a*). 'Liberalism and Assimilation: Lord Durham Revisited.' In *Political Thought in Canada: Contemporary Perspectives*. Ed. S. Brooks. Irwin Publishing, Toronto.

—— (1984*b*). 'Collectivity and Individual Right in "Mainstream" Liberalism: John Arthur Roebuck and the *Patriotes.*' *Journal of Canadian Studies*. Vol. 19.

Alexander, L., and Schwarzschild, M. (1987). 'Liberalism, Neutrality, and Equality of Welfare vs. Equality of Resources.' *Philosophy and Public Affairs*. Vol. 16.

Anderson, M. (1987). 'Law and the Protection of Cultural Communities: The Case of Native American Fishing Rights.' *Law and Politics*. Vol. 9.

Asch, M. (1984). *Home and Native Land: Aboriginal Rights and the Canadian Constitution*. Methuen, Toronto.

—— and Dacks, G. (1985). 'The Relevance of Consociation to the Western Northwest Territories.' In *Partners for the Future*. Ed. S. Iveson. Western Constitutional Forum, Yellowknife, NWT.

Avineri, S. (1968). *The Social and Political Thought of Karl Marx*. Cambridge University Press, Cambridge.

Barber, B. (1984). *Strong Democracy*. University of California Press, Berkeley.

Barry, B. (1973). *The Liberal Theory of Justice*. Oxford University Press, Oxford.

—— (1984). 'Review of *Liberalism and the Limits of Justice.*' *Ethics*. Vol. 94.

Barsh, R. (1983). 'Indigenous North America and Contemporary International Law.' *Oregon Law Review*. Vol. 62.

—— (1986). 'Indigenous Peoples: An Emerging Object of International Law.' *American Journal of International Law*. Vol. 80.

—— and Henderson, J. Y. (1980). *The Road: Indian Tribes and Political Liberty*. University of Toronto Press, Toronto.

—— (1982). 'Aboriginal Rights, Treaty Rights and Human Rights: Indian Tribes and Constitutional Renewal.' *Journal of Canadian Studies.* Vol. 17.

Bartlett, R. (1986). *Subjugation, Self-Management and Self-Government of Aboriginal Lands and Resources in Canada.* Institute of Intergovernmental Relations, Kingston, Ont.

Bentham, J. (1982). *An Introduction to the Principles of Morals and Legislation.* Ed. J. Burns and H. Hart. Methuen, London.

Berger, T. (1981). *Fragile Freedoms: Human Rights and Dissent in Canada.* Clarke Irwin and Co., Toronto.

—— (1984). 'Towards the Regime of Tolerance.' In *Political Thought in Canada: Contemporary Perspectives.* Ed. S. Brooks. Irwin Publishing, Toronto.

Berlin, I. (1969). *Four Essays on Liberty.* Oxford University Press, London.

Bernstein, R. (1987). 'One Step Forward, Two Steps Backward: Richard Rorty on Liberal Democracy and Philosophy.' *Political Theory.* Vol. 15.

Boldt, M., and Long, J. A. (1985a). *The Quest for Justice: Aboriginal Peoples and Aboriginal Rights.* University of Toronto Press, Toronto.

—— (1985b). 'Tribal Philosophies and the Canadian Charter of Rights and Freedoms.' In Boldt and Long (1985a).

—— (1985c). 'Tribal Traditions and European-Western Political Ideologies: The Dilemma of Canada's Native Indians.' In Boldt and Long (1985a).

Boulle, L. (1984). *South Africa and the Consociational Option: A Constitutional Analysis.* Juta and Co., Cape Town.

Bowles, R., Hanley, J., Hodgins, B., and Rawlyk, G. (1972). *The Indian: Assimilation, Integration or Separation?* Prentice-Hall, Scarborough, Ont.

Braverman, H. (1974). *Labor and Monopoly Capital.* Monthly Review Press, New York.

Braybrooke, D. (1979). 'Would the Crisis in Confederation be Resolved More Easily with Less Talk about Rights?' In French (1979).

Broome, J. (1989). 'Fairness and the Random Distribution of Goods.' In *Justice and the Lottery.* Ed. J. Elster. Cambridge University Press, Cambridge (forthcoming).

Buchanan, A. (1982). *Marx and Justice: The Radical Critique of Liberalism.* Methuen, London.

Cameron, D. (1974). *Nationalism, Self-Determination and the Quebec Question.* Macmillan, Toronto.

Campbell, T. (1983). *The Left and Rights: A Conceptual Analysis of the Idea of Socialist Rights.* Routledge and Kegan Paul, London.

Capotorti, F. (1979). *Study on the Rights of Persons Belonging to Ethnic, Religious and Linguistic Minorities.* UN Doc. E/CN 4/Sub. 2/384 Rev. 1.

Cardinal, H. (1969). *The Unjust Society.* Hurtig Publishers, Edmonton.

——— (1977). *The Rebirth of Canada's Indians.* Hurtig Publishers, Edmonton.

Claude, I. (1955). *National Minorities: An International Problem.* Harvard University Press, Cambridge, Mass.

Claydon, J. (1978). 'Internationally Uprooted People and the Transnational Protection of Minority Culture.' *New York Law School Law Review.* Vol. 24.

Cobban, A. (1969). *The Nation-State and National Self-Determination.* Collins, London.

Cohen, G. A. (1985). 'Nozick on Appropriation.' *New Left Review.* No. 150.

——— (1986). 'Self-Ownership, World-Ownership and Equality: Part II.' *Social Philosophy and Policy.* Vol. 3.

Cohen, J. (1986). 'Review of *Spheres of Justice.*' *Journal of Philosophy.* Vol. 83.

Connolly, W. (1984). 'The Dilemma of Legitimacy.' In *Legitimacy and the State.* Ed. W. Connolly. Blackwell, Oxford.

Connor, W. (1972). 'Nation-Building or Nation-Destroying?' *World Politics,* Vol. 24.

——— (1984). *The National Question in Marxist-Leninist Theory and Strategy.* Princeton University Press, Princeton.

Cragg, W. (1986). 'Two Concepts of Community or Moral Theory and Canadian Culture.' *Dialogue.* Vol. 25.

Crowley, B. (1987). *The Self, the Individual, and the Community: Liberalism in the Political Thought of F. A. Hayek and Sidney and Beatrice Webb.* Oxford University Press, Oxford.

Dacks, G. (1981). *A Choice of Futures: Politics in the Canadian North.* Methuen, Toronto.

Damico, A. (1986a). *Liberals on Liberalism.* Rowman and Littlefield, Totowa, NJ.

——— (1986b). 'The Democratic Consequences of Liberalism.' In Damico (1986a).

David-McNeil, J. (1985). 'The Changing Economic Status of the Female Labour Force in Canada.' In *Towards Equity: Proceedings of a Colloquium on the Economic Status of Women in the Labour Market.* Supply and Services Canada, Ottawa.

Davis, S. (1979). 'Language and Human Rights.' In French (1979).

Degenaar, J. (1978). 'Pluralism and the Plural Society.' In *The Government and Politics of South Africa.* Ed. A. de Crespigny and R. Schrire. Juta and Co., Cape Town.

Degenaar, J. (1987). 'Nationalism, Liberalism, and Pluralism.' In *Democratic Liberalism in South Africa: Its History and Prospect.* Ed. J. Butler, R. Elphick, and D. Walsh. Wesleyan University Press, Middletown, Conn.

De Lue, S. (1986). 'The Idea of a Duty to Justice in Ideal Liberal Theory.' In Damico (1986*a*).

Dench, G. (1986). *Minorities in the Open Society: Prisoners of Ambivalence.* Routledge and Kegan Paul, London.

Dene Nation (1977). 'A Proposal to the Government and People of Canada.' In *Dene Nation: The Colony Within.* Ed. M. Watkins. University of Toronto Press, Toronto.

Devlin, P. (1965). *The Enforcement of Morals.* Oxford University Press, London.

Dewey, J. (1928). *The Public and its Problems.* George Allen and Unwin, London.

DIAND (Department of Indian Affairs and Northern Development). (1969). 'A Statement of the Government of Canada on Indian Policy.' In Bowles *et al.* (1972).

—— (1982). 'The Elimination of Sex Discrimination from the Indian Act.' R32–59/1982. Ottawa.

DiQuattro, A. (1983). 'Rawls and Left Criticism.' *Political Theory.* Vol. 11.

Doerr, A. (1974). 'Indian Policy.' In *Issues in Canadian Public Policy.* Ed. G. Doern and V. Wilson. Macmillan, Toronto.

Dunn, J. (1979). *Western Political Theory in the Face of the Future.* Cambridge University Press, Cambridge.

Dunn, M. (1986). *Access to Survival: A Perspective on Aboriginal Self-Government for the Constituency of the Native Council of Canada.* Institute of Intergovernmental Relations, Kingston, Ont.

Dworkin, R. (1977). *Taking Rights Seriously.* Duckworth, London.

—— (1978). 'Liberalism.' In *Public and Private Morality.* Ed. S. Hampshire. Cambridge University Press, Cambridge.

—— (1981). 'What is Equality?' Parts I and II. *Philosophy and Public Affairs.* Vol. 10.

—— (1983*a*). 'In Defense of Equality.' *Social Philosophy and Policy.* Vol. 1.

—— (1983*b*). 'A Reply By Ronald Dworkin.' In *Ronald Dworkin and Contemporary Jurisprudence.* Ed. M. Cohen. Duckworth, London.

—— (1985). *A Matter of Principle.* Harvard University Press, London.

—— (1986). *Law's Empire.* Harvard University Press, Cambridge, Mass.

—— (1987). 'What is Equality?' Part III: 'The Place of Liberty.' *Iowa Law Review.* Vol. 72.

Ehrenreich, B., and English, J. (1973). *Witches, Midwives and Nurses: A History of Women Healers*. Feminist Press, Old Wc:.bury, NY.

Elster, J. (1985). *Making Sense of Marx*. Cambridge University Press, Cambridge.

Erkens, R. (1985). 'Limits and Prospects for a Liberal Policy in a Plural Society: An Essay on the History of South African Liberalism.' In *South Africa: A Chance for Liberalism?* Liberal Verlag, Sankt Augustin.

Fischer, E. (1980). *Minorities and Minority Problems*. Vantage Press, New York.

Fishman, J. (1972). *The Sociology of Language*. Newbury House, Rowley, Mass.

Flathman, R. (1986). 'Liberalism and the Human Good of Freedom.' In Damico (1986a).

French, S. (1979). *Philosophers Look at Canadian Confederation*. Canadian Philosophical Association, Montreal.

Frey, R. (1984). *Utility and Rights*. University of Minnesota Press, Minneapolis.

Friedman, L. (1969). *Argument: The Oral Argument before the Supreme Court in* Brown v. Board of Education of Topeka, *1952–55*. Chelsea House, New York.

Galston, W. (1980). *Justice and the Human Good*. University of Chicago Press, Chicago.

—— (1982). 'Defending Liberalism.' *American Political Science Review*. Vol. 76.

—— (1986a). 'Equality of Opportunity and Liberal Theory.' In *Justice and Equality: Here and Now*. Ed. F. Lucash. Cornell University Press, Ithaca.

—— (1986b). 'Liberalism and Public Morality.' In Damico (1986a).

Gaus, G. (1983). *The Modern Liberal Theory of Man*. Croom Helm, London.

Gellner, E. (1983). *Nations and Nationalism*. Blackwell, Oxford.

Gill, E. (1986). 'Goods, Virtues and the Constitution of the Self.' In Damico (1986a).

Glazer, N. (1975). *Affirmative Discrimination: Ethnic Inequality and Public Policy*. Basic Books, New York.

—— (1978). 'Individual Rights Against Group Rights.' In *Human Rights*. Ed. E. Kamenka and A. Tay. Edward Arnold, London.

—— (1981). 'Minority Protection in Western Democracies: The United States.' In *Protection of Ethnic Minorities: Comparative Perspectives*. Ed. R. Wirsing. Pergamon Press, New York.

—— (1983). *Ethnic Dilemmas: 1964–1982*. Harvard University Press, Cambridge, Mass.

—— and Moynihan, D. (1975). *Ethnicity, Theory and Experience*. Harvard University Press, Cambridge, Mass.

Glover, J. (1977). *Causing Death and Saving Lives*. Penguin, Harmondsworth.

Gordon, M. (1975). 'Toward a General Theory of Racial and Ethnic Group Relations.' In Glazer and Moynihan (1975).

Gordon, S. (1980). *Welfare, Justice and Freedom*. Columbia University Press, New York.

Gould, C. (1978). *Marx's Social Ontology*. MIT Press, Cambridge, Mass.

Gray, J. (1986). *Liberalism*. University of Minnesota Press, Minneapolis.

Green, L. (1988). *The Authority of the State*. Oxford University Press, Oxford.

Green, L. C. (1983). 'Aboriginal Peoples, International Law and the Canadian Charter of Rights and Freedoms.' *Canadian Bar Review*. Vol. 61.

Green, T. H. (1941). *Lectures on the Principles of Political Obligation*. Longman's, Green, and Co., London.

Griffin, J. (1984). 'Towards a Substantive Theory of Rights.' In Frey (1984).

—— (1986). *Well-Being: Its Meaning, Measurement, and Moral Importance*. Oxford University Press, Oxford.

Gross, M. (1973). 'Indian Control for Quality Indian Education.' *North Dakota Law Review*. Vol. 49.

Gutmann, A. (1980). *Liberal Equality*. Cambridge University Press, Cambridge.

—— (1982). 'What's the Use of Going to School?' In *Utilitarianism and Beyond*. Ed. A. Sen and B. Williams. Cambridge University Press, Cambridge.

—— (1985). 'Communitarian Critics of Liberalism.' *Philosophy and Public Affairs*. Vol. 14.

Gwyn, R. (1980). *The Northern Magus: Pierre Trudeau and Canadians*. McClelland and Stewart, Toronto.

Haksar, V. (1979). *Equality, Liberty, and Perfectionism*. Oxford University Press, Oxford.

Hanen, M. (1979). 'Taking Language Rights Seriously.' In French (1979).

Hare, R. M. (1984). 'Rights, Utility and Universalization: Reply to J. L. Mackie.' In Frey (1984).

Harsanyi, J. (1980). *Essays on Ethics, Social Behavior and Scientific Explanation*. Reidel, Dordrecht.

Hart, H. L. A. (1973). 'Rawls on Liberty and Its Priority.' *University of Chicago Law Review*. Vol. 40.

Haslett, D. (1987). *Equal Consideration: A Theory of Moral Justification*. University of Delaware, Newark.

Hauser, R. (1971). 'International Protection of Minorities and the Right of Self-Determination.' *Israel Yearbook on Human Rights*. Vol. 1.

Hegel, G. W. F. (1942). *Philosophy of Right*. Trans. T. M. Knox. Oxford University Press, London.

Herzog, D. (1986). 'Some Questions for Republicans.' *Political Theory*. Vol. 14.

Hirsch, H. (1986). 'The Threnody of Liberalism: Constitutional Liberty and the Renewal of Community.' *Political Theory*. Vol. 14.

Hobhouse, L. T. (1928). *Social Evolution and Political Theory*. Columbia University Press, New York.

—— (1964). *Liberalism*. Oxford University Press, London.

—— (1966). *Social Development: Its Nature and Conditions*. George Allen and Unwin, London.

International Herald Tribune (1985). 'Botha Rejects Plea From Within Party to End Home School Segregation.' 3 Oct.

Jaggar, A. (1983). *Feminist Politics and Human Nature*. Rowman and Allenheld, Totowa, NJ.

Kant, I. (1948). *Groundwork of the Metaphysic of Morals*. Ed. and trans. H. Paton. In *The Moral Law*. Hutchinson, London.

Kaplan, J. (1964). 'Comment on "The Decade of School Desegregation" '. *Columbia Law Review*. Vol. 64.

Kateb, G. (1982). 'Looking for Mr Good Life.' *American Scholar*. Vol. 51.

Kelly, J. (1973). 'National Minorities and International Law.' *Denver Journal of International Law*. Vol. 3.

Knopff, R. (1979). 'Language and Culture in the Canadian Debate: The Battle of the White Papers.' *Canadian Review of Studies in Nationalism*. Vol. 6.

—— (1982). 'Liberal Democracy and the Challenge of Nationalism in Canadian Politics.' *Canadian Review of Studies in Nationalism*. Vol. 9.

Kronowitz, R., Lichtman, J., McSloy, S. and Olsen, M. (1987). 'Toward Consent and Cooperation: Reconsidering The Political Status of Indian Nations.' *Harvard Civil Rights–Civil Liberties Review*. Vol. 22.

Kunz, J. (1955). 'The Present Status of the International Law for the Protection of Minorities.' *American Journal of International Law*. Vol. 48.

Kuper, L. (1969). 'Plural Societies: Perspectives and Problems.' In *Pluralism in Africa*. Ed. L. Kuper and M. Smith. University of California Press, Berkeley.

—— (1984). 'International Protection Against Genocide in Plural Societies.' In Maybury-Lewis (1984a).

Ladenson, R. (1977). 'Mill's Conception of Individuality.' *Social Theory and Practice*. Vol. 4.

Larmore, C. (1987). *Patterns of Moral Complexity*. Cambridge University Press, Cambridge.

Lijphart, A. (1977). *Democracy in Plural Societies: A Comparative Exploration*. Yale University Press, New Haven.

Little Bear, L., Boldt, M., and Long, J. (1984). *Pathways to Self-Determination: Canadian Indians and the Canadian State*. University of Toronto Press, Toronto.

Lomasky, L. (1987). *Persons, Rights, and the Moral Community*. Oxford University Press, New York.

Lukes, S. (1985). *Marxism and Morality*. Oxford University Press, Oxford.

Lustic, I. (1979). 'Stability in Deeply Divided Societies: Consociationalism versus Control.' *World Politics*. Vol. 31.

Lyon, N. (1984). *Aboriginal Self-Government: Rights of Citizenship and Access to Government Services*. Institute of Intergovernmental Relations, Kingston, Ont.

Lyons, D. (1981). 'The New Indian Claims and Original Rights to Land.' In *Reading Nozick: Essays on* Anarchy, State and Utopia. Ed. J. Paul. Rowman and Littlefield, Totowa, NJ.

McDonald, M. (1976). 'Aboriginal Rights.' In *Contemporary Issues in Political Philosophy*. Ed. W. Shea and J. King-Farlow. Science History Publications, New York.

—— (1987). 'Justifying Collective Rights.' Unpublished paper, University of Waterloo.

Machiavelli, N. (1940). *The Prince and The Discourses*. Ed. M. Lerner. Modern Library, New York.

MacIntyre, A. (1981). *After Virtue: A Study in Moral Theory*. Duckworth, London.

Mackie, J. (1984). 'Rights, Utility and Universalization.' In Frey (1984).

MacKinnon, C. (1987). *Feminism Unmodified: Discourses on Life and Law*. Harvard University Press, Cambridge, Mass.

MacMeekin, D. (1969). 'Red, White and *Gray*: Equal Protection and the American Indian.' *Stanford Law Review*. Vol. 21.

McRae, K. (1975). 'The Concept of Consociational Democracy and its Application to Canada.' In *Multilingual Political Systems*. Ed. J. Savard and R. Vigneault. University of Laval Press, Quebec.

—— (1979). 'The Plural Society and the Western Political Tradition.' *Canadian Journal of Political Science*. Vol. 12.

Manyfingers, M. (1986). 'Determination of Indian Band Membership: An Examination of Political Will.' *Canadian Journal of Native Studies*. Vol. 6.

Marx, K. (1843). 'On the Jewish Question.' In Marx (1977).

—— (1844*a*). 'On James Mill.' In Marx (1977).

—— (1844*b*). *Economic and Philosophical Manuscripts*. Lawrence and Wishart, London, 1977.

—— (1858). *Grundrisse*. Ed. M. Nicolaus. Penguin, Harmondsworth, 1973.

—— (1859). *Preface to A Contribution to the Critique of Political Economy*. In Marx and Engels (1968).

—— (1867). *Capital: A Critique of Political Economy*. Vol. 1. Trans. B. Fowkes. Vintage Books, New York, 1977.

—— (1875). 'Critique of the Gotha Programme.' In Marx and Engels (1968).

—— (1977). *Karl Marx: Selected Writing*. Ed. D. McLellan. Oxford University Press, Oxford.

—— and Engels, F. (1846). *The German Ideology*. Ed. C. Arthur. Lawrence and Wishart, London, 1970.

—— (1848). *The Communist Manifesto*. In Marx and Engels (1968).

—— (1968). *Marx/Engels Selected Works in One Volume*. Lawrence and Wishart, London.

Maybury-Lewis, D. (1984*a*). *The Prospects for Plural Societies*. American Ethnological Society, Washington, DC.

—— (1984*b*). 'Living in Leviathan: Ethnic Groups and the State.' In Maybury-Lewis (1984*a*).

Michelman, F. (1986). 'Justification (and Justifiability) of Law in a Contradictory World.' In *Nomos*, vol. 28: *Justification*. Ed. J. Pennock and J. Chapman. New York University Press, New York.

Midgley, M. (1978). *Beast and Man*. New American Library, New York.

Mill, J. S. (1962). *Mill on Bentham and Coleridge*. Ed. F. Leavis. Chatto and Windus, London.

—— (1972). *Utilitarianism, Liberty, Representative Government*. Ed. H. Acton. J. M. Dent and Sons, London.

—— (1987). *The Logic of the Moral Sciences*. Ed. A. Ayer. Duckworth, London.

Miller, R. (1984). *Analyzing Marx*. Princeton University Press, Princeton.

Mkhwanazi, F. (1985). 'Apartheid's Long Winter Sunset.' *National Student*. Vol. 82.

Moore, K. (1984). *The Will to Survive: Native People and the Constitution*. Hyperborea Publishings, Val d'Or, Que.

Morgan, E. (1984). 'Self-Government and the Constitution: A Comparative Look at Native Canadians and American Indians.' *American Indian Law Review*. Vol. 12.

Morton, F. (1985). 'Group Rights versus Individual Rights in the Charter: The Special Cases of Natives and the Quebecois.' In

Minorities and the Canadian State. Ed. N. Nevitte and A. Kornberg. Mosaic Press, Oakville, Ont.

Murphy, J. (1973). 'Marxism and Retribution.' *Philosophy and Public Affairs*. Vol. 2.

Nagel, T. (1980). 'The Limits of Objectivity.' *Tanner Lectures on Human Values*. Vol. 1. University of Utah Press, Salt Lake City.

Neal, P. (1987). 'A Liberal Theory of the Good?' *Canadian Journal of Philosophy*. Vol. 17.

Nicholls, D. (1974). *Three Varieties of Pluralism*. St Martin's Press, New York.

Nielsen, K. (1985). *Equality and Liberty: A Defense of Radical Egalitarianism*. Rowman and Allanheld, Totowa, NJ.

—— (1987). 'Rejecting Egalitarianism: On Miller's Non-egalitarian Marx.' *Political Theory*. Vol. 15.

Nietzsche, F. (1968). *On the Genealogy of Morals*. Trans. W. Kaufman and R. Hollingdale. Vintage Press, New York.

Nozick, R. (1974). *Anarchy, State and Utopia*. Basic Books, New York.

—— (1981). *Philosophical Explanations*. Harvard University Press, Cambridge, Mass.

Okin, S. (1979). *Women in Western Political Thought*. Princeton University Press, Princeton.

—— (1987). 'Justice and Gender.' *Philosophy and Public Affairs*. Vol. 16.

—— (1989a). *Justice v. Gender*. Basic Books, New York.

—— (1989b). 'Reason and Feeling in Thinking About Justice.' *Ethics*. Vol. 99.

Oldenquist, A. (1986). *The Non-Suicidal Society*. Indiana University Press, Bloomington.

Opekokew, D. (1987). *The Political and Legal Inequities among Aboriginal Peoples in Canada*. Institute of Intergovernmental Relations, Kingston, Ont.

Penton, M. (1983). 'Collective versus Individual Rights: The Canadian Tradition and the Charter of Rights and Freedoms.' In *The U.S. Bill of Rights and the Canadian Charter of Rights and Freedoms*. Ed. W. McKercher. Ontario Economic Council, Toronto.

Perry, M. (1987). 'A Critique of the "Liberal" Political-Philosophical Project.' *William and Mary Law Review*. Vol. 28.

Phillips, M. (1983). *The Dilemmas of Individualism: Status, Liberty, and American Constitutional Law*. Greenwood Press, Westport.

Polyviou, P. (1980). *The Equal Protection of the Laws*. Duckworth, London.

Ponting, J., and Gibbins, R. (1980). *Out of Irrelevance: A Socio-political Introduction to Indian Affairs in Canada*. Butterworth, Toronto.

—— (1986). 'An Assessment of the Probable Impact of Aboriginal Self-Government in Canada.' In *The Politics of Gender, Ethnicity and Language in Canada*. Ed. A. Cairns and C. Williams. University of Toronto Press, Toronto.

Porter, J. (1975). 'Ethnic Pluralism in Canada.' In Glazer and Moynihan (1975).

Purich, D. (1986). *Our Land: Native Peoples in Canada*. James Lorimer and Co., Toronto.

Rabushka, A., and Shepsle, K. (1972). *Politics in Plural Societies: A Theory of Democratic Instability*. Charles Merrill, Columbus.

Radcliffe Richards, J. (1980). *The Sceptical Feminist: A Philosophical Enquiry*. Routledge and Kegan Paul, London.

Rawls, J. (1971). *A Theory of Justice*. Oxford University Press, London.

—— (1974). 'Reply to Alexander and Musgrave', *Quarterly Journal of Economics*. Vol. 88.

—— (1978). 'The Basic Structure as Subject.' In *Values and Morals*. Ed. A. Goldman and J. Kim. Reidel, Dordrecht.

—— (1980). 'Kantian Constructivism in Moral Theory.' *Journal of Philosophy*. Vol. 77.

—— (1982). 'Social Unity and Primary Goods.' In *Utilitarianism and Beyond*. Ed. A. Sen and B. Williams. Cambridge University Press, Cambridge.

—— (1985). 'Justice as Fairness: Political not Metaphysical.' *Philosophy and Public Affairs*. Vol. 14.

Raz, J. (1982). 'Liberalism, Autonomy and the Politics of Neutral Concern.' *Midwest Studies in Philosophy*. Vol. 7.

—— (1986). *The Morality of Freedom*. Oxford University Press, Oxford.

Reiman, J. (1986). 'Law, Rights, Community, and the Structure of Liberal Legal Justification.' In *Nomos*, vol. 28: *Justification*. Ed. J. Pennock and J. Chapman. New York University Press, New York.

Rich, P. (1976). 'Liberalism and Ethnicity in South African Politics, 1921–1948.' *African Studies*. Vol. 35.

—— (1984). *White Power and the Liberal Conscience: Racial Segregation and South African Liberalism 1921–60*. Manchester University Press, Manchester.

Richardson, H. (1978). 'Self-Determination, International Law and the South African Bantustan Policy.' *Columbia Journal of Transnational Law*. Vol. 17.

Robinson, E., and Quinney, H. (1985). *The Infested Blanket: Canada's Constitution—Genocide of Indian Nations*. Queenston House, Winnipeg.

Robinson, J. (1971). 'International Protection of Minorities: A Global View.' *Israel Yearbook on Human Rights*. Vol. 1.

Rodewald, R. (1985). 'Does Liberalism Rest on a Mistake?' *Canadian Journal of Philosophy*. Vol. 15.

Roemer, J. (1985). 'Equality of Talent.' *Economics and Philosophy*. Vol. 1.

—— (1986). 'The Marriage of Bargaining Theory and Distributive Justice.' *Ethics*. Vol. 97.

Rorty, R. (1985). 'Postmodernist Bourgeois Liberalism.' In *Hermeneutics and Praxis*. Ed. R. Hollinger. University of Notre Dame Press, Notre Dame, Ind.

Rosenblum, N. (1987). *Another Liberalism: Romanticism and the Reconstruction of Liberal Thought*. Harvard University Press, Cambridge, Mass.

Sandel, M. (1982). *Liberalism and the Limits of Justice*. Cambridge University Press, Cambridge.

—— (1984a). 'The Procedural Republic and the Unencumbered Self.' *Political Theory*. Vol. 12.

—— (1984b). 'Morality and the Liberal Ideal.' *New Republic*. 7 May. Vol. 190.

Sanders, D. (1972). 'The Bill of Rights and Indian Status.' *University of British Columbia Law Review*. Vol. 7.

—— (1983a). 'The Re-Emergence of Indigenous Questions in International Law.' *Canadian Human Rights Yearbook 1983*. Carswell, Toronto.

—— (1983b). 'The Rights of the Aboriginal Peoples of Canada.' *Canadian Bar Review*. Vol. 61.

Scheffler, S. (1979). 'Moral Scepticism and Ideals of the Person.' *Monist*. Vol. 62.

—— (1982). *The Rejection of Consequentialism*. Oxford University Press, Oxford.

Schwartz, B. (1986). *First Principles, Second Thoughts: Aboriginal Peoples, Constitutional Reform and Canadian Statecraft*. The Institute for Research on Public Policy, Montreal.

Scruton, R. (1982). *Kant*. Oxford University Press, Oxford.

Seltzer, A. (1980). 'Acculturation and Mental Disorder in the Inuit.' *Canadian Journal of Psychiatry*. Vol. 25.

Seton-Watson, H. (1977). *Nations and States: An Enquiry into the Origins of Nations and the Politics of Nationalism*. Westview Press, Boulder, Colo.

Shapiro, I. (1986). *The Evolution of Rights in Liberal Theory*. Cambridge University Press, Cambridge.

Shklar, J. (1964). *Legalism*. Harvard University Press, Cambridge, Mass.

Sidgwick, H. (1981). *The Method of Ethics*. 7th edn. Hackett Publishing, Indianapolis.

Sigler, J. (1983). *Minority Rights: A Comparative Analysis*. Greenwood Press, Westport.

Simkins, C. (1986). *Reconstructing South African Liberalism*. South African Institute for Race Relations, Johannesburg.

Singer, P. (1979). *Practical Ethics*. Cambridge University Press, Cambridge.

Smith, M. G. (1969). 'Some Developments in the Analytical Framework of Pluralism.' In *Pluralism in Africa*. Ed. L. Kuper and M. Smith. University of California Press, Berkeley.

—— (1984). 'The Nature and Variety of Plural Unity.' In Maybury-Lewis (1984a).

Smith, R. (1985). *Liberalism and American Constitutional Law*. Harvard University Press, Cambridge, Mass.

Sparham, R. (1978). 'Political Development in the Northwest Territories.' In *Northern Transitions*. Vol. 2. Ed. R. Keith and J. Wright. Canadian Arctic Resource Committee, Ottawa.

Spragens, T. (1986). 'Reconstructing Liberal Theory: Reason and Liberal Culture.' In Damico (1986a).

Strike, K. (1982). *Educational Policy and the Just Society*. University of Chicago Press, Chicago.

Sullivan, W. (1982). *Reconstructing Public Philosophy*. University of California Press, Berkeley.

Svensson, F. (1979). 'Liberal Democracy and Group Rights: The Legacy of Individualism and its Impact on American Indian Tribes.' *Political Studies*. Vol. 27.

Tarnopolsky, W. (1983). 'The Equality Rights in the Canadian Charter of Rights and Freedoms.' *Canadian Bar Review*. Vol. 61.

Taylor, C. (1979). *Hegel and Modern Society*. Cambridge University Press, Cambridge.

—— (1985). *Philosophical Papers*. Vol. 2: *Philosophy and the Human Sciences*. Cambridge University Press, Cambridge.

—— (1986). 'Alternative Futures: Legitimacy, Identity and Alienation in Late-Twentieth Century Canada.' In *Constitutionalism, Citizenship and Society in Canada*. Ed. A. Cairns and C. Williams. University of Toronto Press, Toronto.

—— (1988). *Justice After Virtue*. Legal Theory Workshop Series, Faculty of Law, University of Toronto. WS 1987–8 no. 3.

Taylor, D. (1985). 'Women: An Analysis.' In *Women: A World Report*. Methuen, London.

Thigpen, R., and Downing, L. (1983). 'Liberalism and the Neutrality Principle.' *Political Theory*. Vol. 11.

Thornberry, P. (1980). 'Is there a Phoenix in the Ashes? International Law and Minority Rights.' *Texas International Law Journal*. Vol. 15.

Toronto Star (1986). 'Botha's Warning.' 28 Sept.

Unger, R. (1984). *Knowledge and Politics*. Macmillan, New York.

United Nations Human Rights Committee. (1983). *Considerations of Reports Submitted by States Parties under Article 40 o, the Covenant: Canada*. CCPR/C/1/Add. 62.

van den Berghe, P. (1969). 'Pluralism and the Polity: A Theoretical Explanation.' In *Pluralism in Africa*. Ed. L. Kuper and M. Smith. University of California Press, Berkeley.

—— (1981*a*). 'Protection of Ethnic Minorities: A Critical Appraisal.' In Wirsing (1981).

—— (1981*b*). *The Ethnic Phenomenon*. Elsevier, New York.

Van Dyke, V. (1975). 'Justice as Fairness: For Groups?' *American Political Science Review*. Vol. 69.

—— (1977). 'The Individual, the State, and Ethnic Communities in Political Theory.' *World Politics*. Vol. 29.

—— (1982). 'Collective Entities and Moral Rights: Problems in Liberal–Democratic Thought.' *Journal of Politics*. Vol. 44.

—— (1985). *Human Rights, Ethnicity and Discrimination*. Greenwood Press, Westport.

Waldron, J. (1987). 'Theoretical Foundations of Liberalism.' *Philosophical Quarterly*. Vol. 37.

Wallach, J. (1987). 'Liberals, Communitarians, and the Tasks of Political Theory.' *Political Theory*. Vol. 15.

Walzer, M. (1980). 'The Moral Standing of States.' *Philosophy and Public Affairs*. Vol. 9.

—— (1982). 'Pluralism in Political Perspective.' In *The Politics of Ethnicity*. Ed. M. Walzer *et al.* Harvard University Press, Cambridge, Mass.

—— (1983). *Spheres of Justice: A Defence of Pluralism and Equality*. Blackwell, Oxford.

Ward, E. (1974). 'Minority Rights and American Indians.' *North Dakota Law Review*. Vol. 51.

Weaver, S. (1981). *Making Canadian Indian Policy*. University of Toronto Press, Toronto.

—— (1985). 'Federal Difficulties with Aboriginal Rights Demands.' In Boldt and Long (1985*a*).

Weinfeld, M. (1981). 'Minority Protection in Western Democracies: Canada.' In Wirsing (1981).

Weinstein, J. (1986). *Aboriginal Self-Determination off a Land Base*. Institute of Intergovernmental Relations, Kingston, Ont.

Weinstein, W. (1981). 'Minority Protection in the Third World: Africa.' In Wirsing (1981).

Weston, W. (1981). 'Freedom of Religion and the American Indian.' In *The American Indian: Past and Present*. 2nd edn. Ed. R. Nichols. John Wiley and Sons, New York.

Williams, B. (1981). *Moral Luck*. Cambridge University Press, Cambridge.

—— (1985). *Ethics and the Limits of Philosophy*. Fontana, London.

Wirsing, R. (1980). 'Cultural Minorities: Is the World Ready to Protect them?' *Canadian Review of Studies in Nationalism*. Vol. 7.

—— (1981). *Protection of Ethnic Minorities: Comparative Perspectives*. Pergamon Press, New York.

Wolff, R. (1977). *Understanding Rawls*. Princeton University Press, Princeton.

Wood, A. (1979). 'Marx on Right and Justice.' *Philosophy and Public Affairs*. Vol. 8.

—— (1981). 'Marx and Equality.' In *Issues in Marxist Philosophy*. Vol. 4. Ed. J. Mepham and D. Ruben. Harvester Press, Brighton.

Worsley, P. (1984). 'The Three Modes of Nationalism.' In Maybury-Lewis (1984a).

Young, C. (1976). *The Politics of Cultural Pluralism*. University of Wisconsin Press, Madison.

Young, I. (1981). 'Toward a Critical Theory of Justice.' *Social Theory and Practice*. Vol. 7.

Index